"Jamaal Williams and Timothy Jones do the body of Christ a great service with their book. It allows readers to consider the joys and challenges of creating a multiracial Christian church and ministry. Such ministries are badly needed in a post-Christian America that is racially divided. But these ministries need to be accomplished with careful thought and planning. *In Church as It Is in Heaven* provides great insight that allows for such thinking and planning to take place."

George Yancey, professor of sociology at Baylor University and author of *Beyond Racial Division*

"As the authors express in this book, my heart and hopes for churches on earth have been guided by the eschatological vision of the church in heaven found in Revelation 7. *In Church as It Is in Heaven* helps us get there. It is outstanding; I could not put it down. Any church or Christian captivated by God's promise for his church in eternity will be blessed, convicted, edified, and encouraged by this work. Thank you, my brothers. What a gift you have given us."

Daniel L. Akin, president of Southeastern Baptist Theological Seminary

"Some have given up on a biblical vision of racial justice, morality, and reconciliation. Jamaal Williams and Timothy Paul Jones have not. This book is a practical guide that gives up neither sober realism nor kingdom hope."

Russell Moore, editor in chief of *Christianity Today*

"What I love about this book is how Jamaal Williams and Timothy Paul Jones encourage a communal solution to a communal problem. So many treatments on this topic ask what people can do individually and don't seek larger transformation. Framing the book around liturgy and the habits that form us was a compelling contribution. I encourage all who long for unity instead of division to pick this book up. May it be in the church as it is in heaven."

Patrick Schreiner, associate professor of New Testament and biblical theology at Midwestern Baptist Theological Seminary and author of *Political Gospel: Public Witness in a Politically Crazy World*

"*In Church as It Is in Heaven* casts a biblically and theologically grounded vision of a multiethnic community. Neither Jamaal Williams nor Timothy Paul Jones sugarcoat that vision. For them, being authentically multiethnic means intertwining dreams and broken dreams, rich and nearly impossible-to-maintain crosscultural relationships, promises and betrayal, stereotypes surfaced then broken. Many churches like the idea of being diverse but ditch the process when the road gets too bumpy and costly; a minuscule handful are authentically multiethnic in the fullest sense. *In Church as It Is in Heaven* is the still-unfolding story of one church in Kentucky that is refusing to abandon the process."

Paul Tokunaga, founder and president of MELD: Multi-Ethnic Leadership Development

"People often talk about how divided our churches are when it comes to race and ethnicity, but few local church ministers know where to begin to make practical changes. This is why I'm so thankful for *In Church as It Is in Heaven*. Jamaal Williams and Timothy Paul Jones speak not only from their theological training but their pastoral experience as well. They have lived it together, and we benefit from their wisdom."

Courtney Reissig, author of *Teach Me to Feel: Worshiping Through the Psalms in Every Season of Life*

"In the last ten years, we have seen vivid reminders that we still have extensive work to do for racial reconciliation in our country and in our churches. If we were once able to think that these problems were behind us, recent struggles have made it clear that they are not. As believers, we should not just want a resolution to the racial divides, but we should also want to see the people of God lead the way. As such, this work by Jamaal Williams and Timothy Paul Jones is an important contribution to this ongoing work that deserves a careful reading."

James K. Dew Jr., president and professor of Christian philosophy at New Orleans Baptist Theological Seminary and coauthor of *How Do We Know? An Introduction to Epistemology*

"Conviction, camaraderie, hope—these are just a few things I felt reading *In Church as It Is in Heaven*. Jamaal Williams and Timothy Paul Jones write not as those who have reached the destination but as those inviting us to come along with them on the journey of pursuing multi-ethnic congregations. Best of all, the book is rooted in Scripture and has a lot of practical advice. It brings a conversation often up in the clouds down to the ground. This is a welcome and welcoming guide for all those eager to show the world we are Jesus' disciples by the way we love one another."

Isaac Adams, lead pastor of Iron City Church and founder of United? We Pray

"Questions of diversity, harmony, and reconciliation are unavoidable today. Most of us are somewhere between unprepared and unwilling to have these necessary conversations—which is a problem given that God intends the kingdom of heaven to include people from every tribe, nation, and tongue. To close the gap between God's intention for the kingdom and our personal preparedness, we need experienced Christian leaders with biblical vision and gracious hearts to shepherd us. This is precisely what Jamaal Williams and Timothy Paul Jones offer us with *In Church as It Is in Heaven*. Here's a book with potential for renewing the church's longing for the things God finds beautiful in the kingdom."

Thabiti M. Anyabwile, pastor of Anacostia River Church and author of *What Is a Healthy Church Member?*

"'[Our] destinies are tied together.' Dr. King's insight is true for society as a whole and even more so for the church. This book provides a faithful and practical path for the church to pursue our unity mandate."

Justin E. Giboney, president of the AND Campaign

"Jamaal Williams and Timothy Paul Jones rightfully posit excellent scholarship with heedful nuance inside a framework of biblical ecclesiology. *In Church as It Is in Heaven* is a timely resource interacting with primary sources alongside logical arguments guiding the reader toward healthy application. Although the truth hurts when communicated, we would be remiss in failing to admit it provides a pathway to holistic healing only found in Christ. Williams and Jones are pastoral and prophetic truth tellers unmasking the deceptions of the evil one regarding individual, interpersonal, and local church institutional misunderstanding, sin, and tensions grounded in race. I will be recommending this text for the living stones Jesus redeemed for years to come."

D. A. Horton, associate professor at California Baptist University

"As a fellow kingdom laborer, I value voices that are grounded in biblical truth and straightforward about the realities of building a multicultural church. Pastor Jamaal and Pastor Timothy call us up to God's vision while honestly unpacking the joy, the pain, and the sacrifices in maintaining intentional multiethnic kingdom ministry. I hope many leaders will count the cost and choose to apply the liturgies and practices laid out in this book. Just like the early church in Acts, we can bear a wonderful witness of how the power of the Holy Spirit binds unlikely people together in unity and justice."

Dorena Williamson, speaker and author of *The Celebration Place*

IN CHURCH AS IT IS IN HEAVEN

Cultivating
a Multiethnic
Kingdom Culture

Jamaal E. Williams & Timothy Paul Jones

An imprint of InterVarsity Press
Downers Grove, Illinois

InterVarsity Press
P.O. Box 1400 | Downers Grove, IL 60515-1426
ivpress.com | email@ivpress.com

InterVarsity Press® is the publishing division of InterVarsity Christian Fellowship/USA®. For more information, visit intervarsity.org.

Scripture quotations, unless otherwise noted, have been taken from the Christian Standard Bible®, Copyright © 2017 by Holman Bible Publishers. Used by permission. Christian Standard Bible® and CSB® are federally registered trademarks of Holman Bible Publishers.

This book is published in association with Nappaland Literary Agency, an independent firm dedicated to publishing works that are: Authentic. Relevant. Eternal. Visit us on the web at: http://www.NappalandLiterary.com.

While any stories in this book are true, some names and identifying information may have been changed to protect the privacy of individuals.

The publisher cannot verify the accuracy or functionality of website URLs used in this book beyond the date of publication.

Cover design: David Fassett
Interior design: Jeanna Wiggins

ISBN 978-1-5140-0538-5 (print) | ISBN 978-1-5140-0539-2 (digital)

Printed in the United States of America ∞

Library of Congress Cataloging-in-Publication Data
A catalog record for this book is available from the Library of Congress.

29   28   27   26   25   24   23 | 12   11   10   9   8   7   6   5   4   3   2   1

For our children
who will, we pray,
see the fruit of these labors someday
in churches that look more like heaven.

Nia
Josiah
Kayla
Micah
Judah

Hannah
Skylar
Kylinn
Katrisha

There was a vast multitude from every nation, tribe, people, and language, which no one could number, standing before the throne and before the Lamb.

JOHN THE APOSTLE

Eleven o'clock on Sunday morning is one of the most segregated hours, if not the most segregated hour, in Christian America.

MARTIN LUTHER KING JR.

Your kingdom come. Your will be done on earth as it is in heaven.

JESUS CHRIST

Expect great things from God; attempt great things for God.

WILLIAM CAREY

CONTENTS

Introduction

BROKEN CITY, BROKEN WORLD

You've probably never heard of Shelby Park. It's an ethnically diverse neighborhood here in Louisville, Kentucky, and home to Sojourn Church Midtown. It's where the two of us—one of us Black, the other White—serve as pastors.

You probably *have* heard about an apartment building about nine miles south of us. On March 13, 2020, the Louisville Metro Police Department executed a no-knock warrant on a unit in that building. In the botched raid that followed, twenty-six-year-old medical technician Breonna Taylor was shot to death. None of the suspects named in the warrant were even in the apartment, and the officer who obtained the warrant had fabricated evidence.[1] The resulting wave of demonstrations and counterdemonstrations lasted for months. There were vigils and protests and prayer walks. Most were peaceful, and we participated in some of them. But there was violence as well. Two police officers and seven protesters were shot during the demonstrations, and National Guard troops killed the owner of a popular barbecue stand on the west end of town.[2]

Four blocks from Sojourn Church Midtown stands Little Flock Missionary Baptist Church. It's a historic African American congregation that's served our neighborhood for more than a century. On June 3, 2020, an unidentified group of White males fired at least thirty bullets through its front doors.[3]

This wasn't the first attempted attack on a historic African American church in our city in recent years. Less than two years before the shooting of Breonna Taylor, a White male with a gun tried to force his way into an African American church on the east side of town. When he found the building locked, he drove to a nearby grocery where he murdered a woman and a man—both Black—one of whom was with his grandson, buying supplies for a school project. When the shooter was confronted by another White man, the shooter replied, "Don't shoot me, I won't shoot you. Whites don't kill whites."[4]

The high-profile deaths of Breonna Taylor, Michael Brown, Sandra Bland, Trayvon Martin, Eric Garner, Ahmaud Arbery, George Floyd, and so many others have revealed fault lines in our culture and triggered seismic eruptions in cities across the United States. All of this has left lasting scars in our community, in our church, and in us.

And yet . . .

CHASING GOD'S VISION

. . . we're still here.

A multiethnic band of pastors leading a diverse congregation that loves Jesus, the gospel, and the city of Louisville. We've lamented as we've seen some members leave, we've mourned as many well-intended plans have fallen short, and we've seen our hair grow grayer. Yet we have no plans to give up our vision for this place because we're filled with hope in Christ and hope for you.

Our vision is to pursue a life like heaven.

For us, that means watching this church grow into a diverse, gospel-driven, Scripture-saturated community and equipping other congregations to do the same. What we envision is a future filled with ethnically and socioeconomically diverse churches in every corner of race-torn America. It's a vision that our friend and fellow pastor Jarvis Williams has termed "redemptive kingdom diversity."[5]

Despite the wounds of the past few years, God has been at work among us, turning brokenness into wholeness. At the height of tensions in Louisville, we shepherded our people through a sermon series titled "The Gospel, Race, and Justice" that has had an impact far greater than what we expected. Messages from the series ended up reaching churches far beyond Louisville.[6] Years later, we still hear regularly from pastors who are using these messages to shape their churches' responses to racial injustice.

But this vision isn't merely our vision.

It's also God's vision.

Before time began, God planned to forge humanity into a multiplicity of ethnicities. He crafted Adam and Eve in such a way that their descendants would develop into a kaleidoscope of colors and cultures that would fill the cosmos with reflections of his glory (Genesis 1:28; Acts 17:26).[7] Long before that moment when our primal parents rebelled against him, God's design was to draw a diverse humanity back together in communities that would teem with different colors and cultures.[8] And so, in the shadow of the very tree where the teeth of the first humans tore the flesh of the forbidden fruit, God unveiled his plan to break the power of sin and to create a new kind of community (Genesis 3:15; 22:17; Galatians 3:16). In time, God the Father paved the way for this greater fellowship through the incarnation of his Son.[9] God the Son became the sacrifice for humanity's sin and flung open the door to a glorious love that makes it possible for a multitude of different ethnicities to live together in unity by the power of God the Spirit (1 Corinthians 1:22-24; Galatians 2:11-14; see also John 13:35; Romans 5:5; Galatians 3:13-14).[10] According to Paul, Christian communities that are rich in diversity reveal "the multifaceted wisdom of God" (Ephesians 3:10 NET). Another way of rendering this phrase from Paul's letter to the Ephesians is to say that diverse churches unveil God's "wisdom in its rich variety" (NLT). The term that's translated "rich variety" and "multifaceted" suggests, in the words of one biblical scholar, "'the intricate beauty of an embroidered pattern' . . . or the endless variety of colors in flowers."[11]

Pause and consider the implications of these words for a moment.

According to the apostle Paul, a richly varied church that's united in Christ reflects the richly varied wisdom of our God. To cultivate multiethnic, multigenerational, and multi-socioeconomic cultures in our churches is to declare to the world the riches of God's wisdom in Christ. In the words of D. A. Horton, "diversity was God's idea. He has the patent on it and has licensed his church to do marketing for it."[12]

It's not surprising then that when the apostle John describes the heavenly people of God surrounding the throne of God, he depicts ethnic and cultural diversity. This community is so beautiful that it causes heaven itself to erupt with praise for the wisdom of the one who designed it all. Listen to these words from our brother John:

> There was a vast multitude from every nation, tribe, people, and language, which no one could number. . . . And they cried out in a loud voice: "Salvation belongs to our God, who is seated on the throne, and

to the Lamb!" All the angels stood around the throne, and along with the elders and the four living creatures they fell facedown before the throne and worshiped God, saying, "Amen! Blessing and glory and wisdom and thanksgiving and honor and power and strength be to our God forever and ever." (Revelation 7:9-12)

Perhaps what is most striking about this vision is how God's people *aren't* described in this text.

John could have highlighted their social statuses or their economic standing or their human families—but he didn't. Instead, the Spirit of God led the man of God to spotlight the ethnic and cultural diversity of the people of God.

According to Jesus, marriage and childbearing will not persist into eternity (Matthew 22:30; Mark 12:25; Luke 20:34-36). Our socioeconomic statuses certainly won't last past the coming of God's kingdom. And yet, our ethnic and cultural identities apparently will. That's significant when it comes to how we think about ethnic diversity. As New Testament scholar Esau McCaulley points out, even at the end of time,

> the very diversity of cultures is a manifestation of God's glory. God's eschatological vision for the reconciliation of all things in his Son requires my blackness and my neighbor's Latina identity to endure forever. . . . The vision of the kingdom is incomplete without black and brown persons worshiping alongside white persons as part of one kingdom.[13]

Simply put: You don't need to check your ethnicity at the door of God's kingdom. Your ethnicity and your culture are part of God's plan for his praise.[14]

But what relevance does this have for churches here and now? Sure, John's vision describes a gloriously diverse *future* for God's people. But there's no reason to think that God meant churches to grow in ethnic diversity in the *present*, right?

It all depends on what you think it means to pray, "Your will be done on earth as it is in heaven."

We understand this prayer as a plea for God's revealed will to be practiced on earth no less than it is in the heavens. And so, if it is God's will for "a vast multitude from every nation, tribe, people, and language" (Revelation 7:9) to gather together in the heavens, whenever we ask God's will to be done "on earth as it is in heaven" (Matthew 6:10), part of what we're praying for—even if we don't recognize it—is kingdom diversity here and now.

Of course, the diversity in John's vision will never be completely realized in this life, just like our own holiness won't be completed until God glorifies us at the end of time. Still, that doesn't mean we shouldn't strive for both diversity and holiness now. Just as the promise of perfect holiness in the future compels us to pursue holiness in the present (1 Peter 1:3-15; 2 Peter 3:11-14), the certainty of John's heavenly vision in the future should drive us to strive for a life like heaven here and now.[15]

So is ethnic diversity in the church a future hope? Or is it a present calling? Yes.

IS THIS BOOK FOR ME?

The primary focus of *In Church as It Is in Heaven* is the divide between Black and White believers in the United States of America. That's not because this rupture is somehow more important than other divisions in other locations around the world—it isn't. It's because this split is the starkest one in our social context. At the same time, nearly every concept in this book can be adapted for other circumstances. So don't stop reading just because our context is different from yours! Instead, rework the contents to fit your context.

For some of you, ethnic diversity could look like a church that brings together persons of European descent with Indigenous Australians or Native Americans. For others, it may take the shape of a historic African American church making space for Latino families that are moving into the neighborhood. Still others might find themselves helping a second-generation Korean congregation grow to welcome Anglo neighbors.

But what if you happen to live in a location where there is little or no ethnic diversity? What should you do if everyone within an hour's drive of your address looks like you? If that describes your context, you can still take steps toward multiethnic, multigenerational, and multi-socioeconomic diversity. It could be that, right now, what this looks like for you is simply developing a deeper understanding of differing colors, cultures, and socioeconomic situations that will guide you to greater compassion and understanding. Regardless of your context, you can at least pursue what's possible in your context and seek the opportunities that God provides to do more—and don't underestimate the power of educating the next generation. It may be that your role is to bring up sons and daughters, nieces and nephews, so that they become lifelong seekers of justice who live with compassionate hospitality toward every ethnicity.

And what if you're a Black or Brown brother or sister who's been hurt due to racism, prejudices, and blind spots in the church? One of our goals has been to fill this book with healing and hope for you as well. Our prayer is that by the time you finish *In Church as It Is in Heaven,* you will have grown in your capacity to set Christ-honoring boundaries, to live in the power of God's forgiving grace, and to be confident in the path that God has placed before you.

WHO'S THE STAR?

One last reminder: Sojourn Church Midtown is not the star of this story, and neither are we.

We can't help but talk about the community where God has called us to serve because we love what God is doing here. But please don't focus on Sojourn as you hear these stories. You can visit our church on any Sunday and see clearly that we are on this journey with you and that we still have a long way to go.

The Holy Spirit is the star in this story, not us. He is the person who has brought us this far, and he is the only power who can move us beyond where we are.

It is the triune God who makes possible what seems impossible and who is, even now, opening doors that we cannot yet see. Apart from his power and grace, the entire fabric of our progress in the direction of a life like heaven would unravel in an instant. So don't focus on what God has done at Sojourn Church Midtown. Instead, meditate on what the Spirit of God might do in the place where you are, because he is able to do far more than you could ever ask or think.

Now, if you're ready to join us on this journey, our first stop is a highway in South Carolina.

PART 1

CALL TO WORSHIP

Learning to Love Multiethnic Kingdom Culture

The problem is not that we don't know what's right. The problem is that we don't love what's best.

	What's the problem?	What's the liturgy?	What's the result?
Call to Worship	We don't love God's vision for kingdom diversity.	We practice a liturgy of love that prays for ethnicities and classes of people who aren't present in our church.	We develop a multiethnic kingdom culture that forms us into worshipers who praise our Creator God for the beauty of kingdom diversity.

1

THE EVIDENCE THAT OUR WORLD HAS YET TO SEE

"Ma'am, are you okay? Are you being held against your will?"

Wait. What did that police officer just ask my wife?

I (Jamaal) didn't hear my wife's answer. That's because I was standing behind our Chevrolet Malibu in the January cold. I'd been ordered to be silent and to face the trunk while another officer frowned with suspicion as he examined my driver's license.

Moments before, my wife and I had been cruising across South Carolina with joyous hearts. She was pregnant with our first child, and we were heading east to celebrate a friend's wedding.

Then, seemingly out of nowhere, a patrol car swerved around and pulled alongside us, siren screaming. For a moment, it looked as if the cruiser was preparing to ram us from the left side. I glanced down at the speedometer, heart palpitating.

The police vehicle forced our car onto the shoulder and screeched to a halt behind us. Two White officers stepped out. I had no idea what was going on. Maybe I had slipped a few miles over the speed limit at some point—but why was this happening so aggressively?

Just get over it. Calm down, I told myself. *Maybe you were tired and you swerved without knowing it.*

I lowered my window, palms sweating, rehearsing to myself the instructions I'd heard from my parents since I was nine years old: *Be respectful no matter the circumstance. Keep your hands on the steering wheel, obey, and move calmly.*

The first police officer barked orders through my window. "Grab your license and step out of the car." Then he told me to go to the back and to stand facing the trunk.

"Sir," I asked, "is there anything I did wrong?"

He raised a hand, signaling me to be quiet. He looked up from my Kentucky driver's license. "Why are you even in South Carolina?" he asked. "Where are you headed anyway?"

That was when the second officer asked my wife if she was being held against her will. A few tense moments later, the first officer shoved my wallet into my hand and told me we were free to go. The men returned to their vehicle and reentered the highway with tires squealing.

They never told me why I'd been stopped.

I slid back into my car and sat still for several moments, trying to process what had taken place. As an African American man, it was virtually impossible not to recognize that my ethnicity had played a part in this encounter. This wasn't the first time I'd faced situations with law enforcement that were unexplainable apart from the presence of some form of racism. Study after study has demonstrated that African Americans are pulled over at rates disproportionate both to their numbers on the road and to any propensity to violate traffic laws.[1] And yet, I was too shocked to be enraged, and I had neither time nor space to react. I had a wife and an unborn child to protect and a destination to reach.

WHAT HAPPENED WHEN I TOLD MY STORY

Six years later, I was preaching my second sermon as a new lead pastor at Sojourn Church Midtown in Louisville. A little more than fifteen hundred people gathered each week in buildings strung along the edge of a neighborhood known as Shelby Park. The neighborhood is about half African American and 44 percent White, with a handful of Asian immigrants and Latino families mingled among their White and Black neighbors.

The church was working through the book of Proverbs, and the focus of that week's message was what Proverbs has to say about justice. One of the points I wanted to make was that the pursuit of justice requires compassion and humility toward persons with different life experiences.[2] Specifically, I wanted our majority-White congregation to become sensitive to the challenges faced by their African American sisters and brothers. Understanding these challenges is crucial because every person is created in God's image and we are called to bear one another's burdens.

This awareness was, however, particularly critical in our context at the time. The congregation was still overwhelmingly White, not only in its demographics but also in its culture. I was concerned that if I didn't help our people to cultivate compassion and understanding toward their Black neighbors, we might end up building a church "on top of" the Shelby Park neighborhood instead of growing a church family that reflected and rejoiced in the diversity of its community.

And so when I preached that second sermon at Sojourn Church Midtown, I told the story of my unexpected encounter with the police in South Carolina. Before and after telling what happened, I repeatedly emphasized my gratitude for the vast numbers of honorable law-enforcement officers who work daily for justice, risking their lives to protect others. I assumed the story had landed exactly how I intended; I quickly discovered I was wrong.

In the days that followed, angry emails flooded the church's inbox. Some came from current and retired police officers. A few of them suggested that my disrespect for the police had caused them to reevaluate whether they could stay at Sojourn, sentiments that still haunt me today because of the deep appreciation and respect I have for law-enforcement officers. It wasn't as if I hadn't faced criticism as a pastor before. I had led a historic African American congregation in our city for eight years before I became a lead pastor at Sojourn. At the same time, it was shocking to see members of our church rise in anger simply because I told this story from my own experience. But that was only the beginning.

The next few years turned into a painful crash course for me, my family, and Sojourn Church Midtown. Over and over, issues of race and multiethnic ministry stood at the forefront in these conflicts. Sure, I expected challenges when I became the lead pastor of an overwhelmingly White church in such a diverse neighborhood. But I never anticipated the full depth of these tensions.

On top of everything else, recent years have been marked by political and racial unrest of a sort that our nation hasn't seen since the 1990s.[3]

Some of the most painful unrest took place in our own city in the aftermath of the killing of Breonna Taylor. And yet, working through this difficult time with godly pastors at Sojourn Church Midtown has been an unimaginable blessing. Through these hardships, we've seen over and over that God has placed us in this place at this time for a purpose, just like he's placed you where you are for a purpose too.

Even in these hardships, here's what I see happening right now in churches across the United States where members have refused to be taken captive by the radicalized political rhetoric that has infected our nation: through the power of the gospel, God is opening doors for his people to live lives that are rich in diversity—here in Louisville, on the streets of Chicago and Tulsa and Oakland, from the rural countrysides of Missouri to the coal mines of eastern Kentucky, and thousands of places in between. If this sort of redemptive kingdom culture truly begins to take shape "on earth as it is in heaven," the structures where we gather will begin to look far more like God's eternal vision, teeming with a diversity of generations, colors, cultures, and economic backgrounds. And that's why our prayer is that you will learn to love God's design for a multiethnic and multi-socioeconomic church wherever you are.

HOW MULTIETHNIC KINGDOM CULTURE
PROVIDES A DEFENSE OF THE FAITH

This journey matters deeply to us because of what we believe about the church's witness to the watching world—and that's the primary focus of this book. This is a book about diversity, but it's more than that. It's a work of Christian apologetics, the field of study that focuses on defending the truthfulness of the historic Christian faith.

But this is likely to be unlike any other apologetics book you've read. Most apologetics books harvest data from science or history or logic and then build a case for the rationality of Christian faith. Those types of texts are helpful—but that's not the approach we're taking here. The purpose of this book is to present a defense of God's truth built on the capacity of the gospel to create and cultivate diverse churches.

Our contention is that a diverse church provides a strong apologetic argument for the power of the gospel and the truthfulness of God's Word.

What you'll come to see throughout this book is that secular ideologies struggle to provide any satisfying reason why people from different ethnicities and socioeconomic backgrounds would choose to link their lives together in a community.

"The more mixed the congregation is, especially in 'class' and 'color,'" John R. W. Stott pointed out decades ago, "the greater its opportunity to demonstrate the power of Christ."[4] We think Stott was right. Multiethnic and multi-socioeconomic churches present the world with unique evidence for the truth of the gospel—and that's what makes this message different from so many others that you're likely to hear about diversity in the church. There is a glory glimpsed when God's people gather in all their diversity that's hidden when we remain apart.

HOW THE LIFE OF THE CHURCH
PROVIDES A DEFENSE OF THE FAITH

For Christians today, the idea of the church itself serving as an apologetic for God's truth may seem strange and new—but this is one of the earliest and the most venerable approaches to apologetics in the history of Christianity.[5] Less than a century after the last book of the New Testament was written, a Christian philosopher named Aristides of Athens identified the life of the church as one of the primary evidences for the truth of the gospel. His focus wasn't on the church's diversity; it was on the church's care for the parentless and the poor, but it's clear that Aristides believed the church's way of life functioned as a living apologetic for the gospel.

"Christians," Aristides wrote, "deliver the orphan from anyone who treats the orphan harshly. The Christian who possesses resources gives without boasting to the one who has none."[6] Such countercultural patterns of life couldn't be satisfactorily explained, according to Aristides, unless some divine reality was at work among the Christians: "This is a new type of people, and surely there is something divine mingled among them."[7]

Another second-century Christian named Justin explicitly highlighted how the breaking of barriers between ethnicities provided evidence for the truths that the church proclaimed. "We who once despised and destroyed each other and who refused to hold anything in common with people who were not of the same tribe, due to their differing customs, now live in common with them."[8]

And so, seeing the life of the church as a defense of the faith isn't anything new.[9] It's a return to a practice that's very old. That's one of the reasons why you'll see names from the early centuries of Christianity scattered throughout the pages of this book. We're convinced that the words of ancient Christians are far more relevant to our lives today than the proclamations of the latest political pundits. The practices of the church, both past and present, provide a living witness to the truth of the gospel. "Christian witness requires a community—a church in particular—in which truthful speech is made evident by the quality and character of their practices and life together."[10]

One of the ways that truthful speech can be made most evident in our churches today is by cultivating what we refer to as "multiethnic kingdom culture." What we mean when we talk about such a culture is a context where people develop a gospel-formed identity that simultaneously includes and transcends their ethnic identities. Knowing that whatever is true and beautiful and good in every culture will persist into eternity, multiethnic kingdom culture is able to celebrate a diversity of ethnicities in the same community while simultaneously seeing Christ himself as our supreme and central identity.[11] This pattern of forming a new identity that retains and redeems an individual's ethnic and cultural identity was characteristic of churches in the earliest decades of Christianity.[12] Multiethnic kingdom culture is one way of calling churches back to this pattern today.

When Spirit-empowered love cultivates multiethnic kingdom culture in a church today, the world around us glimpses evidence of God's truth it may never have seen before. Just as the church's care for the marginalized demonstrated the truth of the gospel in centuries past, churches marked by multiethnic kingdom culture today provide rich and renewed evidence of God's power to do what no human power can accomplish. When people outside the faith see a faithful multiethnic, multigenerational, and multi-socioeconomic church, they may still reject the gospel we profess, but they cannot reasonably deny the power of what we practice.

When a North African pastor named Augustine of Hippo considered the impact of the Christian way of life in the fourth century AD, he marveled,

"By their virtues and words, Christians have kindled the fires of divine love in the world."[13]

Through the power of the Spirit and the gospel, we still can.

WHY MULTIETHNIC KINGDOM CULTURE ISN'T OPTIONAL

When we pursue multiethnic kingdom culture, we are persisting in a work that Jesus himself began. Think about how God's work unfolds throughout the New Testament. When Jesus called his first followers, our Savior brought together a band of Jewish males, but he refused to allow this initial community of disciples to remain homogeneous. He led them into the presence of Syrophoenician and Samaritan women, and he expanded his circle to include both women and men (Matthew 27:55; Mark 7:24-26; 15:41; Luke 23:49; John 4:9, 27). Moments before he left the planet, Jesus commissioned his followers to teach every ethnicity to obey his words (Matthew 28:19-20; Acts 1:8). This mission produced leadership and local gatherings that practiced diverse fellowship (Acts 13:1; 20:4).[14]

Even in the first century, these patterns weren't perceived as optional. Once, when Peter and Barnabas backpedaled from their earlier embrace of multiethnic table fellowship, Paul declared that they were "deviating from the truth of the gospel" (Galatians 2:14; see also Acts 10:34).[15] God's Word makes it clear that believers are called to live here and now as a "fellowship of differents"—as a family in which barriers between us are broken because of what God the Father has accomplished through the broken body of his Son.[16] This will look different in every context, but any habits that prevent faithful kingdom diversity in a church signify a divergence from the implications of the gospel.[17]

STILL THE MOST SEGREGATED HOUR

Despite God's plan and our passion for kingdom diversity, the reality is that American churches have fallen far short when it comes to multiplying multiethnic congregations. With few exceptions, American Protestants view multiethnic churches as a desirable ideal, but their actual fellowships remain steadfastly monoethnic.[18]

Consider this: More than eight in ten pastors are convinced that churches should work toward greater ethnic diversity, and nearly

80 percent of church members agree. Well over half of these members claim they would feel comfortable worshiping alongside a multiplicity of ethnicities. And yet, people's actual practices reveal different priorities. Eighty-six percent of these same churchgoers attend churches that consist primarily of a single ethnicity.[19] Even though American Christians say they desire diversity, they consistently choose churches filled with members that look like themselves.[20] American churches are not merely segregated; they are—in the words of one sociologist—"hypersegregated."[21]

What's worse is that this gap can't be blamed on a lack of ethnic and racial diversity in neighborhoods and communities. Although American neighborhoods do tend to be separated along ethnic lines, churches in these communities are about ten times more segregated than the neighborhoods themselves.[22] In other words, even when communities are multiethnic, churches in those communities typically aren't.

The dream of diversity is alive and well. The reality is elusive at best.

Of course, not every neighborhood in North America includes sufficient ethnic diversity for every congregation in that community to be comprehensively multiethnic. If that's the type of context where God has placed you and your family, don't give up! In later chapters, we'll examine how congregations in contexts like yours can still pursue a diverse and redemptive kingdom culture. And yet, there are tens of thousands of churches throughout North America that—despite being in areas that are rich in ethnic and cultural diversity—look less like multiethnic outposts of God's kingdom and more like homogeneous country clubs.

In 1960, Martin Luther King Jr. appeared on *Meet the Press* and popularized a statement that civil rights activists had already been repeating for years: "Eleven o'clock on Sunday morning is one of the most segregated hours, if not the most segregated hour, in Christian America."[23] Decades later, these words still ring true. In fact, they may even be truer now due to political divisions that have worsened racial relations. And yet, if our proclamation of Jesus never forms communities of faith where racial and ethnic barriers are broken down, something is missing in the ways that we're teaching people to live out their faith in Jesus.

But the real problem isn't a gap in our knowledge. It's a gap in our love.

2

THE GAP IN OUR LOVE

A vast number of well-intended approaches to multiethnic ministry focus on increasing the knowledge that people possess about ethnicity and race. This isn't necessarily wrong—multiplying people's awareness of issues can be helpful, and that's part of what we'll do in this book.

But an increase in knowledge is not our primary goal, because a lack of knowledge is not the primary problem.[1]

Research has revealed that most pastors and churchgoers already know the right facts about the desirability of ethnic diversity. And yet, what we do as human beings is not determined solely by what we know. Our actions also arise from what we love.

Think about it: If correct facts and knowledge determined the course of our lives, we would always do what our minds know is best. Brussels sprouts and salad would rule our palates instead of ice cream and bourbon balls. Jogging or Bible reading or time with our families would eclipse the hours we squander scrolling through social media. And yet, every day, our choices demonstrate that *knowing more* about what's right doesn't always translate into *doing more* of what's right.

This chasm between what we know and what we do is not limited to the modern age. It's part of what Augustine of Hippo was getting at when he considered the difference between recognizing the truth and submitting to the truth. "It is one thing," Augustine admitted, "to see the land of peace from a mountain's wooded summit . . . and quite another to stay on the path that leads you there."[2] Often, the reason we don't stay on the path to what's best isn't because we don't know what's best. It's because we don't love what's best. And that's why Jesus doesn't stop with simply depositing new ideas into our minds.[3] Jesus doesn't want merely to inform our thinking. His goal is to transform our longings and our loves.

So what does this have to do with developing churches that are rich in kingdom diversity?

When it comes to developing multiethnic communities, none of us will ever make the sacrifices to remain on this path unless we love God's vision for eternity so much that we can't be satisfied unless we taste that communion here and now. But here's the problem: none of us naturally loves close fellowship with people who are different from us. This is especially true for people who have grown comfortable with social structures that position their color or culture as normative.

We know what's right, but we don't love what's best.

HOW OUR LITURGIES SHAPE OUR LOVES

If increased knowledge isn't enough to change what we love and long for, what is? How do we cultivate a yearning for remaking our lives? Specifically, how do we develop a love and a longing for multiethnic kingdom culture in our churches?

Sometimes, the Spirit of God miraculously provides his people with new longings in an instant—but not always, and not necessarily when or how we expect it. What happens far more frequently in a fallen world is that our habits transform our loves, our longings, and eventually our lives.

Another word for the habits that shape our loves is *liturgy*.[4]

A few of you may be confused by this term. After all, the word *liturgy* may never have crossed your mind when thinking about your daily routines. When you think of liturgy, you might think only about the ways that a church structures its worship services. And yet, *liturgy* means far more than the hymns and creeds and confessions and readings repeated week by week with your church family. The word *liturgy* can also describe the bodily practices at work throughout the week in your daily life.[5] Our loves develop, in part, in response to the routines that take shape through embodied practices.[6]

Sometimes, our lives are shaped by these routines in ways we never even think about. Even then—perhaps *especially* then—these liturgies are still at work, creating the longings that direct our lives. For example, if your first act every morning is to check how many comments and likes you received overnight on social media, you are training your soul to ache for the approval of others. This love will shape how you respond to people around you, even if you never recognize the reason why. If you obsessively check the news throughout the day, you could be feeding a delusion that you are more in control of what happens in your own life if you know everything about every global event as soon as it happens. If that's your liturgy, you're far more likely to become enraged whenever the events of your life don't conform to your expectations. If you see someone whose ethnicity is different from yours and immediately lock your car doors or watch them with a touch of suspicion, these actions don't merely reflect your inner disposition. Your habits are also shaping your loves in such a way that your hospitality becomes limited to people who look like you.[7]

But liturgies can work the other direction too. By God's grace, the liturgies of our lives can also turn our loves away from self-centered delusions and toward God's good design.[8] "Habits form virtues," theologian John Webster has pointed out, "and virtues are the content of character."[9] Routines of fasting can awaken a hunger within our souls for the satisfaction that Jesus alone can provide. Habitual generosity toward those who possess less than us deepens our dependence on God by loosening the stranglehold that a love of money can have. A particular prayer or catechism or confession of faith, recited slowly in moments of anxiety, can eventually redirect how we react to stressful situations.[10] Over time, the liturgies that we repeatedly embody reshape our lives by redirecting our longings and our loves.[11]

HOW LITURGIES CAN LEAD TO A LIFE LIKE HEAVEN

The most powerful liturgies are the ones we practice both individually and with others—and that's why liturgy matters so much when it comes to the formation of multiethnic churches. Diverse churches will never multiply across race-torn America until God's people learn to love God's multiethnic vision for his church. One way to embed this love in our churches is to develop liturgies of life that cultivate new longings and clear away the thorny brambles that choke out multiethnic kingdom culture in our lives.

To put it another way, multiethnic kingdom culture requires the development of different and deeper loves. And so, what you'll discover as you read this book are liturgies of life that can change the culture of your life by producing new longings and new loves.[12] We've arranged these liturgies to follow the outline of our weekly worship service, which reflects an order of worship stretching back in time to the Reformed churches of the sixteenth and seventeenth centuries.[13]

But be forewarned: These liturgies are not simplistic platitudes you can work into your life over the course of a weekend, and they aren't events you can do once and then move on. They are repeated patterns of life that can begin, over time, to break down barriers separating Christians of different colors and cultures. They are time-consuming, and some of them may even seem impossible. In fact, they're sufficiently difficult that we don't intend for you to incorporate all of them. Instead, here's what we hope you'll do: As we describe each habit or liturgy, prayerfully consider how God might be calling you to grow in this area. Then, choose one—just one—of the liturgies in that chapter, and let that habit become a starting point for the development of greater diversity in your life.

So, what do we expect the Spirit of God to do through these habits of life? As we've repeated liturgies like these over and over with the people of Sojourn Church Midtown, we've seen God draw us in the direction of a life like heaven. In the process, the Scriptures and the Spirit have revealed wounds of division in all their awful ugliness, and God has healed people's souls in ways that stand far beyond any human capacities. But please don't get the wrong idea about us or about our church—we are far from where we yearn to be. This book is not a declaration that we've reached a destination. It's an invitation for you to join us on a journey that's far from over. We are still working these liturgies into our own lives and into the lives of the people who gather with us each week. We are still learning what it means to live in a multiethnic kingdom culture. We will still be learning decades from now, and so will you.

HOW LITURGIES PROVIDE US WITH A BETTER PATH TO MULTIETHNIC DIVERSITY

When we recognize the gap is in our love, we see diversity itself should never be our ultimate goal. "We are ambassadors," Jasmine Holmes writes, "not of the amount of melanin in our skin, but of the good news of Christ's redeeming work."[14] Diversity is an *implication* and a *result* of gospel-driven love, not the goal itself.[15] The goal is faithfulness that embraces the unity God has already accomplished in Christ through the power of the gospel.

If we live under the delusion that diversity itself is the goal, we find ourselves worrying about the precise percentages of different ethnicities or socioeconomic classes in our church.[16] The goal of gospel faithfulness sets us free from that anxiety. When our goal is faithfulness, we stop asking, "How do we increase the number of minorities in our church?" or "How do we attract a greater percentage of people from lower-income neighborhoods?" The goal of faithfulness prepares us to ask better questions like, "Is there anything that might keep people from a particular ethnicity from finding a spiritual home in our church?" and "How can we love our neighbors by overcoming the barriers that centuries of separation have placed between us?"

Once we recognize that gospel faithfulness is the goal, we also see that not every approach to multiethnic ministry is equally helpful. There are defective and dangerous approaches to diversity, and part of our goal in this book is to help you to avoid these pitfalls.

One defective approach tries to solve spiritual issues based on un-Christian or even anti-Christian ideas. Sources from the world around us can—and do!—help us understand problems and unpack cultural issues. That's why we have drawn data from resources outside the Christian faith throughout this book, just as Christians have done throughout the ages. "Every good and true Christian should understand that wherever truth may be found, it belongs to his Lord," Augustine wrote in the fourth century. "Christians should learn and receive truth from pagan literature, even as they reject superstitious vanities. . . . We weren't wrong to learn the alphabet just because the pagans said Mercury invented it, nor should we avoid justice and virtue just because pagans have dedicated temples to justice and virtue." Neither should we avoid seeking truth in secular sources today simply because those sources originated in the context of defective worldviews. At the same time, such sources can never provide wholly adequate solutions when it comes to creating diverse, Christ-centered communities. "Whatever is written in Scripture," Augustine also reminds us, "is better and truer than anything we could devise by our own wisdom."[17] Only the Word of God and the Spirit of God are sufficient to provide the people of God with lasting solutions as we make our way toward multiethnic kingdom culture.

Another wrong approach is to pursue a shallow diversity that expects minority cultures to conform to a majority culture. Churches have sometimes been spaces where minority Christians are expected to assimilate into the culture of the majority or have found themselves treated like furniture meant to be seen but never taken seriously. Preachers and scholars alike have warned against these false veneers of diversity.[18] In churches where minorities are expected to conform to a majority culture, the congregation may include more than one color of skin. And yet, such churches—unlike the heavenly multitude described in God's revelation to John—are never truly able to celebrate a diversity of ethnicities because one single human culture reigns supreme. This sort of surface-level diversity is not what we're advocating because it's not what the elders in the book of Revelation were celebrating (Revelation 5:8-9). Deep diversity is beautiful, but it takes time because deep diversity challenges people's assumptions about themselves and their cultures.

HOW GOD GREW OUR CHURCH'S LOVE FOR MULTIETHNIC DIVERSITY

A year or so after I (Jamaal) shared the story about my encounter with the police in South Carolina, it seemed that our congregation was finally beginning to connect with me as their pastor. The church was multiplying in ethnic and cultural diversity like never before. At the same time, some members began growing dissatisfied as the music expanded to include different genres and their preferences no longer dominated our planning for worship. During these struggles, the Spirit of God led us to plan a Sunday that would give our members a glimpse of who we'd become and what we could be in the future.

"Diversity Sunday" overflowed with songs, Scripture readings, and testimonies representing a multitude of different languages and cultures, providing the people with a tiny taste of what worship might look like in God's heavenly kingdom. The result was a Sunday brimming with celebrations of the many backgrounds and ethnicities that God had already placed within our church.

Before the benediction at the end of the service, I invited everyone to close their eyes and to imagine the future with me:

Suppose you pull into the parking lot on Sunday at some point in the future. A few years have passed, and we all look a little older. Imagine the scene as you step out of your vehicle and walk toward the doors.

As you enter the gallery, you're welcomed by a Nigerian brother and a Korean sister. You make your way into a sanctuary where you're surrounded by people from very different social classes and economic circumstances. A Latino worship director is welcoming everyone as you slip into your seat. To your right, there's a single mom with two children lifting her hands in worship. In front of you, there's a homeschooling family of six. Beside you, there's a group of college students; across the aisle, a Pakistani couple and a young African American man named Jay who has a 1990s flat high-top fade, all of them singing with all their might.

Onstage, you see some people who are clean-cut and others who are tattooed out, some who are fashion forward and others who are fashion clueless. Everyone is worshiping as one. You're overcome with emotion, and all you can think is, *Jesus is beautiful, and so is his multiethnic, multi-socioeconomic, multigenerational bride.*

And then you wonder, *When did this happen? How did my church become so transcultural and diverse?*

I then asked everyone to open their eyes and spoke these words of blessing as I looked out and saw the faces of people who had grown more and more precious to me over the past year:

"After this I looked, and there was a vast multitude from every nation, tribe, people, and language, which no one could number, standing before the throne and before the Lamb."

Now, Christians, go into the world, longing for God's kingdom to come and God's will to be done on earth as it is in heaven, in the name of the Father and the Son and the Holy Spirit.

Peace be with you.

In those moments, the Holy Spirit unexpectedly went to work in the lives of his people in ways that were far beyond my power. When the worship service ended, a husband and wife approached me and said, "Brother, we were seriously contemplating leaving because of all the changes over the past year. We just couldn't see where the church was heading or why this is so important. But after imagining what the future might look like, we need to apologize. We're here, and we want to work toward this vision—but we also know that we'll need to grow and sacrifice along the way." They weren't the only ones.

One after another, throughout the week, others shared with us how monumental that service had been for them. This was not the finish line of our movement toward a multiethnic kingdom culture—far from it! That weekend was merely the beginning. It was a crucial moment when many of the members in our congregation finally caught the vision that we had spent years struggling to show them.

In the years since we've been swept up by the Spirit into this ministry of ethnic reconciliation, we've seen testimony after testimony pointing to God's power to produce a kingdom-shaped culture.[19] We've seen White Christians grow in their cultural awareness and repent as they became aware of present biases and past actions that had wounded others. We've watched as Black and Brown believers confessed inner bitterness and recognized how their own wounds had sometimes led them to live with suspicion toward brothers and sisters who sincerely love them.

But these breakthroughs didn't happen merely because people learned more or tried harder. They happened because people pursued habits of life together that narrowed the gaps in what they love. The Spirit of God worked through the liturgies of life we were practicing together, and the people fell in love with a vision for the future that most of them had never seen before. These habits oriented people toward the gospel and enabled them to be honest with themselves and others because God's grace in Christ left them with nothing to lose and nothing to prove.

3

LITURGIES OF LOVE
AND LONGING

Each Sunday, worship services at Sojourn Church Midtown follow a sequence that begins with a call to worship. The purpose of a call to worship is to recapture our imaginations and reorient our desires by reminding us of the beauty of God's character and his ways—and that's precisely what we've tried to do in these opening chapters.

A call to worship may seem like a strange way to set out on a journey toward multiethnic kingdom culture. And yet, anything we do that moves us toward gospel-shaped community is merely a response to what God is already doing. As Mike Cosper points out, "God is the great initiator. He made the world, he made us, and he is remaking us in Jesus. Our gatherings, our songs, our sermons, our fellowship around the table—all of it is a response to his initiation and invitation."[1]

A diverse and faithful congregation is a living response to God's gracious remaking of his world through the gospel—and that's why a call to worship is the best place for us to begin. You will never move toward a life of kingdom diversity until the beauty of this Spirit-initiated reality captures your imagination.

PAY ATTENTION TO WHERE YOU ARE

Throughout the next month, develop a habit—a personal liturgy—that cultivates a love and a longing for kingdom diversity in the place where you are.

Start by paying closer attention to the people you see in your city or community. Each day in the upcoming month, consider what colors or cultures are *not* present among the members of your church. You may see someone at the grocery store whose ethnicity isn't represented in your church. Or you might see someone on the street who belongs to a socioeconomic group that isn't part of your community of faith. Consider carefully why certain colors, cultures, or classes aren't present in your church while others are. Before the end of each day, jot down who isn't represented in your church.

PRAY FOR WHAT COULD BE

Now, here's your daily liturgy to cultivate new longings and loves:

1. Each evening for a month, look at your list of people who aren't represented in your church. As you add new entries, pray for people in the groups you're listing. Pray that members of your church would be faithful and eager to receive the groups you listed.

2. Imagine what your weekly worship would look like if people from this group became part of your church. Or imagine what your life might look like if you became part of a church where Christians from that class or ethnicity were the majority.

3. Praise God as you consider his power to accomplish this.

As you pray through this growing list, there will be times when you think, *That person would never even want to be part of my church*—and you might be right. If so, what does that tell you about your congregation?

You may even find yourself hoping a particular type of person never shows up in your church. Perhaps, when you consider what it would look like for you to join a church where your own color or culture is the minority, the possibility seems so uncomfortable that you can't handle it. When such thoughts arise—and they will!—pay attention to your struggles to envision possibilities that stand beyond your natural expectations. Persist in your habit of praising God and praying for these people until you sincerely long to praise God alongside them in the same congregation. Someday, God will bring all ethnicities together. Let your confidence in God's capacity to do this awaken your soul to worship him now.

HOW MULTIETHNIC KINGDOM CULTURE
DEFENDS THE TRUTH OF THE GOSPEL

One pattern that people noticed about ancient Christian communities was how they embraced an astonishing range of marginalized people.

According to one fourth-century Christian, early churches enfolded persons from "each sex, and every kind and age" together into the same communities of discipleship.[2] We're convinced that God can still grow churches in multiethnic, multigenerational, and multi-socioeconomic diversity today. In the words of civil rights leader John M. Perkins, "There is no institution on earth more equipped and capable of bringing transformation to the cause of reconciliation than the church."[3]

But remember: Christians aren't the only ones who long to bridge the divisions that separate humanity along racial lines. There are people who have never glimpsed the glories of Christ who want it too.

What if these individuals looked at our churches and glimpsed the diverse community their hearts yearn to see? "People need to see," Dallas Willard once pointed out, "individuals living in daily interaction with the kingdom of the heavens."[4] One of the ways the world can glimpse the kingdom of heaven among us is by seeing a type of diversity in the church that their own theories and categories can't explain.

That's when some of them might begin to ask, "How is this happening? What tools are you using? And what on earth do all these different people have in common?" If human beings are nothing more than an accidental result of the survival of the fittest, voluntarily linking our lives with people who aren't like us is inexplicable, especially if doing so could result in losing some of our own social power or safety. From the perspective of naturalistic evolution, what contributes best and most to human survival is "to favor kith and kin, do down our enemies, ignore the starving, and let the weakest go to the wall."[5] A diverse church practices precisely the opposite way of life. Communities marked by multiethnic kingdom culture strengthen the oppressed, turn strangers into friends, and choose a church family over physical kinship.

Such diversity can only happen in its fullness through God's work in Christ. And that's why, when the world sees a multiethnic kingdom culture in the church, we can begin gently tilling ground that God has already prepared to bear fruit, helping these secular wonderers to see how the liturgies that have transformed our loves require a gospel that reconciles our lives. Our primary tools are the riches of the Christian faith throughout the ages, and the gospel is what we hold in common, through which God has flooded our lives with a hope greater than any hope this world can possibly possess. "The gospel," in the words of Carl F. H. Henry,

> resounds with good news for the needy and oppressed. It conveys assurance that injustice, repression, exploitation, discrimination, and poverty are dated and doomed, that no one is forced to accept the crush of evil powers as finally determinative for his existence.[6]

Our confidence that God will someday end every ethnic division doesn't mean that Christians should simply wait for God to act at the end of time. The very fact that God will act in the future provides us with the confidence we need to challenge every evil power even now. When that happens in a church, kingdom culture takes shape and provides a living defense of the power of God at work among his people.

A CORPORATE CALL TO WORSHIP

Blessed are the ones who will eat at the feast
in the kingdom of God.
Blessed are the blind, they will finally see
in the kingdom of God.
Blessed are the poor, oppressed, and abused.
Blessed are the weak, distressed, and accused.
When you strike up the band,
Your house will be full, the walls will shake
With laughter and dance and praise
Every sibling of all time and place.
Your house will be full with praise to the King.
Let all the redeemed come sing
Every promise fulfilled as we wonder aloud.
The stones can stay silent, the people will shout.
Blessed are the ones who will eat at the feast
in the kingdom of God.
Blessed are the prisoners, they will be free
in the kingdom of God.
Blessed are the broken, frightened, ashamed.
Blessed are the slaves—you will shatter their chains.

When you say, "Come and dine,"
Your house will be full, the walls will shake
With laughter and dance and praise.
Every sibling of all time and place
Your house will be full with praise to the King
Let all the redeemed come sing.
Every child who was ever without,
Every dialect joining the shout,
Every promise fulfilled as we wonder aloud.
The stones can stay silent, the people will shout.[7]

PART 2

LAMENT

Grieving What Stands in the Way of Multiethnic Kingdom Culture

We will never long for a life like heaven until we lament the lies from hell that have kept us apart.[1]

	What's the problem?	What's the liturgy?	What's the result?
Call to Worship	We don't love God's vision for kingdom diversity.	We practice a liturgy of love that prays for ethnicities and classes of people who aren't present in our church.	We develop a multiethnic kingdom culture that forms us into worshipers who praise our Creator God for the beauty of kingdom diversity.
Lament	We don't recognize how deeply the heresy of racial superiority has impacted our churches and our lives.	We face the reality and the continuing impact of the heresy of racial superiority, and we lament the ways it has wounded us.	We are formed into mourners who grieve the continuing impact of the heresy of racial superiority.

4

LAMENTING THE WOUND

"Diversity equals white genocide."[1]

That was one of many slogans scrawled on signs in Charlottesville, Virginia, in 2017 when hundreds of alt-right activists converged to protest the removal of a statue constructed to commemorate the Confederacy. The statue had been erected in 1924, at the midpoint of a decade in which the popularity of the Ku Klux Klan peaked and White mobs lynched more than two hundred African Americans.[2]

Before the alt-right rally was over, a White supremacist had rammed his Dodge Charger into a cluster of counter protesters, murdering thirty-two-year-old Heather Heyer and leaving five other counter protesters in critical condition.

The next morning, I (Timothy) stepped behind the pulpit to preach in the first service of the day at Sojourn Church Midtown. A few months had passed since our church's inaugural Diversity Sunday, and the congregation was moving steadily toward becoming a more multiethnic family. I intended to begin the message with a prayer that acknowledged our people's pain by pleading for an end to ethnic division and racial hatred.

And yet, as I took in the faces in front of me, I found that I couldn't speak at all.

I looked into the eyes of people scattered throughout the congregation whose ethnic heritage stretches back to the shores of Africa. I saw people with whom I have shared meals and movies, prayers and tears. One of them was my own daughter, the tight coils of her hair braided and beaded and glistening in the morning sunlight. These are people for whom I would readily risk everything I have and everything I am. And yet those who held the signs in Charlottesville saw such mingling of Black and White as a threat.

"Diversity equals white genocide."

This is a sentiment that grows out of a lust for dominance entangled with deep fear. Diversity only seems like a threat, after all, if your ethnicity gives you a sense of supremacy so central to your identity that you're terrified to let it go.

In that first service, I stood there, so choked by emotion that I was unable to speak the prayer I had planned. The only words that slipped past my lips were, "How did it come to this?" It wasn't that I lacked knowledge of the historical events that brought us to this moment—but some sorrows run deeper than data. What I sensed in that moment was the ache that throbs within us when someone we love is in pain and we are powerless to relieve them of it. It was a yearning for a more righteous world entwined with a deep awareness of how difficult the journey to justice will be.

What I felt was lament. But it wasn't merely the pain of this single event that weighed on me—it was the pain of my own story as well.

I know how easy it is to give in to the fears that breed such prejudice. The first time I can recall personally encountering an African American family, I ran the other way.

I was three years old.

THE STAIN THAT WAS NEVER THERE

It happened beside a row of carts in the aisle of a dry goods store. I (Timothy) was waiting for someone to lift me into a cart when an unfamiliar family stepped into the store, unlike any household I had ever glimpsed in this rural region of Missouri.

As the family passed through the doors, a toddler in a ruffled dress dashed past her parents' grasp and headed in my direction. I had never been so close to anyone whose color was so different from mine. And so, faced with a toddler running toward me, I did the only thing that made sense to me in that moment.

I ran.

But the girl had a head start, and running was never my strength, even as a three-year-old. Before the mother could sweep the giggling runaway into her arms, the child's tiny hand grasped my elbow.

In the days that followed, I suspect the toddler's parents enjoyed some well-deserved laughs at the memory of me tearing down the aisle in unrestrained terror. And yet, what I remember most vividly about this incident was what happened afterward.

Once I was situated in the seat of my family's cart, I turned over my arm and strained for several seconds to see the spot where the child had touched me. I wanted to know whether the hue of her flesh had left a mark on mine.

At three years old, I had somehow absorbed a sense that blackness was a cause for concern.[3]

That moment has crossed my mind more than once over the past decade, in the times when I embrace my youngest daughter's chestnut skin. I cannot escape the lump in my throat when I recall how a younger version of me somehow feared being stained by a reality in which I now see nothing but beauty.

But where does a child pick up such misconceptions? Had the images on news broadcasts that I glimpsed while playing on the floor in front of the television already skewed my view of darker hues of flesh? Had I picked up conversations even then that spoke of "the Blacks" as a social problem? Had I noticed that certain epithets for African Americans were used in some social situations but not in others?

I don't know.

What I do know is that less than a half decade after I arrived on this planet, what I felt in proximity to a different color of flesh was not awe at God's creativity but fear at the possibility of being stained.

Whenever I recall that turning of my elbow as a three-year-old, I am left with the same question that passed through my lips as I stood before my church in the aftermath of a rally that equated ethnic diversity with genocide: *How did it come to this?*

THE WOUND THAT REALLY WAS THERE

There was no stain on my skin that day, but there was a wound that ran deeper than any human eye can see. It was, in the words of my fellow Kentuckian Wendell Berry, "a historical wound, prepared centuries ago to come alive in me at my birth like a hereditary disease, and to be augmented and deepened by my life."[4] This wound began in the past, but certain defects from the past have a pernicious tendency to seep into the present. Such wounds remind us, as William Faulkner famously pointed out, that "the past is never dead. It's not even past."[5]

The lack of ethnic diversity in American churches is simply one visible sign of the living traces of racism in American culture.[6] But even here, there is hope because these wounds can never speak the final word in the lives of those who follow a Savior who will heal every wound and wash every blemish away (1 Peter 2:24; Jude 24).[7] It is, in fact, precisely at this point that the Word of God supplies the people of God with a better response than the world around us can ever provide.

That better way begins with lament.

WHY I NEED LAMENT—AND SO DO YOU

Each week at Sojourn Church Midtown, we set aside a few moments for confession and lament. These moments may seem meaningless to some, but this space has provided some of the most meaningful times of worship I've experienced over the years. There have been so many times when these precious pauses were precisely what I (Timothy) needed. I remember aching for this space to grieve when our oldest daughter spent weeks on a ventilator with virtually no chance of survival. When another of our children experienced a severe concussion and spiraled downward into months of mental-health struggles and suicidal ideation, I needed these dedicated moments to cry out to God. In each of these instances and so many more when I have found myself clawing at the walls of a pit of pain, my soul has yearned for these spaces in the service to cry out to God.

I need lament and, even if you don't know it, so do you.

Lament is "the honest cry of a hurting heart wrestling with the paradox of pain and the promise of God's goodness."[8] It's a prayer spoken in pain that leads to trust. Much like the spirituals that African captives sang in the American South, biblical laments are "tones, loud, long and deep, breathing the prayer and complaint of souls boiling over with the bitterest anguish."[9] Lament floods the pages of Scripture. The practice of lament is so crucial that if one part of the church is grieving, the rest of the church is called to enter that pain (Romans 12:15).[10] "The Bible exhorts us to weep with those who weep," H. B. Charles has pointed out. "It doesn't tell us to judge whether they should be weeping."[11]

Sometimes, it's the weight of our own sin that drives us to anguish (2 Corinthians 7:9-10), but personal sin isn't the only reason for believers to lament.[12] Jesus was sinless, yet his own sorrows and the pain of those who rejected him drew lament from his lips more than once (Matthew 23:37-39; 27:46; Mark 15:34). When the prophet Daniel surveyed his people's history, he lamented not only his own sins but also the sins of his ancestors (Daniel 9:8). More than one-third of the Psalms are laments, and these songs grieved not only sin but also injustice, suffering, and despair (Psalm 13:1-2; 94:3-7).

Despite the prominence of lament in Scripture, "this intense—almost violent—embodied form of prayer . . . is not practiced today with the intensity that the Psalms seem to convey."[13] Lamenting together is hard because, in the words of our friend John Onwuchekwa, it means "inhaling the secondhand smoke of each other's hard times."[14] And yet, we need lament in the church today no less than the saints of the Old and New Testaments did.

Lament is for the wife and husband who weep as they wander through empty bedrooms, longing for children who never arrive.

Lament is for those who struggle daily through the shadowlands of depression.

Lament is for those whose hearts are broken by more than sixty million preborn victims of legal abortions and by the circumstances of mothers-to-be who see this systemic evil as their only option.[15]

And lament is for all of us who grieve the ways that wounds of racial prejudice have torn the body of Christ into congregations separated by ethnicity.

Until Christians learn to lament these lacerations in the body of Christ, we're unlikely to make any meaningful movement in the direction of a life like heaven. And that brings us back to the question I whispered that morning as I stood before these people I love: *How did it come to this?*

Lament calls us to seek an answer to that question.

Here's why: You are unlikely to weep with the sister who weeps unless you're willing to hear the experiences that brought her to tears in the first place. You won't bear your brother's burden well if you refuse to take the time to listen to the story behind it. And your church will not make any meaningful movement toward a life like heaven unless you face the reality of how we have been scarred by this separation in the first place. In some sense, if you haven't learned to lament, you haven't learned to love.[16]

Ethnic separation has become a habit in our churches and in our lives. Lament helps us uproot this habit—but we can't remove what we don't recognize, and we can't lament a story we've never heard.

HOW DID IT COME TO THIS?

When we look at the New Testament, we glimpse multiethnic and multi-socioeconomic gatherings that were unprecedented in their social contexts. The Word of God and the Spirit of God provided the people of God with everything they needed not only to celebrate a wide array of cultures but also to elevate a multiplicity of ethnicities to positions of leadership—and that's precisely what they did. Peter and John followed the example of Jesus and bridged the divide that separated Samaritans from persons of Jewish descent (Acts 8:25).[17] The church in Antioch unified Jewish believers with Gentiles from an array of different contexts and cultures (Acts 11:19-20). Later in the book of Acts, we discover that one of the leaders of the church in Antioch was "Simeon . . . called Niger," a nickname that unmistakably described a man whose flesh and features were African (Acts 13:1). Simeon served alongside Lucius of Cyrene, an immigrant from the region in Africa known today as Libya. Over the space of a few decades, these churches multiplied into an empire-wide network of close-knit communities that resisted rankings rooted in ethnic origins or socioeconomic status. And this multiplication in kingdom diversity persisted long past the final chapter of the book of Acts.

This isn't to suggest, of course, that early Christians never erred in the ways that they engaged with social and cultural differences. Even in the first century, Christians struggled at times to welcome every social class (1 Corinthians 12:14-26; James 2:1–5:6). Anti-Jewish sentiments arose very early in the history of Christianity with ghastly consequences in the centuries that followed.[18] Nevertheless, by the end of the second century, even those outside the churches noticed the astonishing cultural and socioeconomic diversity of early Christian communities. Pagan philoso-phers and humorists mocked Christians because of the ways churches treated members from every rank of society as equals.[19] In this context, it didn't take long before church leaders began to rethink long-standing social structures. Church leaders like Augustine of Hippo argued that no human being can be a slave by nature.[20] Fourth-century pastor Gregory of Nyssa went even further, condemning the institution of slavery itself.[21] Gregory's perspective was exceptional in his own day, but it does show how one Christian worked out the implications of Scripture in his context.

So what happened? How is it that later generations of professing Christians began to see an entire cluster of ethnicities as inferior and able to be owned as property? What enabled them to justify acts that now horrify us? How was God's truth distorted to sustain the lie that one ethnicity can be inferior to another?

In other words, how did it come to this?

Thousands of books and articles have already recounted the bare historical facts of this story. And so, our plan for the next chapter is to pick our way along a slightly different path, focusing on a series of snapshots highlighting specific theological structures that framed this story. Doing history with integrity requires us to interpret elements of the past within the worlds of the people living at that time, not according to the expectations of the present.[22] And so, even in this very brief exploration, the goal is to understand past beliefs on their own terms, avoiding the temptation to read the experiences of today into other times and places.

As we walk together through the answers to these questions, our hope is that you will learn to weep with those who have wept.

5

THE LIES THAT BLIND US TO THE TIES THAT BIND US

"I know. I know you probably think that."[1]

It's one of the most powerful lines in the 2016 film *Hidden Figures*.

Dorothy Vaughan is a gifted mathematician tasked with providing calculations for the space program in the 1960s. She is also African American. Her White supervisor is condescending and contemptuous toward African American employees at the National Advisory Committee for Aeronautics. The supervisor seems especially put off by Dorothy's desire to receive a promotion that she has clearly earned.

Then, by chance, Dorothy and the supervisor encounter one another in a restroom.

That's when the supervisor feels compelled to say to Dorothy, "Despite what you may think, I have nothing against y'all."

The very tone of the supervisor's declaration reveals a disdain that she herself doesn't seem to know.

Dorothy pauses for a moment before she replies, "I know. I know you probably think that."

It's a poignant scene because it highlights how skilled we are at deceiving ourselves. Prejudice, bitterness, pride, love of praise—all these sins and so many more can slither unseen beneath the surface of our souls. "Sin," nineteenth-century pastor Charles Haddon Spurgeon observed, "injures us most by taking from us the capacity to know how much we are injured."[2]

Social-scientific research has repeatedly suggested that prejudices lurk in our implicit attitudes,[3] but the authors of Scripture knew our propensity for self-deception long before the social sciences—and they knew it far better. It's what drove David to cry out in desperation, "Who perceives his unintentional sins?" (Psalm 19:12). It's part of what God was getting at when he reminded Jeremiah, "The heart is more deceitful than anything else, and incurable—who can understand it?" (Jeremiah 17:9).

Sin has so pervaded human nature that we are capable of sinning involuntarily and even unknowingly. "I have deep anxiety regarding my hidden faults, of which your eyes are aware but mine are not," North African pastor Augustine of Hippo admitted when he reflected on his struggles with sins in his senses that he sometimes didn't recognize. "There remains within me a lamentable darkness in which my own proclivities lie hidden from me."[4] It's as if—after glimpsing his earlier self in the bathroom mirror and seeing all his earlier overconfidence about the purity of his motivations—Augustine says to his younger self, "I know. I know you probably think that."

The disordering effect of humanity's fall from innocence can blind our thinking so much that we can touch something beautiful and wonder if it has left a stain. It can poison the ways we read Scripture so that we use the Bible to justify grievous wrongs. What's worse, we are even capable of contorting our theologies to cover our sins by convincing ourselves no wrong is being done.[5]

Racial supremacy in any form is a heresy that ignores the biblical truth that every human being has the same essential nature.[6] And yet, generations of church members lived and died convinced that Scripture supported their commitment to this heresy. The problem was not with Scripture. The problem wasn't even with the creeds their churches confessed. People who embraced the same confessions of faith frequently landed on opposite sides of this heresy. The difficulty had to do with the ways that people misconstrued God's Word to sustain practices of prejudice and oppression.

Today, it's easy to read our present ways of thinking into the past and to condemn these individuals without a second thought. And yet, history is not a dualistic fantasy with villains and heroes clearly distinguished by the colors of their lightsabers. History leaves us with texts that reveal a messy mixture of motives and actions more complex than any of us would prefer. And so, even though I will not excuse those who misconstrued the Scriptures to sustain heresies of racial superiority, neither do I despise them. Instead, I am driven to consider whether there are similar short-comings in my own thinking today—if there are, perhaps, areas where my own context has so deeply blinded me that I have failed to be convicted by a truth God has revealed in his Word.

The causes of these misinterpretations of Scripture encompassed a tangled snarl of different impulses of which the people themselves were probably never fully aware. Some who professed Christ defended the sub-jugation of Africans on the basis of biblical verses that give guidelines to masters and bond-slaves, either unaware or unwilling to see that the prac-tices described in Scripture were not the same as the racialized trade in human souls taking place along the coasts of Africa.[7] Others claimed their purchase of African captives was justified because it would provide these individuals with an opportunity to become Christians.

Still others contrived their theological support for racial superiority from the biblical story of Noah in Genesis 9. This story was far from the only text used to sustain the claim that Africans were destined for slavery. It has, however, been one of the most widespread distortions of Scripture in modern history. And so, if we want to understand the claims dividing the body of Christ along lines of color and culture, it could be helpful to take a look at the curse a drunken ex-sailor directed at his grandson.

SCRIPTURE AND THE WOUNDS OF RACIAL SUPERIORITY

In case you're not familiar with what happened to Noah after the flood, the closing credits of his life aren't particularly pleasant. Sometime after he beached his boat on a mountaintop, he planted a vineyard (Genesis 9:20). Soon after he discovered viticulture, Noah discovered fermentation. Soon after discovering fermentation, he discovered intoxication. Soon after discovering intoxication, he discovered the floor of his tent and somehow managed to lose his loincloth along the way. That's when Noah's son Ham chose to mock his father's failures instead of covering his nakedness. The other two sons refused to join in their brother's lampoonery. Instead, they found a robe and spread it over their father without so much as a glance in his direction.

Once Noah woke up from what may have been the first hangover in history, the memory of Ham's mockery still echoed in the pounding haze of his headache. And that's when the captain of the ark lost more than his loincloth. The patriarch called down a series of curses on Ham's son Canaan, declaring that the son would someday be enslaved (Genesis 9:25-27).

Clearly, there was some serious dysfunction in Noah's family.

The point of this curse in its canonical context was probably to prophesy a future time when the descendants of Noah's son Shem would conquer Canaan's posterity (Joshua 9:23; Judges 4:23; 1 Kings 9:21).[8] But that's not the only way this text has been interpreted. Sometime in the Middle Ages, this text began to be distorted. Ham and Canaan were recast as the ancestors of Africa, and Noah's curse was reinterpreted so that it damned all supposed descendants of Canaan to slavery.[9]

This misinterpretation didn't cause the enslavement of sub-Saharan Africans. Slavery had existed in Africa for centuries, and souls had been stolen from Africa since ancient times. The trade in African bodies accelerated and multiplied throughout the late medieval and early modern eras, particularly following the rise of Islam.[10] By the time the age of exploration drew European carracks and caravels around the globe, human beings in sub-Saharan Africa were widely seen as commodities to be enslaved—sometimes with the sanction of church authorities and sometimes in defiance of them.[11] Over centuries, a cluster of African ethnicities was identified as "Black," and a caste system formed pressing the darkest flesh to the lowest rung of the ladder.[12] The resulting ranking of races impacted not only persons of African descent but also other darker-complexioned ethnicities around the globe.[13]

In time, the words of Noah rose to prominence as one rationale for the patterns of exploitation from which captors and traders were already profiting.[14] This twisting of Noah's curse did not *cause* "black" and "white" to be positioned on opposite ends of a scale of social value.[15] What the heresy of a Hamitic curse did was provide a rationalization for the enslavement of Africans that tied racialization to an authority greater than humanity.

And yet, this misinterpretation of Noah's curse wasn't the only option, even in the eighteenth and nineteenth centuries. Bible-believing theologians—including one son of a slaveholding pastor named Jonathan

Edwards—provided alternative interpretations of Scripture that attacked this distortion.[16] Yet, in many contexts, church and civic leaders gravitated toward a misuse of the Scriptures that degraded an entire ethnicity instead. "The Negro is not equal to the white man," one Presbyterian leader of the Confederacy declared. "Slavery—subordination to the superior race—is his natural and normal condition. . . . He is either by nature or by the curse against Canaan fitted for that condition."[17] "From Ham were descended the nations that occupied the land of Canaan and those that now constitute the African or Negro race," Baptist leader Patrick Mell opined. "Their inheritance, according to prophecy, has been and will continue to be slavery."[18] The same Bible in which the earliest Christians found what they needed to form diverse communities was now used to degrade persons of African descent.

When the Old Testament prophet Daniel glimpsed his people's sin, he responded by lamenting the ongoing impact of these iniquities (Daniel 9:7-8).

So should we.

"Lord, public shame belongs to us and to our ancestors because we have sinned against you."

The ranking of races ran so deep in American churches that, even when Black Christians joined White congregations after the Civil War, spiritual unity never developed into equality. Regardless of godliness or gifting, African American believers were typically not recognized as equals. And so, with few exceptions, they formed their own congregations and left White churches behind.[19]

The heresy of the Hamitic curse continued to provide a pretense for the degradation of African Americans well into the twentieth century, and this distortion of Scripture wasn't limited to theologians or politicians. It was thoroughly entwined in the minds of ordinary Americans. Early twentieth-century traveling carnivals included attractions known as "Son of Ham Shows." In these grotesque games, patrons paid for the opportunity to hurl baseballs at the head of a Black man, sometimes resulting in the injury or death of a person created in the image of God.[20]

"Lord, public shame belongs to us and to our ancestors because we have sinned against you."

At times, Christian rhetoric and rituals could even accompany acts of unspeakable violence. When two African American men were lynched in Starkville, Mississippi, the crowd sang the Isaac Watts hymn "There Is a Land of Pure Delight" and spread blankets so that their families could enjoy a picnic while watching the men die. Vendors hawked peanuts and bottled sodas as nooses choked the life from the men on the gallows.[21]

When an African American farmhand named Samuel Wilkes was lynched in Georgia, the mob delayed the murder until Sunday afternoon so that churchgoers wouldn't miss the spectacle. After church services had ended and the crowd gathered, men from the mob chopped off the victim's ears, fingers, and genitals before dousing him with kerosene and burning him alive. As Wilkes screamed in agony, one observer cried out, "Glory to God! God bless every man who had a hand in this. Thank God for vengeance!"[22] The crowd that roared its approval saw no contradiction between the hymns they sang on Sunday morning and the torture of a human being on Sunday afternoon. When I (Timothy) visited the site of this lynching a few years ago, I could find no remembrance that this had been site of the torture and murder of Samuel Thomas Wilkes. There was, however, an engraved stone slab across the street that marked the spot where a popular barbecue joint went out of business in 1981. The memory of a restaurant merited a marble marker while, at least as far as I could tell, a man's murder remained unremembered and little mourned.

"Lord, public shame belongs to us and to our ancestors because we have sinned against you."

Far more could be said, but what should be clear is that many persons who claimed to be Christians tried to cover heinous iniquities with veneers of religiosity. Even here, there were exceptions. Certain denominations repeatedly condemned lynching, and there were times when White pastors risked their lives to speak against racial atrocities.[23] But racism of one sort or another remained prevalent among White Americans for centuries, and it didn't stop when people walked through the doors of their churches.[24] As Christians in America, these threads are part of our story, and it's a story that invites all of us to lament. This lament is far from the final word, but it's an essential step for those who want to move toward multiethnic kingdom culture.

THE SCARS ARE NEARER THAN YOU KNOW

After hearing how racial prejudice has been entwined with religious rhetoric over the centuries, some may want to sidestep any hint of lament by saying, "Why should I lament things that I didn't do? Yes, that was terrible, but it's in the past!" And yet, our continuing separation along racial lines betrays a lesion in the social order that's still with us. Furthermore, even though none of us can or should *repent* of any sin we didn't personally commit (Ezekiel 18:20), every Christian should be ready to *lament* wrongs committed by our ancestors in the faith.[25]

What's more, the heresies that sustained these wounds in the past are not nearly as distant as you might think. The "curse of Ham" continued to shape people's perceptions of African Americans even in the late twentieth and early twenty-first centuries. According to a textbook that I (Timothy) was assigned in a church-based high school in the late 1980s, the achievements of persons of African descent have been displaced by the superior "intellectual and philosophical acumen of the Japhethites and the religious zeal of the Semites." This displacement occurred, according to the textbook, due to the "innate nature" of Africans predicted in Noah's curse. This textbook remains available today with these claims still intact.[26]

I received another jolting reminder of the persistence of this heresy in 2016 when a series of unsolicited messages began landing in my inbox. These emails were not sent blindly to a random list of recipients. They were targeted specifically at families like ours, White parents who have adopted children of color. One of these messages referred to White fathers who adopt African American children as "race-cucks" who "pollute Western civilization" by raising "children of Ham"—and those quotations come from some of the least offensive lines in one single email. Most disturbing was the fact that almost every one of the racist messages was steeped in Christian rhetoric. I don't know what sort of person takes the time to inflict such vile vitriol on adoptive families, but I've learned from other parents of multiracial households that I'm not the only one who has received them.

My experiences may not be the same as yours, but this much should be clear: Although the heresy of racial supremacy carries far less power than it did in the past, it's not an artifact that's been abandoned somewhere in the attic of history. Shadows of Jim Crow reside among us, and his wardrobe is filled with an abundance of less conspicuous disguises.

HOW THE SCARS STILL SEPARATE US

But what if these lies suddenly evaporated and no one believed them anymore? As wonderful as that would be, the truth is that some of their impact would persist because the effects of racist policies outlast the lives of racist people.[27]

Here's one simple example: One of the reasons why Black and White Christians rarely gather in the same churches is because they tend not to live in the same neighborhoods, which isn't a result of happenstance. Decades of government policies created spatial and social separations cutting off African Americans from experiencing the same opportunities as White Americans.

For nearly a century, African Americans were excluded from many jobs where advancement was likely, from neighborhoods where housing values multiplied, and from home loans that resulted in significant growth in equity.[28] These prejudicial policies crippled opportunities for some families while cultivating privileges for others. In many cases, White churches didn't merely accept these patterns of prejudice. There were White pastors and churches that actively worked to prevent Black families from moving into their neighborhoods.[29]

The American middle class of the twentieth century was, to a certain extent, created and expanded through gains in home equity.[30] And yet, these opportunities did not become available to African Americans until it was too late to enjoy their full benefit. Even if an African American household possessed perfect credit, the practice of redlining excluded virtually all African American families from receiving federally insured home loans. After the Second World War, low-interest home loans became freely available to returning veterans—but not to every veteran. Despite bleeding on the same battlefields as White soldiers, African American veterans still couldn't live in the same neighborhoods as their White counterparts, and they never received the same benefits. By the time these benefits became widely accessible to African American families, millions of White households were already migrating to larger homes on the outskirts of the cities, and the distance between Black and White grew ever greater.[31]

These separations continue to impact people's perceptions and opportunities today, even in places where the policies that produced them no longer exist. Research reveals, for example, that racial understanding grows when African Americans live in the same neighborhoods as White families and when Whites develop friendships with African Americans who have equal or higher socioeconomic status.[32] And yet, due in part to discriminatory patterns that reshaped urban demographics in the twentieth century, White households rarely locate themselves in places where this is possible.[33] Even in highly diverse metropolitan areas, White families typically choose to reside in locations where fewer than 10 percent of their neighbors are African American and around 70 percent are White.[34] Past policies turned racial separation into a social habit with effects that have persisted long past the time when the unjust statutes went away.

But monoethnic lives are far from the only problem these policies produced. Despite significant gains, a typical African American family's resources amount to about 12 percent of the household wealth possessed by a median White family.[35] At least some of this gap may be traceable to historic patterns of injustice that fractured family stability and home equity while limiting opportunities for advancement.[36] Lesser resources translated into lower tax revenues, which impacted education, employment, and opportunities for economic advancement.[37]

Every individual is responsible for his or her own choices, and no one in a free society will or should possess precisely the same resources as everyone else. And yet, what we're describing here is what happens when prejudice is empowered to *withhold* opportunities for advancement for decades. "The worker is worthy of his wages" (1 Timothy 5:18), but the benefits that many African Americans earned were withheld, and this has had a lasting impact.[38]

SEEING WHERE WE HAVE BEEN BLIND

Regardless of what you think the precise solutions to these problems should be, all of us should be able to agree that African American communities have been wronged in ways that have had lasting potency. The heresy of racial superiority has robbed families of opportunities to flourish. It has torn apart the lives of mothers and fathers, daughters and sons. Until we learn to lament these wounds, our churches will never grow into communities that are rich in multiethnic kingdom culture.

And so, slow down and ask yourself, Have I taken seriously the many ways that racism has affected my soul? Have I paused to lament how this struggle has wearied me and stolen years from my life? Have I wept over the future my children will face, knowing ethnic prejudices will last long past the years God has allotted me on this earth? Have I mourned the ways Black bodies have been treated as objects to be stolen, auctioned, flogged, lynched, mutilated, raped, choked, and riddled with bullets instead of being cherished as exquisite images of God? Have I considered how much joy I have missed that I would have experienced if my life had been enriched with more people who don't look like me?

All of us are far more wounded by the heresy of racial superiority than we know. You might never carry a sign that declares, "Diversity equals white genocide," and you may never vocalize bitterness and hate toward people who have treated you unjustly. But there can still be hidden corners in your heart where you harbor hatred that God alone knows or hurts that you've never brought to him for healing. You may never turn your elbow to look for a stain on your skin—but you can still bear a scar in your soul.

"Our sins don't just keep our mind from seeing the light," Augustine of Hippo once pointed out. "They keep our mind from seeing itself."[39] And that's why we need habits of lament, to make space for God to show us the sins and the scars we don't even know.

6

LITURGIES
OF LAMENT

In the last chapter, we lamented the sins and structures that have divided Black and White communities.

But lament isn't only for what happened in the past.

It's also for the present, and this call to lament is not only for White Christians but also for Black and Brown brothers and sisters.

What I (Jamaal) want to do in this chapter is minister to Christians of color by acknowledging your pain. I know firsthand many of the emotions that you may have experienced, so I want to lead you on a journey of honest reflection, admitting and lamenting my experiences and yours.

If you don't regularly take the time to lament those moments, your pain will pile up until it eventually crashes down like the wooden pieces in a game of Jenga. Pain that's not transformed will eventually be transferred, and that transfer of pain will inevitably hurt you and those around you.

But I want to do this with a spirit of gentleness. And so, before I ask you as a Christian of color to face your story, I'll share my own story. Along the way, you will see how God worked through a simple article to slow me down enough to admit the depth of my own pain so that I could boast in my weakness and experience Christ's joy.

THE LAMENT OF AN ESTRANGED PIONEER

Early in my time as a pastor at Sojourn, I experienced a period of intense emotional struggle, and I wasn't sure why. There were times of deep joy, but I also felt an ongoing sense of sadness.

It was during one of those seasons that I ran across a study by Korie Edwards and Rebecca Kim titled "Estranged Pioneers: The Case of African

American and Asian American Multiracial Church Pastors." Their article drew together data from more than one hundred interviews and revealed many African American and Asian American pastors in multiethnic congregations experience a deep sense of alienation as they navigate a racialized society where they are frequently seen as inferior to White peers.[1] Edwards and Kim refer to these pastors as "estranged pioneers." They have left behind what is familiar

> to explore a new way of doing church, but their ventures are not valued or celebrated as something that will potentially benefit the communities they come from. What's more, their sense of identity is challenged or destabilized in the process. Alienation characterizes their journey. . . . Their authority is questioned. . . . Some feel they have to work harder to be accepted. And some fear that their race is a liability for their church.[2]

Reading this study was a breakthrough for me as a Black pastor in a predominantly White yet increasingly multiethnic church. There was something about reading the words of Black and Brown brothers who had similar experiences that provided me with freedom to pause and acknowledge my pain. The article brought me to tears, and I don't cry easily. I recognized I wasn't unspiritual or overly sentimental. Instead, I had experienced deep hurt and I needed to accept that reality and face the wounds.

I needed to take the time to lament.

"Lamentation . . . forces us to slow down," Dominique Dubois Gilliard recognizes.

> We lament because, paradoxically, the cure for the pain is in the pain. Lamentation begets revelation. . . . Lamentation is a spiritual practice that softens hardened hearts, a revolutionary act that ushers us into uncensored communion with God. As a Christian, to live without lament is to live an unexamined life.[3]

What this looked like for me was sitting down and writing out some of the ways I had been wounded in majority-White contexts. Here are just a few of the experiences I hadn't fully faced until this point:

- I had been threatened by having a shotgun shell and a note placed on my Bible while I was on a break between keynote talks at a conference. The note said, "Pray that I don't use this today." It happened in a rural region where ethnic minorities were few and far between.[4]

- I had been asked if any of my family members were in prison and, if so, could I work that into my sermon to give the congregation "a more Black experience."

- I had been asked if I could preach in a baseball cap and gym shoes so that an all-White audience could have an experience of "life in the hood."

- I had been told by a White fellow pastor I should stop voicing my opinions and be happy with the way things are because "there are a thousand other Jamaals who could do what you do."[5]

- I had been sidelined in theological conversations and asked to chime in only if the conversation included issues of race and ethnicity.

When I read "Estranged Pioneers," I recognized I'm not an anomaly, and I don't need to hide the pain of these experiences. When I lamented this pain and took it to the cross of Christ, God gave me grace to boast in my weaknesses, knowing that his "power is perfected in weakness" (2 Corinthians 12:9-10).

But the need for lament didn't end there. The next step was to enter into lament with others.

WHAT HAPPENS WHEN WE LAMENT THE PAIN TOGETHER

I was nervous watching the faces of more than a dozen pastors seated around the table. As they read the document before them, they were glimpsing the inward toils and struggles of Black and Brown participants in the ministries of Sojourn Church Midtown. The moment was the culmination of months of work, and I had no idea what their response might be.

Months earlier, I had asked a couple that leads professional focus groups if they would conduct some focus groups for our church. After accepting my invitation, they gathered three groups, mostly from the growing number of Black and Brown attendees and members. Group participants responded to a series of open-ended questions about their experiences as members of ethnic minorities at Sojourn or as a White person married to someone from an ethnic minority. Around the same time, the pastors also heard the experiences of an interracial Christian couple who had visited Sojourn Church Midtown multiple times as "secret shoppers." This couple provided us with answers to a series of questions such as, "What was your experience at Sojourn as an interracial couple?" "What can you celebrate about Sojourn and our pursuit of a multiethnic vision?" "What things would keep you from seeing this space as your church home?"—and so on.

The resulting reports revealed deep racial stereotyping and condescension in our church that caused ethnic minorities and interracial couples to become hypervigilant about how others viewed them. People described how they were stared at and even given awkward nicknames. Some of these individuals experienced a lack of social reciprocity from other members, which left them disconnected from the church community.[6]

As I sat watching our leaders review these reports, a sacred silence filled the room.

I saw pastors choke up as they realized how many of our Black and Brown members were hanging on by a thread. We lamented together as brothers, and doors began to open between us that had never been opened before.

This movement of the Holy Spirit hadn't happened overnight. Four years earlier, many of these same pastors started persistently asking God to raise up Black and Brown leaders to shepherd this church. Their liturgies of prayer had shaped what they loved and longed for. And so, when God provided the leadership, they were ready to do the work even when that meant facing hard truths. Watching our pastors soak in these experiences was the most significant moment in my tenure at Sojourn up to that point. Their lament gave me hope.

Unfortunately, this posture of tenderness is often the exception, not the norm. Sometimes, White evangelical churches find themselves unprepared to understand what many African American members have experienced. One of the results has been an exodus of Black and Brown believers from White churches. Some have exited quietly while others have "left loud" by airing their grievances on social media.

WHEN LAMENT CAUSES MORE PAIN THAN IT HEALS

Despite how our pastors learned to lament well in that sacred gathering, Sojourn Church Midtown has made plenty of missteps along the way. In fact, a few months before that meeting with the pastors, the church attempted a service of lament in the aftermath of the shooting of Philando Castile. The problem was that even though the service brought up the pain that Black and Brown members felt, the experience applied no clear gospel hope.

Perhaps the worst part of the evening happened near the end of the service. An African American sister was accosted by a White member who pointed to a nearby police officer and demanded, "Do you see that officer? You should go over there and give him a hug." This was deeply painful for the African American sister because she was looking for a place to "weep with those who weep" (Romans 12:15). Instead of finding a space to weep, her pain was ignored, and she was told what to do with her body. What's more, while we should all be thankful for men and women who serve with honor in law enforcement, this demand set up a false dichotomy. Christians can and should honor law-enforcement officers, but that doesn't mean we can't also mourn moments when power may have been misused.

That service of lament failed primarily because it didn't prepare people to share their pain in ways that pointed them to Christ. Biblical lament doesn't simply dredge up the darkness. Throughout the Scriptures, lament also opens a door to the light. If lament doesn't lead us to the light of Christ, it's not gospel lament.[7]

A PERSONAL LITURGY OF LAMENT

The Scriptures "describe lamentation as a liturgical act that reorients and transforms us."[8] So how can you develop healthy liturgies of lament in your life that reorient you to the transforming light of Christ?

Carve out some time during your times of prayer and Bible reading during the upcoming month to lament, following these four movements.[9]

- *Turn:* Take a physical posture to remind yourself that you're turning in prayer to your heavenly Father. Return to the same posture each time. What we do with our bodies shapes what we love and what we long for.

- *Groan:* Lament the reality that Sunday morning remains one of the most segregated hours of the week. Cry out to God about the sheer sadness of ethnic divisions in the United States of America. Grieve the ways that our dinner tables each night of the week are often as monoethnic as our churches. Do not rush through these moments of groaning and lament; receive them as opportunities to experience God's grace. If you're uncertain what to say during these personal liturgies of lament, consider personalizing and paraphrasing portions of this lament that are applicable to you:

  > We lament and repudiate historic acts of evil such as slavery from which we continue to reap a bitter harvest, and we recognize that the racism which yet plagues our culture today is inextricably tied to the past. . . . We apologize . . . for . . . perpetuating individual and systemic racism in our lifetime; and we genuinely repent of racism of which we have been guilty, whether consciously (Psalm 19:13) or unconsciously (Leviticus 4:27).[10]

- *Ask:* Plead with God for peace, justice, and reconciliation in your community. Pray that God would provide opportunities for your church to share the gospel with more people from a greater range of ethnic and economic backgrounds. Pray for Black and Brown believers who work in predominantly White spaces. Pray that the Spirit would help them to reflect the light of Christ as they persevere in spaces where they might feel like they don't fit.

- *Trust:* As you plead and pray, grip your hand tightly in a fist as you consider your own pain and the pain of others, then very slowly release your fist into an open hand. As you feel this release of tension, pray, "Your kingdom come, your will be done, on earth as it is in heaven."

Yes, there are burdens to lament, but when our burdens become our Savior's burdens, there is freedom and hope. "Every other burden oppresses you and seems heavy, but Christ's burden lifts you up," Augustine of Hippo once pointed out to the people of his church. "Any other burden is a crushing weight, but Christ's burden gives you wings."[11]

HOW LAMENT POINTS TO THE EXISTENCE OF A CREATOR

Your laments have cosmic implications.

To lament racial injustice is to provide evidence—whether intentionally or not—that something greater than nature has been at work in the development of the cosmos. If human beings are nothing more than highly evolved animals, it's difficult to explain why we'd choose to lament for other people. Doing so exacts an emotional cost, after all, and it is unlikely that purely materialistic natural selection would favor such a habit.[12] To put it another way, lament requires a self-sacrificial disposition that is incompatible with a universe resulting from naturalistic evolution.

According to British philosopher Anthony O'Hear, traits that work against natural selection include "respect for the rights of others, self-sacrifice, honor, and this is without mentioning the theological virtues of faith, hope, and charity"—all of which are required when we engage in gospel-driven lament for one another.[13] Whenever someone grieves injustices inflicted on others, they're doing something that a godless cosmos cannot satisfactorily explain. And that's why your laments have cosmic implications.

A CORPORATE LAMENT

Convict us, Lord, we dance and laugh
Ignoring those who weep.
Correct us, Lord, our golden calf
Has lulled our hearts to sleep.
The gap between the rich and poor
Grows ever wider shore to shore.
There's racial hate, religious war
And wolves among the sheep.
Let justice roll like a river,
Like a river, let it roll.
Let justice roll like a river,
Like a river, let it roll.
Indwell us, Lord, and purify
Our hands to work for you.
Enlist us, Lord, to serve nearby

And cross the waters too.
Your image-bearers on the earth
Will never know how much they're worth
Unless we love and help them first
And show the way to you.
Let justice roll like a river,
Like a river, let it roll.
Let justice roll like a river,
Like a river, let it roll.
Let it roll.[14]

PART 3

OFFERING

Giving for the Sake of Multiethnic Kingdom Culture

Generosity happens when we release preferences, privileges, or possessions for the sake of someone else. And yet, we are unlikely to discover what we need to give until we pay attention to what the other person truly needs.

	What's the problem?	What's the liturgy?	What's the result?
Call to Worship	We don't love God's vision for kingdom diversity.	We pray for ethnicities and classes of people who aren't present in our church.	We develop a multiethnic kingdom culture that forms us into worshipers who praise our Creator God for the beauty of kingdom diversity.
Lament	We don't recognize how deeply the heresy of racial superiority has impacted our churches and our lives.	We face the reality and the continuing impact of the heresy of racial superiority, and we lament the ways it has wounded us.	We are formed into mourners who grieve the continuing impact of the heresy of racial superiority.
Giving	We are not ready to recognize or to release our own preferences.	We practice gratitude for the wisdom and the ways of worship practiced by faithful churches in other cultural contexts.	We are formed into servants who sacrifice preferences, privileges, and possessions for the sake of a multiethnic kingdom culture.

7

SEEING BOTH SIDES OF THE BALL

"What color is the ball?"

The gymnasium was packed. The tension in the room was thick and adrenaline was running hot. The speaker was holding up a small paddle ball so the audience could see.

"Red," the crowd responded, a bit baffled.

"No," the speaker responded.

Perplexed members from the audience began to shout, "Red!"

"No, you're wrong," the speaker repeated and then turned his head to see the side of the ball. Then, he rotated the sphere.

His side of the ball was green.

The speaker spoke in the measured tones of a teacher and a sage, "If I'm willing to come around here and see how it looks to you, and if you're willing to come around here and see how it looks to me, we can start to get somewhere."[1]

The name of the speaker was Dr. Dudley E. Flood, an African American civil rights activist, educator, and author. He was one of the most influential figures in the movement to desegregate public schools in North Carolina. He's gained widespread respect over the years, and it's easy to see why. It takes confidence to pull a sleight of hand trick with a ball at any meeting. It took immense courage to try it at meetings in the late 1960s and early 1970s that included angry parents, members of the Ku Klux Klan, and the Black Panthers. And yet, that's when Dr. Flood traveled throughout North Carolina, courageously calling for the state to integrate its schools.

More than a decade after the Supreme Court ruled that segregated schools were unconstitutional in the landmark case *Brown v. Board of*

Education of Topeka, many schools in North Carolina remained segregated. The Ku Klux Klan held rallies describing desegregation as "communistic" and "anti-Christian." Some school districts actively blocked desegregation, and the state legislature authorized grants to support "segregation academies" for White students.[2] When the federal government threatened school districts with a loss of funding, some schools implemented "one-way desegregation," closing down schools for African Americans and assigning the students to locations that had previously been all-White.[3]

And where were White churches when all of this was taking place? Did they step around to the other side of the ball to see how this situation looked from someone else's perspective? Were White Christians willing to leverage their privilege and power to provide educational opportunities for young African Americans, formed in the image of God?[4]

Not very often.

Sadly, in many school districts throughout the American South, members of White churches took the lead in sidestepping desegregation.[5] These misuses of privilege and power embedded divisions in social structures and frustrated opportunities for African American students to flourish.[6]

Education isn't the only place where power and privilege have been used to maintain structures limiting opportunities for minority ethnicities. There are other places where people have been unwilling to step around to see the other side of the ball. Sometimes, this unwillingness to see the other side shows up in church. One of the primary places it happens is in people's assumptions about what preaching, leadership, and worship ought to look like. If your church moves in the direction of multiethnic kingdom culture, this is likely to be one of the key spots where you will experience tension and conflict.

What I (Jamaal) want to do for you is what Dudley Flood did for the crowd in that gymnasium in North Carolina.

I want to invite all of us to look at the other side of the ball.

Regardless of whether you're a longtime member of a historic African American church or your church is working to unite first- and second-generation Chinese Americans or you've never attended any church other than a small congregation in the rural Midwest, you can still grow by learning to look at the church's life and worship from someone else's perspective.[7]

In all of this, the goal is mutual generosity. When our lives are rich in generosity, we are prepared to give up not only our possessions but also our preferences because we see "others as more important" than ourselves (Philippians 2:3). Our model for this kind of giving is Jesus himself, who "did not consider equality with God as something to be exploited. Instead, he emptied himself" for the glory of his Father and the love of his people (Philippians 2:6-7).

HOW JESUS USED HIS POWER TO GIVE

It's easy to assume that a lack of cultural awareness is limited to mission fields on the other side of the world, but it isn't. It happens here and now when churches assume the superiority of their own preferences and look down on the preferences of other churches. This isn't to say preferences are wrong. It's simply to point out that our own cultural preferences were not handed down by Jesus and Paul, and they aren't superior to any other cultural preferences. To put it another way, no human culture is intrinsically superior to any other. The patterns of beauty and brokenness, of common grace and common sin, simply fall in different places in different cultures.

When churches don't recognize how their practices have been shaped by cultural preferences, certain styles of leadership and worship can become cultural idols baptized in Christianized assumptions. This doesn't happen only in majority-culture congregations. It can happen anywhere since all of us tend to favor our own preferences and traditions.

At the same time, due to the power dynamics entwined with ethnicity in America, ethnic minorities can sometimes experience a particular pain when we're pressured to leave behind practices that differ from the majority, even though our practices may be well within the bounds of Scripture. When that happens, the result can be increased distance and division between Christians of different ethnicities. Once again, the standard for how Christians should leverage their privilege and influence is Jesus himself. Jesus used his power to draw near to us. His very incarnation was an act of accommodation, and he chose to experience our struggles from our point of view (Hebrews 4:15).[8]

Particularly if you're a White brother or sister who longs for a multi-ethnic kingdom culture, would you be willing to step around to see the other side of the ball by listening to my story?

LEARNING GENEROSITY IN OUR PREFERENCES ABOUT PREACHING

About two years into my pastorate at Sojourn, I found myself engaged in multiple meetings with congregants that followed a similar pattern. What became clear is that people can develop all sorts of workarounds— sometimes knowingly, usually unknowingly—to avoid admitting their own cultural preferences. As I listened to these individuals' stories, many of our conversations ended up in the same place:

Member: We're seriously thinking about leaving the church.

Me: What's brought you to this point?

Member: A lot of people don't feel like the Bible is being preached here anymore.

After a few of these conversations, I began to bring a copy of our preaching calendar with me. The sermons have always been expository messages, usually working verse-by-verse through books of the Bible. When I showed these members the preaching schedule from the past few months and asked for a specific example of a Sunday when the Bible hadn't been preached, they typically couldn't point to a single moment where we might have left biblical exposition behind. That's when the conversations frequently turned racial. At this point, I had preached only one sermon at Sojourn that emphasized racial and ethnic issues. And yet, the repeated criticism was that I was focusing on racial issues instead of preaching the Bible.

When I finally stepped around to their side of the ball, what dawned on me was that sitting under the preaching of a Black man was a new experience for nearly all of these White congregants. Since I was a Black man, every sermon I preached seemed to some of them like a sermon on race. Because of this change in *who* was preaching the Bible, they felt as if *what* was being preached had changed too. It saddens me to say that some members were never able to see why they felt the way they did about the preaching. Over time, however, many others recognized their feelings did not match reality. These were the members who learned to step around to see the other side of the ball, and they've grown into the strongest supporters of what we're doing at Sojourn Church Midtown.

LEARNING GENEROSITY IN OUR ASSUMPTIONS ABOUT LEADERSHIP

Unrecognized cultural assumptions can also extend to *who* is assumed to be the leader. A few years ago, I traveled with Nathan, one of our White pastors, to California for a roundtable with some of the top missiologists in North America. While we were at this gathering, several conversations followed an almost identical pattern.

The other participants introduced themselves, inquired about our church, and then asked each of us about our role on the church's staff. I identified my role as lead pastor and Nathan introduced himself as a missions pastor. After a few moments, there would be a pause in the conversation, and that's when the questions would begin.

"So, what's your role again?" they asked, looking at me.

"I'm the lead pastor."

"You mean, like the head pastor? The senior pastor?"

When I answered in the affirmative, they either asked the question again or turned to talk to Nathan in apparent disbelief. One time, the other individual even asked Nathan to explain our church's polity and organizational chart. Nathan obliged, but I could see the confusion on his face.

"Interesting," the gentleman said and walked away.

When the two of us were alone, I asked Nathan, "Are you confused about how some of these interactions have gone today?"

"Yeah," he replied. "I can't understand why people keep asking us to repeat our roles and explain our polity. That's never happened to me before."

That's when I pointed out that in this primarily White evangelical context, it was difficult for some of these men to believe that I, an African American male, could be the lead pastor or that Nathan reported to me. Nathan's eyes became enormous.

"Oh my," he said. "That's what's been happening? I've been trying to figure out why something seemed so off in all these conversations."

Even before that trip, Nathan cared deeply about the ways racism impacted Black and Brown brothers and sisters. After the roundtable, he clearly glimpsed the other side of the ball, and he grew to be a vital ally in our church's movement toward multiethnic kingdom culture.

LEARNING GENEROSITY IN OUR
PREFERENCES ABOUT WORSHIP

But by far the hardest part of helping the people to see their preferences had to do with music and worship. Moving in the direction of a multiethnic community at Sojourn Church Midtown meant expanding the congregation's musical repertoire. For years, we had produced deeply theological compositions for the church by developing contemporary arrangements of the hymns of Isaac Watts.[9] We never stopped singing those songs alongside classic hymns and an occasional popular chorus, but we did begin adding other music, mostly Black gospel songs and arrangements from the historic African American church.

The "worship wars" of the 1990s were primarily generational, with younger church members wanting to move beyond the hymnals. If your church moves in the direction of becoming a multiethnic community, you're likely to face a different type of worship war—but the conflict won't be between younger and older generations. This worship war will be more of a class and culture divide that dismisses the musical styles of certain cultures because they don't fit the church's prevailing expectations.[10]

When the music of the Black church started showing up in worship services, the pushback came quickly. Some members claimed that Black gospel music wasn't gospel-centered. Others said the songs were too repetitive and not deep enough theologically.

When the question of repetition came to me, I saw it as an opportunity to teach the people. First off, I gently pointed people's attention to Psalm 136, where the psalmist's divinely inspired song repeats the simple sentence "his faithful love endures forever" more than two dozen times.[11] I then moved past this basic point and invited members into the stories that shaped African American worship. I asked listeners to imagine the cotton fields where my enslaved ancestors sang short, memorable songs while they worked. These songs sometimes carried double meanings, recalling the stories of Scripture while sharing coded messages with other enslaved persons, while their captors listened only a few feet away. It was an exercise in hope expressed through embodied worship.

Still today, worship in historic African American churches makes space to celebrate God's goodness with whole hearts, minds, and bodies. For many African Americans over the years, Sunday morning worship became a time of communal counseling. For people who faced incessant dehumanization and trauma, worship was "therapy" in the best and most biblical sense of the word.[12] "Gospel music is always considered a collective response to Blacks' oppressed status and experience. The medium aesthetically expresses the trials and yearnings of a distinctive group bearing under similar social constraints."[13]

Historically, many African American worshipers had little or no access to counseling or ongoing care for their souls. Still today, when you speak about the African American community, you are speaking about families that, taken as a whole, will require more than two centuries of economic growth at current rates to catch up to the average White family in the United States.[14] The corporate worship moment on Sunday mornings can serve as a form of care for people who lack the resources to afford a counselor.

The music in African American churches is frequently structured to encourage the oppressed to cast their cares on a caring God. The "spirituals" in particular pour out people's hearts to God, crying out to the one who sees the oppressed and makes a way for them (Genesis 16:7-14; Isaiah 43:16). Within these songs, "God stands out as the all knowing, powerful, and omnipresent creator, to whom those in need make appeal."[15] Moments of repetition make space for the Holy Spirit to work some things out in the worshiper's soul. Sometimes, those outside historic African American churches struggle to understand these processes of healing and care that can happen during worship. And yet if a church longs to be truly multiethnic, it's crucial for this expression of worship to be valued and championed alongside other expressions of worship.

I've come to realize that many people claim they want a diverse church, but it quickly becomes clear they don't want multiethnic kingdom culture. They want Black and Brown people to be present in their worship services, but they don't want anything to change. Much like the communities that grudgingly desegregated public schools in ways that maintained the power of the dominant cultures, such churches are open to diversity only if it happens on their terms and according to their preferences. They have no interest in stepping around to see the other side of the ball. In some cases, they discount Black preaching, dismiss Black leadership, and look down on the music of the Black church. The result is a "gentrification of sanctification"[16] —an assumption that spiritual growth is only accessible through practices associated with a particular class and culture.

These negative perspectives on the heritage of African American Christians have seemed widespread, at least in my experience. Fifteen years after living in the dormitory of a largely White seminary, I still remember some of the negative remarks that were made about African American practices of Christianity—almost always by students who had never set foot in an African American church. We prayed differently, sang differently, and preached differently.[17] Personally, I saw deep value in these diverse expressions of "God's multi-faceted wisdom" (Ephesians 3:10). And yet, it was clear not everyone saw the value in expressions of worship and discipleship that were different from their own.

But consider this: the habits that historic African American churches worked into people's lives have resulted in remarkably resilient religious commitments, even as American society has grown increasingly secular. According to statistics from Pew Research,

- *Members of historic African American congregations read their Bibles:* "61% of those who are members of the historically black Protestant tradition (more than half of all black Americans) read Scripture at least weekly. . . . Relatively few black people (24%) say they *seldom or never* read the Bible, compared with 50% of whites and 40% of Hispanics."

- *Members of historic African American congregations believe their Bibles:* "A sizable share of all black people (77%) also say the Bible is the word of God . . . compared with 57% of whites and 65% of

Hispanics. Among those in the historically black Protestant tradition, 85% say they believe the Bible is the word of God."[18]

Of course, a high view of Scripture doesn't inevitably translate into theological orthodoxy and reading the Bible doesn't guarantee that someone obeys the Bible—but that's true of Christianity in every cultural context, not just among African Americans. And none of this is meant to suggest the historic habits of African American churches are superior or beyond critique. What's more, I have no desire to leave behind styles of worship that are more characteristic of other ethnicities. The church needs the richness of the ancient creeds and the hymns of Isaac Watts every bit as much as we need the vibrant exuberance of Black gospel music. Doing away with the Gloria Patri or "When I Survey the Wondrous Cross" would simply put the same problems in a different package by sidelining a different set of cultural preferences.

With all of that being said, here are the questions I would ask you to consider as you look at both sides of the ball: If the practices of historic African American churches correlate with high levels of biblical confidence and engagement with God's Word, why not look for ways to build up these practices alongside others instead of trying to replace them? Why not, at the very least, try to understand the importance of this heritage for African Americans?

POWER, PREFERENCES, AND THE OTHER SIDE OF THE BALL

That's how it looks from my side of the ball.

Now that you and I have stepped around to see the ball from both sides, let's consider together why it's so hard for churches to rethink their cultural preferences. Sometimes, it's simply because people struggle to recognize their own preferences for what feels familiar and comfortable, and I get that. Other times, however, it's because people are unwilling to release their expectation for the church to conform to their inclinations. And yet, if we refuse to release our preferences, our refusal reveals that we may not be ready to follow the example of Jesus who placed the needs of others above his own (Romans 15:1-3; Philippians 2:2).

The problem in all of this is that we all naturally want our own way—and the more power we possess, the harder it can be to let our preferences go. At the root of this desire is a phenomenon that Augustine of Hippo called *libido dominandi* or "lust for dominance."[19] What overthrows our lust for dominance is Spirit-empowered generosity that transforms the ways we see preferences, privilege, and power.[20] And so, in the next chapter, we'll examine a few examples from God's Word that show how a life of gospel-driven generosity can crush our lust for dominance.

8

HOW GOD MADE A HOLY MESS AND TURNED IT INTO A HEAVENLY MOVEMENT

All of us, by nature, desire to be in control.

It's been that way ever since Eve and Adam entertained the serpent's lies in the Garden of Eden.

That's when our primeval parents chose what they thought was the ultimate upgrade: to "be like God" (Genesis 3:5). What happened instead was that their souls were distorted by a self-centered desire to be in control. One result of this distortion was that human beings began to seek dominion over one another (Genesis 3:12-16). "Our nature became so deeply curved in on itself by the corruption of the first sin that it not only bends God's best gifts toward itself," the Protestant Reformer Martin Luther said, "but it also fails to realize that it so wickedly, curvedly, and viciously seeks all things for its own sake."[1]

Every dehumanizing act in history is simply one more sequel in a series of events that began with this primal demand for sovereignty, the desire Augustine called humanity's *libido dominandi*.[2] This lust drives peoples, tribes, and nations to idealize what they find desirable and to degrade anything that differs from this ideal. It's the root of nearly every rivalry that tears humanity apart, including racism.

Most important for our purposes in this chapter, whenever a lust for dominance takes over, generosity is almost always one of its first victims.

A HOLY MESS AT THE TOWER OF BABEL

Infected with an insatiable lust for dominance, primal humanity wasn't interested in developing cultures that would enable images of God to flourish across the face of the earth. One group of men and women settled in Shinar and decided they would stay in a single valley where they would construct a monument for themselves. "Let's make a name for ourselves," they said. "Otherwise, we will be scattered throughout the earth" (Genesis 11:4).

When the ancient Israelites read these words in the writings of Moses, they most likely felt a twofold twinge in their spirits. In the first place, God never called any of us to make a name for ourselves—so the determination to "make a name" would have brought about the first twinge.

Far more importantly, these words at Babel represented a rejection of God's command for humanity to "fill the earth" with communities and cultures (Genesis 1:28)—and that's why the Israelites would have felt the second twinge. God's desire was for the multihued beauty of many cultures to reveal the manifold glory of his perfect design; these cultures would develop as humanity filled the earth. Then, one day, God would draw the many ethnicities back together in Christ (John 12:20, 32). Yet that's not what these rebels wanted.

Diseased with a lust for dominance, the people in the plain of Shinar demanded to dictate their own destinies by staying in a single location and seeking their own glory. They wanted to bring humanity together as one, but not in God's time or God's way. And that's why God wrecked their plans by confusing their languages (Genesis 11:9). "Since the tongue is the instrument of domination, it was by the tongue that their pride was punished," Augustine wrote in *The City of God,* "so that humanity—who would not listen to God when he gave his commands—should be misunderstood when they themselves gave orders."[3] And thus humanity's self-seeking plans at Babel became a symbol of our rebellion against God's design.

Unfortunately, when churches are unwilling to move toward becoming communities marked by multiethnic kingdom culture, they can end up looking more like the monocultural kingdom of Babel than the multiethnic, multigenerational, and multi-socioeconomic kingdom of Christ. Their physical structures may be stunning, but many times the families that fill these structures represent the same socioeconomic classes, social cultures, and political affiliations—all of this, despite the rich diversity of humanity that surrounds the church's physical structures.

There is a better way, and it begins with radical generosity—generosity that releases personal preferences and refuses to hoard privileges and power. In the book of Acts, God gives us a glimpse of this better way that only his Word and Spirit can bring about.

A HEAVENLY MOVEMENT IN JERUSALEM AND BEYOND

The sequel to Luke's Gospel is identified in most of our Bibles as "the Acts of the Apostles," but the book could be named just as easily "the Acts of the Holy Spirit." Luke mentions the Spirit more than fifty times in this book.[4] From beginning to end, Luke stresses that the Holy Spirit is the power behind God's mission (Acts 1:8; 13:9; 15:8, 28; 16:6, 7; 20:28; 28:25).[5]

And what does this have to do with the path of generosity that makes multiethnic kingdom culture possible? What God did at the tower of Babel was make a holy mess that his Holy Spirit would turn into a heavenly movement marked by social and cultural generosity.

God begins his reversal of the curse of Babel with the sound of a rushing wind signifying the outpouring of the Holy Spirit. When the Spirit fills the disciples, what happens is the exact opposite of the chaos at Babel.[6] "How is it that each of us can hear them in our own native language?" the Jewish hearers begin asking one another. "Parthians, Medes, Elamites; those who live in Mesopotamia, in Judea and Cappadocia, Pontus and Asia, Phrygia and Pamphylia, Egypt and the parts of Libya near Cyrene; visitors from Rome (both Jews and converts), Cretans and Arabs" (Acts 2:8-11).

Here's how Jarvis Williams summarizes the implications of this scene for redemptive kingdom diversity:

> The curse of the linguistic division of the tower of Babel is reversed, and God's supernatural Holy Spirit begins to unify the nations once separated. . . . The beautiful diversity that God originally created for the people to live in harmony with one another is now beginning the process of restoration and unification in Christ by the power of the Spirit because of his resurrection. As Luke demonstrates throughout the rest of Acts, the Holy Spirit comes to both Jews and Gentiles by

faith in Christ, and he forms these diverse groups into one people of God.[7]

At the beginning of time, God commanded humanity to multiply throughout the earth (Genesis 1:26-28). What no human being could have imagined at that time was God already knew humanity would rebel against him. In eternity past, God had already determined that he would unveil a greater design later by uniting the one and the many in Christ. This was all part of God's plan, and God's planning never writes a check that his power won't cash.

God's glorious reuniting of humanity in Christ begins when the Spirit shows up at Pentecost. In the weeks that followed Pentecost, Spirit-empowered generosity enabled these men and women to release their possessions and prepared them to release their preferences. "All the believers were together and had everything in common," Luke informs us. "They sold their possessions and property and distributed the proceeds to all, as any had need. Every day they devoted themselves to meeting together in the temple, and broke bread from house to house" (Acts 2:44-46; see also 4:32).

The church developed habits of material generosity in the opening chapters of Acts. And so, it's not surprising that, when the first church-wide crisis erupted, the first Christians were able to face the conflict in a way that was marked by social and cultural generosity as well.

HOW HEAVENLY MOVEMENTS GIVE POWER AWAY

The Jerusalem church brought together Jesus-following Jews from a multiplicity of cultures. Some of these individuals—"Grecian" or "Hellenistic" Jews—were born far from Jerusalem in places where Greek was their first language. Others—the "Hebraic" Jews, in some translations of the Bible—seem to have been raised in Aramaic-speaking families, and their culture was bound more closely to the regions around Jerusalem (Acts 6:1). These Aramaic-speaking Jews were probably the majority in the Jerusalem church, and they may also have been more influential. The apostles were part of this group, after all, and this strand of Jewish culture had shaped Jesus' earthly life as well.

Given the social dominance of the Hebraic Jews in Jerusalem, it shouldn't surprise us that some of the widows from among the Grecian Jews ended up being overlooked in the church's distributions of funds and food (Acts 6:1). There's no indication that anyone intended to dismiss the needs of Grecian Jews, but simply because it was unintended didn't mean the situation could be ignored. Some of the Hebraic Jews might have held "a prejudicial sense of superiority over the Grecian Jews" that contributed to the inequity, but the text doesn't provide us with those details.[8]

The focus of the Spirit-inspired text is on the apostles' response. And what was it that the apostles did? They gave away power they could have held for themselves. The apostles released the administration of finances and food to a group of qualified servants selected by the people of the church (Acts 6:2-5).[9] The church seems to have selected these servants from those who were in the minority in the church.[10] "Those chosen for the role all have Greek names. This does not prove that they were all Hellenists, . . . though, given the situation, it is likely that they were."[11] One of them— Nicolaus of Antioch—was even a Gentile who had converted to the Jewish way of life (Acts 6:5).

Spirit-guided apostles acted with Spirit-empowered generosity, to which the people responded by selecting Spirit-filled men from the very culture that had been overlooked. Immediately after this act of generosity, "the word of God spread, the disciples in Jerusalem increased greatly in number" (Acts 6:7).

But this wouldn't be the last conflict of this sort that the church faced in the book of Acts.

A few years later, some influential men "came down from Judea and began to teach the brothers, 'Unless you are circumcised according to the custom prescribed by Moses, you cannot be saved'" (Acts 15:1). What these teachers were claiming was that before non-Jews could follow Jesus, they first had to convert to a Jewish way of life. Many people apparently accepted this false teaching, resulting in church leaders gathering in Jerusalem for a crucial discussion and decision.

In that first church council, Simon Peter stayed in the same gospel groove God had initiated on the day of Pentecost and reinforced through a rooftop vision in Joppa (Acts 2:1-41; 10:9-43). "God, who knows the heart," Peter argued before his fellow pastors, "bore witness to [the Gentiles] by giving them the Holy Spirit," apart from any conversion to Jewish customs (15:8). And thus, cultural customs should be yielded for the sake of God's mission among the Gentiles, even though those customs were marks of the covenant God had cut with Abraham and his descendants. The other elders and apostles agreed with Simon Peter, and the Christians in Syria rejoiced at the news (Acts 15:31). With this full inclusion of the nations in God's covenant of salvation, the holy mess God made by confusing the people's speech at Babel became a holy movement that included and empowered believers in every culture.

At Pentecost, the Holy Spirit had united Jewish worshipers from different cultures throughout the Roman Empire into one church that gathered in dozens of communities throughout Jerusalem. The generosity that the Spirit formed in these communities prepared the fledgling church to welcome men and women from every ethnicity when the time came.

When it comes to multiethnic ministry today, much differs from what the church faced at the council in Jerusalem, and we're fully aware the situations are not identical. The division between Jews and Gentiles was not only cultural but also covenantal. Still, certain aspects of these earlier challenges are at least partially analogous to some of the cultural challenges we face today.

At first, in some segments of the early church, the dominant group was not willing to yield its cultural values, and that still happens today.[12] Today, Christians can sometimes assume a multiethnic church is one in which a multiplicity of ethnicities yield to the customs of a dominant culture. When that takes place in contemporary Western contexts, it often means the assimilation of the cultures of Black and Brown believers in contexts where the standard reference is White.[13] Whether intentionally or not, when majority cultures meet minority cultures, majority cultures almost always end up dominating the conversations.[14]

When that happens, the result is not a multiethnic community that celebrates the beauty of many classes and cultures. Instead, it's a gathering where every ethnicity is expected to sustain the preferences of a dominant majority. These expectations shape what songs we think the church should sing, what form we assume the sermons should take, and what type of person we're willing to embrace as a leader. When such assumptions are pressed into a culture that has struggled for centuries against all odds simply to maintain basic human dignity, it can easily crush any "sense of selfhood, producing self-hatred, alienation, powerlessness, and dependency."[15]

But once again, gospel-driven generosity shows us a better way revealed through the incarnation of Jesus Christ.

THE RADICAL GENEROSITY OF A LIFE LIKE HEAVEN

Our God is a generous God who is on a mission, and he is forming a people for his glory who are generous and on a mission. But godly generosity is never something we can produce in our own power. It's empowered by the Holy Spirit, and it's motivated by God's free and generous gift to us through the life, death, burial, and resurrection of Jesus Christ. That gift is so great that, as my grandmother used to say, "You can't out-give God."

The immensity of God's gift to us helps us to understand Paul's words to the Corinthian church about giving. Despite severe trials and extreme poverty, the churches of Macedonia had given with joy to the Christians in Jerusalem. Yet Paul made it clear that the Macedonian Christians did not forge their own path of generosity. They were simply following the greater example of Jesus himself. "For you know the grace of our Lord Jesus Christ," Paul wrote. "Though he was rich, for your sake he became poor, so that by his poverty you might become rich" (2 Corinthians 8:9).

Go back and reread those words, slowly. What were the riches Jesus gave up? It wasn't a wealth of money that Jesus released in his incarnation. He didn't give up denarii or drachmae, dollars or cents.

What he gave up was a wealth of privilege.

Jesus possessed every power of the Godhead throughout every moment of his existence in flesh on the earth. His humanity never diminished his deity, and his incarnation never negated his omnipotence. Yet he chose to release the privilege of using these powers throughout his earthly life and death. And thus, Paul's challenge to the Corinthians was, "With that tremendous example of generosity before you, how can you hold back?"[16] If Jesus showed his generosity by releasing his privilege, shouldn't we be willing to do the same for one another? To put it in our terms today, whether our privileges are economic, educational, cultural, or racial, shouldn't we be willing to leverage what we possess to provide opportunities for others?

That's what the church in Jerusalem did in response to the cries of the Grecian Jews, and it's what the church did again when they released cultural customs for the sake of the gospel. And yet, even then, the apostles weren't forging their own path of generosity. They were simply following the example of their Savior. Churches that pursue this pathway of radical generosity

> unambiguously proclaim God's goodness and wisdom in his creation, his continuing sovereignty over his creation, his victory over every kind of sin (even the sin of racism) through the work of his Son, and his promises to empower them continually to live out Christ's victory and deliverance in this world and in the world to come. Such churches recognize and affirm the wonderful variety and diversity of the membership of the body of Christ, while at the same time rejoicing in its unity in Christ.[17]

What this pattern produces in the church is not an assimilated culture where minorities adapt to the majority. Neither is it a pluralistic culture in which each culture or ethnicity pursues its ministries separately. The result is, instead, a community with a common identity that mingles elements from a multiplicity of ethnicities in a culture that celebrates differences while joining in a unified proclamation of the gospel and pursuit of God's kingdom. In such a community, every believer is equal before the throne of Christ, no human culture is prized as superior, and structures of power aren't limited to any particular culture or ethnicity.[18] Members from differing ethnic, cultural, and social backgrounds retain these identities while practicing the shared habits of their overarching identity in Christ.[19] As a result, members from every ethnicity become willing to release their preferences for particular songs or preaching styles for the sake of a diverse and faithful church.

But this requires an attitude of radical generosity in which God's people are prepared to imitate their Savior by releasing preferences, privileges, and resources for the glory of God and the good of his people. When that happens, our lust for dominance is swept away by a longing for authentic communion and a kingdom greater than our own.

9

LITURGIES OF GIVING

"It's now time for the joy of giving. That's where God's people bring God's money to God's storehouse for God's ministry."

When I (Jamaal) was the pastor of Forest Baptist Church, these words from a previous pastor were a part of the liturgy of giving most Sundays.

After a short word of encouragement about why we give, I asked the congregation to follow the "direction of the ushers." That's when the entire community of faith rose and marched from their seats to the front of the sanctuary. With tithes or offerings in hand, the people were prepared to drop their gift in the offering bucket. And what about those who had nothing to give that week? Well, that was okay too. They passed by with everyone else, smiling at me as they tapped the bucket. To ensure that members knew they were called to give from a place of cheerfulness (2 Corinthians 9:7), the organist always played upbeat music during these moments. "This is the day—hallelujah!—that the Lord has made, that the Lord has made. I will rejoice, I will rejoice and be glad in it, and be glad in it."

At Forest Baptist Church, giving was a communal habit of practicing joy.

Like Israel leaving Egypt with wealth and songs of praise, members left their seats with joy because God had delivered them from slavery to sin. This joy also marked their journey to the front of the sanctuary because they recalled how God had rescued them and their ancestors from centuries of slavery, subjugation, segregation, and Jim Crow. The sight of those little baskets overflowing with checks and offering envelopes was a miniature picture of the people's hearts overflowing with gratitude to the Lord.

Gospel-driven generosity begins with an attitude of gratitude for God's generosity to us. This attitude of gladness decimates our lust for dominance and overflows into a willingness to give up our possessions and privileges for the sake of God's greater mission.

With that in mind, let's look at a couple of habits that can aim our souls in the direction of greater generosity.

HOW YOU CAN RECEIVE THE GIFT OF ANOTHER CULTURE'S PRACTICES OF WORSHIP

Here's a habit to help you to move toward multiethnic generosity: Plan to visit a faithful, gospel-driven church outside your own ethnicity or culture once every three months. Embrace this habit as an opportunity to learn from sisters and brothers in other cultures.

But don't start this liturgy just yet.

Before this habit begins, we want to prepare you to be aware of your own cultural preferences so that you can be generous in the ways you respond to others. Here's how:

1. *Consider your own preferences.* The night before you visit, list the aspects of your home church's worship service that you find most meaningful. Thank God for these parts of your church's practices of worship.

2. *Visit the other church.* This could happen on a Sunday, but it might also take place at some other time that doesn't remove you from worship in your local church. As you worship, be receptive to the differences in the other church's practices of worship. Afterward, take time to record your thoughts in a journal. How did the service challenge you to be more like Jesus? What did you enjoy? What seemed uncomfortable? What didn't make sense to you?

3. *Be grateful for your preferences—and be willing to lay them down.* Compare what you experienced with your list of the most meaningful facets of your own church's worship service. There's nothing wrong with having preferences! Be grateful for the ways God has shaped you through these patterns of worship. At the same time, pray you will be able to appreciate these aspects of your church's

worship without turning them into idols by refusing to recognize the value in other expressions of worship. When you're simultaneously grateful for your preferences and ready to lay them down, you're cultivating a heart that's open to ethnic and cultural diversity. This attitude enables us—in the words of my friend Derwin Gray— to "put down our preferences and pick up our crosses."[1]

I can't tell you how much of a joy it can be for African American believers to see White Christians being led in worship by African American brothers and sisters in genres characteristic of the historic Black church. Being a believer who's responsive to styles of worship outside your cultural preferences is a gift to others because it's an act of Christlike humility (Philippians 2:3-4; see also Romans 14:19). And yet, it's amazing to me how many Christians are unwilling to worship in any cultural contexts outside what's familiar to them.

A few years ago, I was speaking at a church-planting conference, and a woman stepped to the microphone in a question-and-answer session.

"I'm passionate about helping my church to become more multiethnic, but every person in my church is White. How can I convince my Black friend to leave her church and come to my church?" she asked.

"Since you're passionate about multiethnic churches," I replied, "have you considered going to her church?"

The look of shock that accompanied her response left me with little hope that she ever visited her friend's church.[2]

But this call to lay down our preferences doesn't apply only to White Christians. It extends to all of us, Black and Brown believers as well. A few years ago, I asked our music minister at the time—who was Latino—to begin including bluegrass music in our worship services from time to time. Kentucky is known as the Bluegrass State, after all, and many of our members had sacrificed their own preferences to stay at Sojourn Church Midtown. The first time we worshiped in a bluegrass style, I told the congregation that this service was for my "less melanated brothers and sisters," and we all enjoyed a good laugh together. There's a joy shared when we overcome the divisions between us not only by rejoicing in someone else's cultural preferences but also by being willing to lay down our own. Here's how Tim Keller makes this point:

One of the ways to bear fruits of repentance is for the members of more and more churches to make the sacrifices of power and comfort needed to form churches that show how in Christ the racial and cultural barriers that divide the world outside the church do not divide them inside, because of the power of the gospel.[3]

HOW YOU CAN RECEIVE THE GIFT OF ANOTHER CULTURE'S WISDOM

Here's another question to ask yourself as you develop a more generous attitude toward other cultures: Do you regularly learn from Christians whose ethnicity or culture is different from your own? If not, make a list of a dozen or so books written by faithful Christians from ethnic backgrounds other than your own. Read one of these books each month throughout the upcoming year—or, better yet, engage more of your senses in this process by obtaining the books in audio formats and habitually listening to them in the same location or on the same commute.

Sometimes, the first step toward a life that looks like heaven is a reading list that's more representative of heaven. I earned a master's degree and a doctorate in educational ministry at a majority-White seminary. Throughout those two degrees, I cannot recall even one instance when a White professor assigned a book or even an article written by an African American scholar. Today, many of the professors are more likely to recommend the work of faithful African American scholars, and I'm glad. Ethnically diverse reading lists are good for everyone. When institutions and pastors limit their reading to their own ethnic demographics, it's easy to open the door to ethnic idolatry, even if no one intends to do so.

The gospel remains unchanged regardless of culture, and the truth remains the same in every context. Yet each culture and ethnicity accentuates different aspects of this glorious gospel, and there is beauty in hearing different ways of expressing the same truth. Unfortunately, there are many Christians who have never considered the multifaceted ways their brothers and sisters from other ethnicities have understood the Scriptures over the centuries.[4] As a result, they miss the benefit of seeing the same truths from different perspectives.[5]

But once again, this applies to me as well! As an African American pastor of a multiethnic church, I may be fluent in Black and White cultures, but I still need to listen and learn whenever I step outside these cultures. That's why I intentionally spend time reading the works of Asian and Latino theologians and seek out coaching in multiethnic leadership.

For some of you, this liturgy of listening may require more than an expanded reading list. It may mean serving under the leadership of a Black or Brown pastor in an urban neighborhood instead of trying to plant a church there. When I teach about multiethnic church planting, I'm sometimes approached by all-White church-planting teams with a question that runs something like this: "We want to plant a church in a predominantly African American neighborhood because we're burdened for that community. Do you have any tips for us?"

I do have a tip for most of them: "Don't—at least not yet."

Unless you've already lived for an extended time in such a community or served under African American pastoral leadership, the best thing you can do might be to spend some time learning to see the other side of the ball first.[6] Move into the neighborhood, work in the community, join a faithful local church, build friendships, and be a servant there before trying to plant a church.

GENEROSITY ISN'T ALWAYS ABOUT MONEY—BUT SOMETIMES IT IS

These liturgies are meant to cultivate gratitude for other cultures and ethnicities. What grows from this gratitude is a willingness to give generously, and what we've emphasized has been releasing preferences, power, and privilege.

But what about more tangible ways you can express generosity?

Maybe you have a position of influence you can leverage to open doors for others. This could take the form of connections to influential social networks or recommendations for leadership roles. It might include an offer to speak at a conference or an invitation to contribute a chapter to a book.

For some of you, however, generosity *does* mean giving money—and it would be difficult for me to overemphasize how important this can be.[7] The first few years of our church's movement toward multiethnic ministry coincided with the difficult departure of the founding pastor and moral failures among a couple of leaders. One result of this turmoil was a loss of three hundred or so members, including key financial stakeholders. And yet, God raised up others who ensured our ministries were able to continue—including one family that gave multiple six-figure gifts. After this family pledged their first gift, I met with them to make certain no strings were attached. I told them about our commitment to boldly address racial injustice in ways that would never waver from a commitment to the Scriptures as God's sufficient and inerrant Word.

"Is there anything about this that would make you cancel your pledge?" I asked—and they assured me they were completely on board with these commitments. Their gifts enabled our church to move toward financial stability, make key transitions, and pursue our God-given mission without anxiety. Much of what we have described in this book would never have been possible without that family's radical generosity.

In the Old Testament, God called landowners to share their resources with those who were poor, remembering that everything they possessed was theirs only because of God's grace (Deuteronomy 17:19-22). Early Christians similarly saw wealth as a means to pursue justice. "The truest advantage of riches," one fourth-century Christian wrote, "is to use wealth not for anyone's particular pleasure but for the welfare of many; not for one's own immediate enjoyment, but for justice, which alone does not perish."[8] Two contemporary authors make much the same point with these words: "Most of us think of our options as either saving or spending. But the biblical witness and Christian tradition suggest that there's another option: sharing."[9]

If you're a Christian with access to significant resources, what if God is calling you to stabilize a faithful church in a financially distressed neighborhood? Could you assist an African American church planter by relieving student loan debt or by starting a scholarship fund for their children? Many Black and Brown church planters in multiethnic neighborhoods long to deepen their roots in the community by becoming homeowners. And yet, they lack financial resources to purchase a home. If you believe in the beauty of a life like heaven, could you assist one of these church planters with a down payment so their family can live in the neighborhood where God has called them to serve?

HOW GENEROSITY POINTS TO GOD'S TRUTH

In the earliest centuries of Christianity, generosity was a mark of the Christian life pointing to a power greater than any human purpose or plan.

According to a second-century writing known as *Epistle to Diognetus*, the ultimate evidence for the truth of the Christian faith was giving one's life: "Don't you see them exposed to wild beasts, that they may be persuaded to deny the Lord, and yet they are not overcome? . . . This doesn't seem to be a human work, does it? This is the power of God, and these are evidences of his presence."[10]

But what about Christians who never have a chance to prove the truth of the faith through martyrdom?

That's where generosity comes in.

According to the author of this ancient epistle, generosity is an apologetic for God's truth. That's because Christian generosity is a living imitation of the sacrificial love God revealed through the incarnation and death of Jesus Christ. This pattern of giving includes caring for the physical needs of one's neighbors, but it isn't limited to the giving of goods or money.[11] It includes the ways a Christian uses power and privilege too. In the words of *Epistle to Diognetus*, "happiness is not a matter . . . of ruling over one's neighbors, desiring to have supremacy over those that are weaker, or possessing wealth and using force." Hoarding of wealth and lording of power are, according to the author of this ancient epistle, "alien to the greatness" that belongs to God because such practices do not reflect God's self-giving love.[12] Generosity awakens an openness to martyrdom that prepares the Christian to be faithful even to the point of death.

Sacrificial giving is, in some sense, a rehearsal for martyrdom that points to the self-giving nature of God. Sharing power, giving freely to those who have been oppressed, feeding the poor, tending the sick, visiting the incarcerated—all of these are habits that no purely natural category is able to explain.[13] I am not suggesting, of course, that everyone who practices unreciprocated generosity is a Christian. There are, after all, plenty of philanthropic atheists in the world. What I am contending is that no one would pursue such generosity unless there is more to the cosmos than mere matter and naturalistic causes. Certainly, there would be no communities practicing radical generosity together.

Much like the apologetic arguments that we've provided in earlier chapters, this argument from generosity doesn't get us all the way to the truth of the gospel, but it does help us to falsify the secular narrative that claims everything is explainable on the basis of naturalistic evolution. Unreciprocated human generosity defies almost every naturalistic explanation.

In the thinking of early Christians, the church's acts of generosity functioned as miniature martyrdoms that provided the world with living evidence for the truth of the gospel.

They still can, and they still do.

A CORPORATE HYMN OF OFFERING

Creator, giver of all things,
All I have is yours.
Accept my humble offering,
All I have is yours.
When I was chained to greed and pride,
Tight-fisted, destined just to die,
You paid my debt and bought my life.
All I have is yours
All I have,
All I have,
All I have is yours.
This offering is a means of grace,
All I have is yours.
You show me this to grow my faith,
All I have is yours.
The more I give the less I need,
I learn that you'll provide for me.
'Twas blind to this but now I see that
All I have is yours.
All I have,
All I have,
All I have is yours.[14]

PART 4

PASSING THE PEACE

Welcoming One Another in a Multiethnic Kingdom Culture

God's peace is not the absence of conflict; it's the presence of welcome.

	What's the problem?	What's the liturgy?	What's the result?
Call to Worship	We don't love God's vision for kingdom diversity.	We pray for ethnicities and classes of people who aren't present in our church.	We develop a multiethnic kingdom culture that forms us into worshipers who praise our Creator God for the beauty of kingdom diversity.
Lament	We don't recognize how deeply the heresy of racial superiority has impacted our churches and our lives.	We face the reality and the continuing impact of the heresy of racial superiority, and we lament the ways it has wounded us.	We are formed into mourners who grieve the continuing impact of the heresy of racial superiority.
Giving	We are not ready to recognize or to release our own preferences.	We practice gratitude for the wisdom and the ways of worship practiced by faithful churches in other cultural contexts.	We are formed into servants who sacrifice preferences, privileges, and possessions for the sake of a multiethnic kingdom culture.
Passing the Peace	We preserve our own preferences by practicing partiality or by trying to ignore ethnicity.	We learn to see beauty in other colors and cultures by practicing intentional multiethnic hospitality.	We are formed into a family in which our lives regularly include Christians from other cultures and colors.

10

GOING TO WAR BY PASSING THE PEACE

"Peace be with you."

"And also with you."

It's a request and response repeated thousands of times each Sunday at Sojourn Church Midtown. The words are spoken most frequently during "the passing of the peace," the moments in the middle of the service when newcomers are welcomed, old-timers are greeted, and lunch plans are confirmed.

Churches around the world practice a similar custom every week, and it's something believers have been doing for centuries. Long before Jesus set foot on planet earth, "peace be with you" was already repeated in the liturgies of the children of Abraham (Genesis 43:23; Numbers 6:26; Judges 6:23). Jesus himself spoke this declaration to his disciples after he turned a tomb into a temporary hotel and checked himself out alive and well (John 20:19-21).

In the years following the resurrection, the first generations of Christians marked the passing of peace with a "holy kiss" (Romans 16:16; 1 Corinthians 16:20; 2 Corinthians 13:12; 1 Thessalonians 5:26).[1] This kiss declared that each church member was an equal heir of one Father and an equal recipient of one Spirit—a rather shocking declaration considering the social diversity of early Christian communities.[2] Women and men, citizens and aliens, the wealthy and the enslaved from a range of different ethnicities—each shared the kiss of peace and proclaimed the power of the gospel to turn rivals into sisters and brothers.

But the impact of this liturgy among ancient Christians didn't end with the kiss itself.[3]

"What is indicated by the lips should happen in the conscience," Augustine of Hippo declared when he explained the kiss of peace to a band of new believers. "Just as your lips approach the lips of your brothers or sisters, so your heart should not be withdrawn from theirs."[4] For Augustine and other early Christians, passing the peace was not merely a meeting of bodies on Sunday; it was the weekly mark of a daily way of life. The people of the church had been adopted by God himself and transformed into a family that knew and cared for one another's needs. What they did with their bodies shaped and signified what was happening in their consciences and in their hearts.

HOW PASSING THE PEACE TURNS STRANGERS INTO FAMILY

Ideally, that's still what happens when we pass peace today.

In contemporary Western contexts, we're less likely to signify this peace with a kiss. Changes in the meaning of lip-to-lip affection have combined with health concerns to replace holy kisses with handshakes and hugs.[5] And yet, even though the *sign* of passing peace may have shifted, the *significance* of the liturgy persists.[6]

For us no less than for ancient Christians, the passing of peace on Sunday should never stand alone. When we pass peace on Sundays, we are declaring that divine adoption has transformed us into something different than we were before. We are admitting that none of us can follow Jesus alone. What we need to follow Jesus is a particular body of believers we might never have selected on our own but in whom the glory of Christ still manages to shine amid the crazy mess of our lives. A particular local church has become our first family, and we cannot be who we are without this church.

At this point, perhaps you're wondering why we're talking about passing the peace in this book. After all, isn't it about multiethnic kingdom culture? What could the passing of peace possibly have to do with multiethnicity and racism and moving our lives in the direction of a life like heaven?

Far more than you might think.

Consider this: In a multiethnic and multi-socioeconomic church, the passing of peace represents an uprising against the societal divisions this world's wisdom has been unable to heal. When you see peace passed among people whose voting patterns place them at different positions on the political spectrum, whose tax returns list incomes hundreds of thousands of dollars apart, and whose ethnicities are those the world is incapable of bringing together, you are watching the peace of Christ go to war against racism, classism, and every political idolatry. Such peace cannot be brought about by any purely human power. It can only be accomplished through the power of the gospel. And that's why learning to pass the peace daily is crucial for any church that longs to grow in kingdom diversity.

In the earliest centuries of Christianity, transcending social differences by practicing habits of hospitality with persons from different backgrounds stood as a key proof of the truth of Christian faith.[7] We think it still can. The passing of peace among people whom the world is unable to unify is an apologetic for the power of the gospel. Through these expressions of peace, we show the world the kind of king and kingdom we represent.[8] When we watch this diverse community of sisters and brothers welcome one another each week at Sojourn Church Midtown, our souls brim with gratitude as we witness the ways Christ has torn down the walls of hostility that once separated us (Ephesians 2:14).

Our fellowship is far from perfect. And yet, we've seen enough of the stories that surround us to know these hugs and handshakes and high-fives represent the overflow of peace that's been passed throughout the week. This liturgy is the epitome of peace shared through text messages and telephone calls, coffee shop conversations and game nights, shared meals and shared lives forming a diverse community into brothers and sisters. What we're seeing is the passing of a peace that passes human understanding.

WHAT HAPPENED WHEN PEACE WASN'T PASSED IN THE PASSING OF PEACE

I (Timothy) must admit, however, there are times when I've felt a touch of sadness mingled with these moments of joy.

This sadness is not because of the passing of peace I see around me.

It's because I remember a very different time of welcome in another time and another place.

That passing of the peace took place in a congregation I served more than two decades ago, at a time when Princess Diana's death was still fresh on people's minds and the first singles from *The Miseducation of Lauryn Hill* were climbing the pop charts. Decades later, the memory of that moment still scrapes uncomfortably across the surface of my soul. What was passed in that place wasn't peace. It was prejudice and pain, and it changed the direction of my life.

When I scanned the congregation in front of me on that Sunday, I saw a pair of faces I'd never seen before, and I felt a surge of joy. Newcomers were a rarity in that tiny town of four hundred or so people in the rural Midwest, and it had been quite some time since anyone new had visited our church. A good Sunday drew forty or fifty folks into the church's sanctuary. On sparser Sundays when wintry weather made senior citizens hesitant to venture out, I took comfort in the fact that even Jesus only had a dozen disciples who showed up consistently, and at least we had a few more people than that.

But my joy ran deeper than the mere fact that someone new had visited our church.

The newcomers were an African American couple, older than I was at the time but younger than the congregation's average age. In the five years I'd served this church, no one whose ethnicity was anything other than White had ever set foot in the building. I was thrilled to see this couple in the pews, and I was filled with hope they might become part of our fellowship.

When the time came to pass the peace, I headed toward the visitors, planning to welcome them. Before I made it to their pew, a church member approached me with some questions about an upcoming Christmas program. The time of welcome was over before I was able to finish that conversation, but I wasn't worried. As I returned to the platform, I glimpsed two longtime members of the church greeting the couple.

Or at least that's what I assumed the two men were doing.

I preached the sermon and offered an invitation. During the time of invitation, the man and woman knelt at their pew with their heads bowed. After the closing prayer, I opened my eyes, planning to invite the visitors to join my wife and me for lunch.

But the couple had already left the building.

And no wonder.

When I began to ask if anyone had obtained their information so I could contact them, I discovered what had happened during the time of welcome wasn't welcoming at all. According to an attender who overheard the conversation, the two men of the church had informed the man and his wife that, while it was fine for them to stay in the sanctuary for the rest of this service, they needed to find a place where they could worship with their own "kind of people." The two church members then provided the couple with the location of a historic African American church fifteen miles or so away and told them not to come back to our church.

All week, I tried to discover who these two visitors had been so I could apologize for what had taken place, but nobody seemed to know who they were or where they came from. What made it worse was that, even though none of the other church members condoned what had happened, no one was willing to confront what had happened. The most frequent response I received was an embarrassed chuckle followed by, "Well, that's just the way those two men are." A few months later, I left the church.

I still don't know where the visiting couple came from. They hadn't moved into town because everyone in this community knew immediately whenever someone moved in. Perhaps the couple had moved into the rural regions surrounding the town, or perhaps they were from another nearby community. Or maybe they were visiting angels of whom we were unaware (Hebrews 13:2).[9]

I don't know. I never saw them again.

But I am confident I will one day.

When God's chosen people from every tribe, language, and ethnicity gather around his throne, that couple will be there. When I see them, I plan to do at that time what I couldn't in this life. I will embrace them and let them know how glad I am to see them.

For now, however, I'm left to grieve what happened that day.

In retrospect, I recognize how much courage it required for them to walk through the doors of an all-White church in the first place. I'm still amazed they remained for the rest of the service after being told not to return. To this day, I wonder what happened when they knelt to pray during the invitation hymn. Somehow, I've always suspected they were praying, "Father, forgive them"—but an imprecatory prayer, asking God to pour out his wrath on this church, might have been equally appropriate.

My grief for this couple is not, however, the only sadness I feel when I remember that Sunday.

I also lament all the church missed.

What if other church members had stepped in to show hospitality to this couple? What if the church had regarded the heresy of racial supremacy as a serious sin instead of laughing it off as a harmless quirk in two older men's personalities? What if the church had truly passed peace?

The church could have grown that Sunday—and not merely by enfolding two additional people into its fellowship. The congregation could have expanded its perspective by learning to rejoice in the wisdom of people who believed the same gospel but brought different experiences to the table. What happened instead was a failure to pursue God's design for his people. The church fumbled a divinely given opportunity to display living evidence for the truth of the gospel in that community.

The events of that Sunday marked me deeply. Over time, the ache I felt within me grew into a yearning to pursue ministry that was intentionally multi-socioeconomic and multiethnic. This calling landed me first in an economically challenged neighborhood on the east side of Tulsa and eventually led me to Sojourn Church Midtown in Louisville with dozens of urban mission trips and work with Native American congregations in South Dakota scattered in between.

While working to bridge ethnic and economic divisions all along the way, I've seen over and over how hard it is for congregations to welcome people who don't fit their church's dominant cultures. Even for the most well-intentioned Christians, passing the peace day by day with people from different backgrounds doesn't happen naturally. It happens supernaturally, as God works through his church by the power of his Word and the presence of his Spirit. Even then, it's a painful process of learning to pass the peace with people who may see the situations of life in different ways than you do.

Chances are, if you're reading this book, you aren't the type of person who asks visitors not to come back to your church because of the color of their skin. And yet, telling newcomers to find a place for their own "kind of people" is far from the only way churches fail to pass the peace with minority believers. Without knowing it, almost any church can develop an inward culture that implicitly tells those who aren't in the majority they might be better off in a different congregation—and that brings us to one of the more painful parts of our story at Sojourn Church Midtown.

THE PRICE YOU HAVE TO PAY

In 2011, a White congregation with a love for the arts renovated a historic cathedral in Shelby Park and moved into the neighborhood, oblivious to what passing the peace in a multiethnic context would require. The church was only a decade old at the time, and most of its history up to that point had happened in a hipster community known as Germantown. Mike Cosper, one of the founding pastors of Sojourn Church, had this to say as he reflected on the church's disposition during those years,

> It isn't arrogance that makes you think, "This is it, we've figured it out." It's innocence. The innocence of your own hearts, whose corruption and weakness has yet to be tested and revealed under the ordinary pressures of marriage, work, family, and suffering.[10]

Mike wasn't speaking about the church's movement toward ethnic diversity, but his words certainly apply to that part of our story as well. This process has unmasked more corruption and weakness in us than anyone imagined when the journey began, but God is still doing something beautiful amid these many shortcomings.

"Restored church served as a catalyst for Shelby Park neighborhood revitalization"—those are the words embossed on the sign that the Kentucky Historical Society placed in our church's parking lot, and it's mostly true. But that single sentence can't capture the many missteps along the way or the continuing struggle to avoid building a congregation "on top of" this community. What quickly became clear was that merely moving across the railroad tracks that sequester Shelby Park from the rest of the city wasn't enough. When it came to welcoming ethnic minorities, Sojourn was wired from top to bottom with unacknowledged assumptions that short-circuited any real movement toward multiethnic kingdom culture.

Three years after Sojourn Church Midtown relocated in Shelby Park, Mike Cosper preached a sermon titled "Jesus, Race, and the Wall of Hostility." His message took a hard look at the challenges that African Americans have historically faced, and it marked a crucial moment for many members of Sojourn Church Midtown. A decade later, the content of that sermon doesn't seem particularly radical. At the time, however, it was a powerful and prophetic message that challenged the ways the church thought about ethnic diversity and racial division.

A few months later, the leadership of the church called Jamaal Williams as the church's lead pastor, and the congregation took its first tentative steps toward becoming a multiethnic refuge for Christians in this location. Over the space of a couple of years, the church's worship expanded to encompass a mélange of musical genres. Liturgies increasingly acknowledged the realities of racial prejudice. Sunday sermons remained steadfastly grounded in Scripture, but the styles of preaching expanded.

And it hurt.

Another pastor of a multiethnic church put it this way when he reflected on his own congregation's movement toward authentic diversity: "When the novelty wears off, you really see the price you have to pay."[11] He's right. There's a price your church will pay to pass peace among people from different ethnicities and socioeconomic strata.

WHY IT HURT SO MUCH

"Sometimes on the way to better, things get worse for a while," a novelist once pointed out, and she's right.[12] On the way to multiethnic kingdom culture, things got worse for a time. Tensions and loss tinged every step of our transition. Dozens of members moved on to other churches, and we answered more angry emails than any of us cares to recall. There were conflicts over styles of worship, along with the service of lament that opened more wounds than it healed. And yet, the pain of this process has been one of the tools God has used to press our church in the direction of a life like heaven. During this week's passing of the peace, I barely moved from my seat, and I shook hands with persons from at least four different ethnic backgrounds, and it was beautiful.

We have lost much and we still have far to go, but we have also gained.

But *why* has this process been so painful? Why is it still painful for us at times? And why is it likely to be painful for you and your church as well?

One key reason for the pain was that the dominant culture was losing its dominance in our church.

Cultural change is always stressful, but there are some transitions that bring more stress than others. In an American context, any change that diminishes the dominance of the majority culture tends to be particularly traumatic. In a nation with a past marked by racialization and racism, any attempt to bring multiple cultures together as equals means bracing your shoulder against centuries of crushing pressure that have pushed downward against cultures of color. This process is even more painful when people aren't aware of the ways their own backgrounds have shaped their preferences—and that's what happened for many members at Sojourn Church Midtown. A life of passing peace sometimes requires us to acknowledge patterns of prejudice and partiality within us we never even knew, and this is hard to do.

One of the primary patterns that stood in our way at Sojourn was the assumption that white is a neutral color.

11

WHITE IS NOT A NEUTRAL COLOR

"I don't see why anyone needs to be talking about race at church anyway!" she said. "I'm not racist, and I don't know anyone who is. If Black people want to start coming to Sojourn, no one's going to stop them. Why can't we just keep doing things the normal way?"

The woman at the next table in the coffee shop had been a member of Sojourn Church Midtown for years. But now, faced with the changes that had accompanied our movement toward a more multiethnic community, she was entertaining the possibility of looking for another church. I (Timothy) had arrived at the coffee shop intending to catch up on some reading, but my unplanned proximity to this woman had quickly developed into an impromptu pastoral meeting.[1]

Like most members during the church's first decade, her family was young and White. Now, the leadership and demographics of Sojourn were starting to shift. By God's grace, hundreds of men and women were catching a multiethnic vision for the church's future. But not everyone glimpsed this new future simultaneously, and some people never caught the vision at all. At this point, a couple of years after Jamaal became a lead pastor, more than a few members were struggling to see why any changes might be needed.

The church's previous patterns of worship and leadership had been—in this individual's thinking—neutral, normative, and no less welcoming to Black and Brown believers than to White Christians.[2] From her perspective, the celebration of different cultures and ethnicities that had happened on Diversity Sunday was unnecessary, and so were the shifts in preaching styles. She was open to having African American pastors on staff as long as they served under the authority of "a regular pastor."

As far as she could see, her preferences were normal and neutral for everyone, while the practices of other ethnicities and cultures were abnormal intrusions. What she couldn't seem to recognize was that her preferences were no less shaped by her cultural background than anyone else's.[3]

She wasn't alone. Whenever one cluster of ethnicities lives as a dominant majority for generations, those who share that background tend to view their own preferences as the impartial default for everyone. This blindness is one of the most difficult barriers you're likely to face when your church begins to move toward a more diverse future.[4] One of the primary reasons why this barrier is difficult in the United States is because so many White Americans don't notice the dominance of their own cultural preferences all around them.[5]

HOW DOMINANCE BLINDS US TO OURSELVES

Churches are not immune to this blindness.

It's easy for those of us who are part of a dominant culture never to notice how our cultural background shapes our preferences in worship and discipleship. If you're rarely exposed to other cultures, you may simply assume that your preferences aren't cultural at all; your preferences may feel to you as if they're the normal and neutral default. That's one reason why, whenever a church begins to move in a multiethnic direction, some members may struggle to recognize the ways their own certain preferences stand in the way of full-fledged faithfulness to Jesus. Here's how pastor John Piper describes the dilemma:

> Your church and your ministry (and your whole life) are through-and-through culturally shaped. You may not feel it, in the same way that fish don't feel wet. Wet is all they have ever known. Wet is just the way it is.... My exhortation, especially to dominant-culture churches, is that we recognize that all of us have a culture interwoven with our ethnicity, and the more dominant a culture is, the more invisible it seems to us. And it would be helpful if brothers and sisters of color could see that we are owning the tension that exists between our majority-white culture and the radical call of Jesus.[6]

What this means in American churches is that White perspectives and practices can be unintentionally perceived as normal and neutral for everyone. And that's why it can be hard for those of us who are members of majority cultures to recognize how ethnicity affects our lives—or even to cultivate any sort of ethnic self-awareness.[7]

This may be a new concept for you. If it is, pause for a moment and reread John Piper's words. Notice, he's not suggesting that any cultures ought to be completely cast aside. Instead, he's calling each of us to be aware of our own cultural preferences so we can recognize any tendencies that might stand in tension with the kingship of Jesus. The goal of this awareness is to open the door for the Word of God and the Spirit of God to form the church into a multiethnic, multigenerational, multi-socioeconomic family.

For many of us in majority cultures, part of the journey toward a life like heaven is simply learning to recognize the many ways the dominance of White culture impacts people's lives. To live as part of the majority culture in the United States is to be able to organize your life so you can spend almost all your time with people whose ethnicity matches your own if you so choose. It means you can easily purchase toys, books, movies, and greeting cards featuring people who look like you anywhere you go. For the most part, you can even ignore experiences, writings, and ideas that come from persons of color—and all of this can happen with very little effort.[8]

When that happens, disregarding minority perspectives can seem like the "normal way" of doing life. Such disregard inadvertently treats the majority ethnicity as dominant and central.[9] And yet, even if a monoethnic existence seems normal to you, God has provided everything you need to experience a life that's so much better. This better life is a life that leaves partiality behind.

HOW PARTIALITY PREVENTS US FROM PASSING PEACE

Of course, the specific patterns of cultural dominance we see today haven't always existed. These patterns have only taken shape over the past few centuries, and some portions are less than a century old.

At the same time, the sin of viewing one culture or class as better than another is *not* something new. It's far older than any modern social system. In fact, this tendency was so common in the first century that early

Christians coined a term to describe the habit of treating a particular type of person as superior.[10] This term is translated in most of our English Bibles as "favoritism" or "partiality."[11]

The sin of partiality happened among first-century Christians when wealthier visitors were placed in seats of honor during the church's worship services (James 2:1-9). Partiality happens today when a church gives more honor to a visiting politician than to the homeless family that shows up looking for refuge from the cold. Partiality is when a church's activities come with a cost only middle- and upper-income families can afford. Partiality can devastate the holiness of our congregations if we fail to correct well-to-do members of the church because we fear what will happen if they stop giving. Such partialities prevent us from passing the peace day by day in ways that form us into a family. Partiality is sin because it is a failure to love our neighbors, and God's condemnation of partiality is a reminder that we cannot simultaneously rank one another and love one another.

But socioeconomic differences weren't the only reasons for partiality, even in the first century.[12] Partiality can also be cultural and ethnic. Less than a generation after Jesus ascended into the heavens, some Christians were already defying God's design by valuing those who shared their culture above those who didn't (see Acts 6:1; 10:1-35; Galatians 2:11-14). Although sins of cultural partiality have taken different shapes over the centuries, they've never completely passed away. One of the primary forms they have taken in contemporary Western society is prejudice against persons of African descent. And yet, even here, explicit racism isn't the only form that partiality can take. Ethnic and cultural partialities can poison our thinking in subtler ways as well, so that we value certain cultures above others in ways that we may not immediately see.

When that happens, partiality can distort what we see as the right songs to sing, how we think they ought to be sung, which leaders we're willing to follow, and what we assume must be the normal way to preach. Ethnic partiality can affect which tragedies we lament and which ones we try to ignore. It influences the pictures we hang in the lobby and the books we stock in our bookstores. In White-dominant cultures, partiality can be innocently reinforced in everything from peach-colored headset microphones to Sunday school posters depicting Jewish biblical characters with pale flesh and European facial features.[13] The result is ethnic and cultural dominance many of us may not even notice.

HOW COLORBLINDNESS BLINDS US
TO ALL THE WRONG THINGS

So what can churches do to change these patterns of partiality? This is one of the many places where it's clear that the world's solutions to ethnic division simply aren't sufficient to accomplish the blood-bought unity to which Christ has called his people. "If we're driven by what the world says success regarding race looks like rather than what the Word says faithfulness looks like, we'll be crushed, because the world's demands can never be met," Isaac Adams writes. "That beast is never satisfied."[14]

One of the most common responses Christians have borrowed from the world around them is to try to ignore colors and cultures altogether. "I don't see Black people as Black," someone might claim. "I just see them as people." Another way of saying the same thing happens when a church member declares, "Why can't we all just be colorblind?"

Most of the time, the people making these appeals to ethnic colorblindness mean well, and there is some truth behind what they're saying.[15] No one should be granted or denied privileges on the sheer basis of ethnicity.[16] That's part of what Martin Luther King Jr. was getting at when he proclaimed, "I have a dream that my four little children will one day live in a nation where they will not be judged by the color of their skin but by the content of their character."[17] And yet, making certain that ethnicity doesn't stand in the way of equality doesn't mean trying to act as if ethnicity doesn't exist.[18]

In practice, approaches that try to ignore ethnicity have not been successful in diminishing racism, according to a wide range of sociological studies.[19] But these social-scientific studies are not our primary concern, because the primary problem with colorblind solutions is not sociological.

It's theological.

The most pressing problem with attempting to live a colorblind life is that, when we try to ignore someone's ethnicity, we are downplaying a reality in which our heavenly Father delights. In the beginning, our sovereign Creator crafted humanity to develop into a vibrant palette of different colors and cultures.[20] God delights in this, and so should we.[21]

And how do we know that God delights in different colors and cultures? The same way we discover any other objective truth about God: we find it in his inspired Word.

If the triune God wanted us to be blind when it comes to someone's ethnicity, why did the Holy Spirit guide Luke to highlight the ethnic origins of the seeker that Philip baptized in the desert (Acts 8:27)? If colorblindness is God's design, why did Luke's Spirit-inspired words specify the African origins of two teachers in the church of Antioch? And why did God guide Luke to select a word to describe one of them that specifically highlighted Simeon's darker flesh (Acts 13:1)? If God doesn't delight in different colors and cultures, why did he display his glory by spinning a vision of numberless multitudes from every ethnicity before the eyes of the apostle John (Revelation 5:9; 7:9-10)? And why would he superintend John's writing in such a way that the apostle mentioned how the glory and honor of every ethnicity would be part of the consummation of God's kingdom (Revelation 21:26)? In these and dozens of other instances throughout the New Testament, God's Word refuses to be blind to ethnicity. Instead, the Scriptures consistently celebrate the many colors and cultures of those whom God has called to himself. Christian hip-hop artist Shai Linne puts the point like this:

> To my white brothers and sisters in Christ, please don't tell me that you don't see color. I know what you mean. You're trying to communicate that you treat all people equally and that you judge people based on the content of their character rather than the color of their skin. That's great. We should all do that. But God was intentional when He gave me brown skin. He didn't give it to me that it might be ignored. He gave it to me that it would be appreciated and that He might be praised for His creative genius. So don't rob God of His praise by ignoring it![22]

There is no partiality in the gospel (Acts 10:34), but gospel impartiality was never meant to dull our eyes to the exquisite colors and cultural rhythms that surround us in a multiethnic community.[23]

God isn't colorblind, and neither should we be.

The gospel isn't designed to make us colorblind; it keeps us from being color bound and shows us the many ways we have been color blessed. God did not create a colorless world, and he did not intend his people to be blind to others' colors or cultures. If you try to live a colorblind life, you're missing glimpses of splendor that God designed for his praise.

The gospel makes us one, but it doesn't make us the same.[24] The hue of our flesh, the features of our faces, the structures of our bodies, the cultural stories that history has entwined with our ethnicities—these beautiful differences have taken shape within the scope of our Father's sovereign plan. No color or culture is better or more beautiful than another because each one is part of a global mosaic that has been crafted for our Creator's glory. "God's vision for his people is not for the elimination of ethnicity to form a colorblind uniformity of sanctified blandness," New Testament scholar Esau McCaulley has noted. Instead,

> God sees the creation of a community of different cultures united by faith in his Son as a manifestation of the expansive nature of his grace. This expansiveness is unfulfilled unless the differences are seen and celebrated, not as ends unto themselves, but as particular manifestations of the power of the Spirit to bring forth the same holiness among different peoples and cultures for the glory of God.[25]

There are further problems with a colorblind strategy for ethnic reconciliation as well. The abuse and dehumanization inflicted on African American communities for centuries still shape the world today. Living under the pretense of colorblindness can blind us to the results of these injustices that still surround us. When that happens, claiming to be colorblind doesn't bring about impartiality. Instead, it provides a pretext, whether intentionally or not, for ignoring the persistent effects of past partialities.

YOUR ETHNICITY MATTERS . . . BUT YOUR ETHNICITY IS NOT WHAT MATTERS MOST

But if the answer isn't colorblindness, what is it?

Colorblindness clearly can't produce a peace that transforms a multiplicity of ethnicities into one family in Christ. But neither can another popular secular solution known as "multiculturalism." Instead of downplaying the differences in cultures, multiculturalism takes the opposite approach, focusing on the positive distinctives and contributions of minority cultures.[26] And yet, multiculturalism will always fall short when it comes to cultivating multiethnic kingdom culture because multiculturalism tends to focus only on perceived distinctives of minority ethnicities and to turn diversity itself into the primary goal.[27]

Another secular approach incapable of cultivating multiethnic kingdom culture is "antiracism." Secular antiracists have contended in many cases that racism is a permanent and indestructible component of the social order in America, which leaves people without hope.[28] In some expressions of antiracism, people are classified as "oppressed" or "oppressors" on the basis of their ethnicity, without regard for anything they've actually done. Such a perspective short-circuits the collaborative conversations that are necessary for us to welcome one another with hospitality and joy, and it's not been proven to work in practice.[29] Even worse from a Christian perspective, antiracism makes ethnicity central to our identities in a way that Scripture doesn't.[30]

Colors and cultures matter, and they are part of God's plan for his eternal glory. And yet, these realities are never our most central identities as followers of Jesus Christ. What matters most about us as Christians is our creation in God's image and our re-creation through union with Christ.

To embrace the gospel is to be adopted in Christ (Ephesians 1:5–2:22). When that happens, Christ himself becomes our central identity, transcending our ethnic and cultural identities without replacing them.[31] That's how God formed early Christians into a new kind of humanity in which an astonishing multiplicity of ethnicities reflected God's beauty together in gospel-shaped communities. This way of life is what drove one second-century writer to look at the church and wonder, "Why has this new genus of humanity . . . come into the world now and not before?"[32]

Neither colorblindness nor multiculturalism nor secular antiracism can transform the people of God into a "new genus of humanity" that exemplifies multiethnic kingdom culture. What we need instead is a solution that delights in the beauty of our differences while refusing to allow these differences to divide us or define us—and that brings us back to the process of learning to pass the peace day by day.[33]

God's peace is not the absence of conflict; it's the presence of welcome. When we pass peace day by day, we welcome fellow believers into our lives with all of their disparate stories and struggles, burdens and joys (Romans 12:15-16; Galatians 6:1-10; Ephesians 4:2-3). That's part of what Paul was getting at when he penned these words for a church family where the fellowship was fracturing due to cultural differences: "Welcome one another, just as Christ also welcomed you, to the glory of God" (Romans 15:7).

As a follower of Jesus Christ, the family you welcome shouldn't be limited to persons who come from the same ethnic, cultural, and socioeconomic background as you. That's why the welcome Paul described required giving up personal preferences and partialities so others can experience peace (Romans 15:1-7).[34] "For even Christ," Paul pointed out, "did not please himself" (Romans 15:3). Welcoming one another in this way means embracing fellow believers as human beings embedded in particular cultures and embodied in certain ethnicities. It means acknowledging the differences between us as opportunities to reflect the glory of God's plan more fully, not *in spite of* our differences but *because of* these differences. When that happens in our churches, the world around us will witness a new kind of family that's rich with diverse fellowship and divine righteousness.

DO YOU LOVE GOD'S VISION?

Sojourn Church Midtown moved into Shelby Park as a congregation with a culture that was not hospitable to minority cultures. Much has changed since then, but this transformation hasn't happened because we blinded ourselves to people's ethnicities. It also didn't happen because we traded one cultural dominance for the dominance of some other human culture or color. Solutions of this sort simply rearrange the same problems in a different package.

Our goal isn't Black or Brown culture. It's a kingdom culture that unites in the worship of one King and learns to pass the peace by delighting in all that is beautiful and good in every color, culture, and class. Here's how Tony Evans describes the values of this kingdom:

> God's kingdom is not white. God's kingdom is not Hispanic. Nor is it Asian, Middle Eastern, or Indian. God did not come to take sides. God

came to take over. And until we bow beneath the overarching rules set forth by the Ruler in his realm, we will continue to live defeated lives in the face of walls too thick to crumble and an enemy looming too large for us to overcome.[35]

Kingdom culture may look different in your church than it does in ours. For you, cultivating a kingdom culture might mean learning to pass peace with displaced Somali refugees or Latino immigrants. It may entail some difficult adjustments to make a congregation of twentysomethings more welcoming to senior citizens. It could require you asking yourself what's preventing nearby members of the Lakota tribe from seeking fellowship in your church. It might mean adjusting your ministries to accommodate low-income families in a nearby trailer park. It could even mean helping your church to plant a congregation that will grow to become multiethnic in a way your church can't at this time. Regardless of what kingdom culture looks like in your context, remember this: you cannot develop kingdom culture without cultivating a love that welcomes a greater breadth of people. Become deeply aware of the palette of different cultures around you and learn to love the glimmers of beauty in all that you see. And remember, gaps in kingdom culture aren't primarily the result of what we know or don't know; they're usually due to deficiencies in what we love.

And that's why I responded in the way that I did to the church member in the coffee shop who couldn't see why anything might need to change.

"When you hear about John's vision of a multitude that includes every ethnicity and language," I said, "do you love that vision?"

"Well," she hesitated. "I guess so."

I paused and pressed further, "Do you love that vision enough to give up some of your preferences so we can see a hint of it in our church?"

"But that's in heaven," she shot back, sidestepping the question. "Not here."

"And don't we pray for God's will to be done 'on earth as it is in heaven'?" I replied. "If we ask God's will to be done on earth as in heaven, shouldn't we do what we can to move in that direction here and now?"

A few minutes later, our conversation ended. Our parting was cordial and kind, but the church member was still struggling to see why growing in ethnic and cultural diversity might require anything to change.

Once again, the gap isn't primarily in what we know; it's in what we love. What we love is formed in part by what we repeatedly do, and that brings us back to liturgies. The liturgies of our lives—the physical acts and responses we repeat until they become habits—direct our longings and our loves.

When it comes to passing the peace across cultures and ethnicities, what we need are liturgies of hospitality.

12

LITURGIES OF HOSPITALITY

For many of us today, hospitality is "a nice extra if we have the time or the resources, but we rarely view it as a spiritual obligation or as a dynamic expression of vibrant Christianity."[1]

It wasn't always this way.

In the earliest decades of Christian faith, hospitality was not seen as an optional add-on. The apostle Peter commanded Christians in Asia Minor to "be hospitable to one another without complaining" (1 Peter 4:9; see also Romans 12:13; 1 Timothy 3:2; Titus 1:8). The author of Hebrews raised the stakes even higher. According to this writer, mortal beings aren't the only possible recipients of Christian hospitality: "Don't neglect to show hospitality, for by doing this some have welcomed angels as guests without knowing it" (Hebrews 13:2).

Practices of hospitality seem to have been one of the reasons why ancient pagans were attracted to Christianity. In the fourth century, the emperor Julian shared this complaint about Christians with his fellow pagans: "Why don't we notice that it is their benevolence to strangers, their care for the graves of the dead, and the supposed holiness of their lives that have done the most to increase their number?"[2] A few decades later, in the aftermath of the sacking of Rome, Augustine of Hippo urged his North African congregation to welcome refugees from the Italian province with "hospitality and good works." "Let but Christians do what Christ enjoins," Augustine told his church members, "and so will the heathen blaspheme only to their own hurt."[3]

WHAT HOSPITALITY IS—AND ISN'T

Unfortunately, many of us today have confused hospitality with entertainment. When we hear the word *hospitality*, we think of inviting a church member over to our house to enjoy a perfect meal that we've prepared after meticulously cleaning our apartment and hiding every mess behind closed doors—after which we aren't particularly sure we even like the family we've invited, and we're certainly never going to ask them again, unless they ask us to dinner at their house, in which case we'll be obligated to reciprocate and the cycle of stress will start all over again.

That's not the type of hospitality described in the New Testament.

To practice New Testament hospitality is to pass the peace day by day in such a way that strangers are transformed into family.[4] Hospitality is not merely having someone over for dinner—although that may be one place to start. Hospitality is radical welcome coupled with Christlike generosity. Understood in this way, "hospitality is not something you do as much as it is someone you become."[5] Such generous welcome is frightening for many of us because it means there will be people who discover not only the messiness of our homes but also the messiness in our hearts.

"Although we often think of hospitality as a tame and pleasant practice, Christian hospitality has always had a subversive, countercultural dimension"[6]—and we see this most clearly when we welcome those who are unlike us. Hospitality doesn't pretend differences don't exist, as in colorblindness. Instead, it rejoices in the diversities of gifts and stories, recognizing there are facets of God's glorious work I would never have noticed apart from the gifts and stories of people who are different from me. A lifestyle of generous welcome means glimpsing God's creativity in the very things that make others different from us.

When our lives expand to embrace the differences that once separated us from our fellow believers, divine hospitality goes to war against human partiality. This sort of welcome is an essential part of growing as a Christian. When C. S. Lewis began attending church with people from different socioeconomic classes, he had this to say about how the experience affected him: "I came up against different people of quite different outlooks and different education, and then gradually my conceit just began peeling off."[7] That's what happens when we welcome people who are different from us. It's even truer when we invest our lives in a community where peace is passed among people from a diversity of ethnicities and economic backgrounds.

HOW HOSPITALITY TREATS THE WOUND
OF ETHNIC PARTIALITY

Multiethnic hospitality crushes the conceited assumption that we have nothing to learn from cultures other than our own. When I welcome believers whose culture or color is different from mine, I am admitting that the resources I need to be what God created me to be are not the exclusive property of people who look like me. Such hospitality can help us see the beauty and the brokenness woven into other ethnicities' experiences along with our own, which can strip away the delusion that our own preferences are neutral or normative for everyone.[8]

But how do we start this growth toward lives that are rich with multiethnic hospitality?

One way to grow toward multiethnic hospitality is to cultivate habits that connect us with persons whose culture or ethnicity is different from our own. Let's consider a couple of very ordinary habits that can develop into life-changing liturgies of hospitality.

Prepare your life for multiethnic hospitality. When I (Timothy) am walking down a sidewalk with a group of African American brothers, I sometimes notice a sound I've never heard in the company of White brothers.

It's a series of clicks, and it comes from the cars along the curb.

The occupants of these vehicles would likely never describe themselves as racists. And yet when they glimpse a group that's mostly composed of African American men, their first instinct is to lock their doors. What I hear in those moments is the sound of fear, and it comes from people who probably don't even know they're afraid. Even if you aren't prone to lock your doors when you see people whose ethnicity is unlike your own, you probably have anxieties provoked by the presence of particular cultures or colors. Fear is one of the key factors that keeps ethnicities divided, because love can never flourish in a heart filled with fear (1 John 4:18). And that's why one of the first steps toward living a life of multiethnic hospitality is learning to hand over our fears to our Father in heaven.

Here's one way to prime your heart to fight these fears: At least once each week, shop in a place where the primary ethnicity differs from your own. For some of you, that may mean purchasing a few items each week at a Latino grocery or in an Asian market. For others, it might look like making a habit of purchasing milk or some other weekly staple in a part of town where the residents are mostly African American. A few of you may be able to shop in a neighborhood filled with Middle Eastern immigrants. Regardless of what context you choose, select a particular day and time and go to the same spot every week. As you do, seek opportunities to build friendships with the people you see repeatedly. If you're in a context where English isn't people's first language, learn to greet the people you meet in their own tongue.

When you return home each week, write down anything that frightened or frustrated you about this experience. During your daily devotional time, work through your list of fears and frustrations. As you do, ask God to reveal any tendencies toward ethnic partiality hidden in your heart. Persist in these habits week by week until you're no longer anxious when you head to the place you've selected. "Men often hate each other because they fear each other," Martin Luther King Jr. said, "they fear each other because they do not know each other; they do not know each other because they cannot communicate; they cannot communicate because they are separated."[9] When we choose not to be separated, fear fades.

For some of you, shopping in a place where the primary ethnicity is different from your own may seem impossible. If that's because you live in a location that's too distant from any other ethnicities, explore the question of why there is so little ethnic diversity in your location. Are there other ways you could narrow this separation? If the reason this habit seems impossible is because of your own fears and anxieties, consider what this hesitancy reveals about your soul. Is it possible your fear masks partiality toward certain places or people? If you automatically assume it's unsafe to shop in a spot where your own ethnicity isn't predominant, what does this assumption suggest about your perceptions of others? What liturgies might God use to transform your fears into hospitality?

Practice a life of multiethnic hospitality. "When we talk about racial reconciliation, we often want the fruit of reconciliation without the relationships," Chicago pastor Jon Kelly commented in a recent panel discussion. "But until our dinner tables become diversified, . . . we won't make any progress."[10]

But how do we help this to happen? The answer is *not* to approach someone during the passing of the peace at church and ask, "Since your ethnicity is different from mine, could you come to our house for dinner so my family can learn how to be less prejudiced?" I watched a well-intended but less-than-thoughtful individual do this once. It was awkward, to say the least. No one wants to be reduced to a tool in someone else's personal improvement project.[11]

A better response is hospitality arising from prayerful intentionality. If we believe prayer changes things, shouldn't prayer be central in such a complex process of transformation? Ask God to bring about opportunities for authentic multiethnic relationships, and trust that God will provide an answer in his time. When that begins to happen, be intentional about cultivating habits of free and authentic hospitality.[12] Work toward sharing a meal together in your home at least once each month.[13] Your heart grows more sensitive to the sin of ethnic partiality when your home becomes a location for multiethnic hospitality.

When practicing these habits, don't treat other people as your personal experts on whiteness, blackness, or any other ethnic or socioeconomic experience. Particularly in the early stages of your relationship, be willing to practice a discipline of listening (James 1:19).[14] For those of us in the dominant majority, it's easy to see our role as solving the problems in other people's perspectives. And yet, it's impossible to practice Christian hospitality if you consistently treat other people's viewpoints as problems your opinions can fix. Whether or not it's intended, the root of this attitude may be ungodly pride, and pride prevents us from listening. Ultimately, ungodly pride—in the words of Augustine—"abhors equality with other human beings."[15] When that happens, there is no capacity to see the other person as a gift from whom we can learn.[16]

If you're a church leader, your congregation can also pursue multiethnic hospitality as a community. Consider partnering with a nearby congregation where the confession of faith is the same as yours but the primary ethnicities in the church are not. Prepare your people beforehand by working through this book or one like it. Begin hosting the other congregation on a regular basis for a special evening of worship with your church, inviting their pastor to preach the sermon. Particularly if your church is a majority-culture congregation, be sure that the other church is treated as an equal, not as a group that requires your guidance and correction.[17] In some cases, it may be helpful for you to partner with a church that's larger than your own, so you don't unintentionally overwhelm your brothers and sisters. After these special times of worship, eat together and enjoy times of fellowship.

The finished work of Christ has already guaranteed the adoption of every person whom God has chosen (Ephesians 2:19). Hospitality puts this adoption into practice. The gospel makes us a family. Hospitality develops the habits of living together as a family here and now.[18] But be prepared: Whenever a household mingles together a multiplicity of ethnicities, it's likely to seem strange to the world around us. It's true in families, and it's true in churches. I was reminded of this reality a few years ago when I (Timothy) heard someone ask my child, "Is she *really* your sister?"

HOW GOD SHAPES US INTO A FAMILY

The glow of the setting sun shimmers across the surface of the pool and brushes across the flesh of my three younger daughters. Their older sister reclines on a nearby chaise, soaking in the sun's last rays. It's been a long drive from Kentucky to Florida. The children are bursting with energy, my wife and I are ready to rest, and the hotel pool provides an opportunity for both.

Eyes half-closed, I watch the children as they bounce a beach ball between them and dance to the music that's thumping through a speaker above their heads. Another girl—alone and perhaps nine or ten years old—watches their frolicking from the edge of the pool. After a few minutes of watching from a distance, she dog paddles in their direction and asks to join the game. Space is made, rules are declared, and soon all of them are giggling and gyrating and bouncing the ball between them.

During a lull in the danceable music, the girls begin introducing themselves—and that's when the conversation takes a turn.

"So how do you all know each other?" the newfound acquaintance asks.

"We're sisters," my youngest child replies without the slightest hesitation.

The new participant's eyebrow arches as she stares at the three girls surrounding her. The youngest has dark chestnut skin and pitch-black curls, the next child's braided weave and latte-hued flesh hint at a heritage that encompasses Black and White and perhaps Native American, while the third child's straight hair frames a peach-colored face. Adoption has made them sisters, but their new friend is clearly not considering this possibility.

"That's funny," the girl says, but no one laughs. She presses further, "You're joking, right?"

All three of my daughters shake their heads. The next-to-youngest points to the chaise where their olive-skinned Romanian sibling has fallen asleep, "And that's our sister too. She's the oldest."

"So you're stepsisters?"

"No," the youngest insists. "We're all the same family, and that's our mom and dad." She casually gestures in my direction. This attempt to clarify the issue does nothing to reduce the other child's confusion. When she turns, she sees a man and a woman who are both very White and very middle-aged, and both of the child's eyebrows arch in surprise.

"Seriously," the new friend says to our youngest child while pointing at her lightest-skinned sibling, "is she your sister for real?"

"Of course she's real!" our next-to-youngest child interjects with her typical literal-mindedness, apparently offended her sister's very existence is now up for debate.

"No, no, no," the friend persists in her interrogation, now more confused than ever. "What I mean is, is she *really* your sister?"

Our next-to-youngest replies with utmost seriousness, "Yes, we're all really sisters." A few moments later, the new acquaintance gives up on the conversation and joins in my children's games, still unconvinced the four of them are members of the same family.

That evening, I had a good conversation with my younger children about how to answer people's questions about our family. At the same time, I was proud of their relentless insistence they were real sisters. Adoption decrees have made them sisters by law, and they know that. But legal decrees are not what make them sisters in life. What transforms them from strangers into sisters is the life we live together. It's because of meals eaten at the same table, hours spent together in the same car, games played together in the back yard, and conflict after conflict resolved. It's the love of the same imperfect parents mingled with ordinary habits of hospitality that have shaped their souls until they will fight with dogged determination for their relationships with one another.

That's how God turns his people into a family too. He decreed our adoption by his sovereign will in eternity past (Romans 8:14-16), but he also shapes us into brothers and sisters through the time we spend together here and now. That's the power of gospel-driven hospitality.

HOW HOSPITALITY HEALS THE WOUNDS OF PARTIALITY AND PROVIDES EVIDENCE FOR GOD'S TRUTH

The best the world's approaches to diversity can do is decrease the tensions between different ethnicities, and these approaches typically fail even to do that. The gospel enables the church to do far more than merely curtailing conflict. When a church's hospitality becomes multi-socioeconomic and multiethnic, we and the world around us see the glistening of a reality that can only be described as supernatural.

Naturalistic evolution might be able to explain hospitality directed only toward those who can benefit you or who are related to you. Yet a godless cosmos cannot comprehensively explain a lifestyle of hospitality that welcomes those who are different as equals. Such habits defy Darwinian explanations.[19] Particularly when practiced by an entire community, multiethnic hospitality provides an apologetic argument that calls into question every materialist account of human social behaviors.

But sometimes, the same hospitality that helps us live as a family also brings hurt because it draws us into the reality of another person's pain.

When an African American pastor mentions the clicking of car locks as we walk together down the street, what needles my soul is not merely what this reveals about the persistent prejudice in our nation. I hurt when I hear the locks clicking because this is my brother, and the time we've spent together has made his life inseparable from mine.

When a young Black woman is gunned down in her apartment because of a no-knock warrant that should never have been issued, I am saddened by this unjust loss of a living image of God. And yet, my grief runs far deeper than that. I cannot think of her life without also thinking of the dozens of beautiful African American sisters who have been guests at my table over the years and how they teach my younger daughters to see the beauty in their skin and to enjoy their hair and to remember to sing the Stevie Wonder birthday song on their birthdays. They are my family, and their presence in my life has transformed how I see the value and the beauty of Black lives. For much of my adult life, ethnic partiality bothered me, but it never brought me pain. After years of multiethnic hospitality, the wounds of ethnic partiality hurt more deeply than words can describe.

That's the power—and the price—of passing the peace.

A CORPORATE PASSING OF THE PEACE

Come, weary and tired, worn out from life,
Step out of the shadows, walk into the light.
Come sinner or saint, slave man or free,
Bring blessings and offerings, then you shall see.
Bring blessings and offerings, then you shall see.
There's a peace to settle your soul.
There is a peace that is calling you home.
You've been tempted and shaken, tested and failed,
You've been so far from Jesus, too close to hell.
Your vision's been clouded by this world's delight,
But I tell you you're not of this world, so stand up and fight.
You're not of this world so stand up and fight.
There's a peace to settle your soul.
There is a peace that is calling you home.[20]

PART 5

COMMUNION

Feasting Together on the Victory Jesus Won

Live like Jesus has already broken down the walls between us—because he has.

	What's the problem?	What's the liturgy?	What's the result?
Call to Worship	We don't love God's vision for kingdom diversity.	We pray for ethnicities and classes of people who aren't present in our church.	We develop a multi-ethnic kingdom culture that forms us into worshipers who praise our Creator God for the beauty of kingdom diversity.
Lament	We don't recognize how deeply the heresy of racial superiority has impacted our churches and our lives.	We face the reality and the continuing impact of the heresy of racial superiority, and we lament the ways it has wounded us.	We are formed into mourners who grieve the continuing impact of the heresy of racial superiority.
Giving	We are not ready to recognize or to release our own preferences.	We practice gratitude for the wisdom and the ways of worship practiced by faithful churches in other cultural contexts.	We are formed into servants who sacrifice preferences, privileges, and possessions for the sake of a multiethnic kingdom culture.

	What's the problem?	What's the liturgy?	What's the result?
Passing the Peace	We preserve our own preferences by practicing partiality or by trying to ignore ethnicity.	We learn to see beauty in other colors and cultures by practicing intentional multiethnic hospitality.	We are formed into a family in which our lives regularly include Christians from other cultures and colors.
Communion	We expect fellowship and forgiveness to happen without acknowledging the pain that's present in our place.	We physically engage the stories of the place where God has planted us.	We are formed into disciples who love the people in our neighborhoods more fully because we know the stories that have shaped them.
Benediction	We see reconciliation as a goal that we must achieve.	We are reminded through benedictions that every blessing is already ours in Christ.	We recognize reconciliation as a blessing that we receive, and we live as sons and daughters of God with nothing to earn and nothing to prove.

13

KNOWING
YOUR PLACE

If you've followed the flow of this narrative carefully, you recognize we have patterned each section after the structure of our worship services. At this point, it's time for the sermon.

WHY DO THE SERMON AND THE LORD'S SUPPER MATTER SO MUCH?

The Word rightly proclaimed and the sacraments—or "ordinances"—rightly administered are the marks of a church that's faithful to Jesus.[1] That's why we take both habits so seriously. Preaching invites people into communion with God through his Word as the preacher recounts God's redemptive works. And so, every Sunday at Sojourn Church Midtown, the preacher stands behind an old-school wooden podium and works line by line through the Scriptures, pointing people's attention to Jesus Christ. We wouldn't have it any other way. "To preach Christ," Martin Luther once said, "is to feed the soul, to justify it, to set it free, and to save it, if it believes the preaching"—and that's what we endeavor to do.[2] After every sermon, we share the Lord's Supper and physically remember how the sacrifice of Jesus broke down the barriers between us.

Previous chapters in this book have explored how the gospel shatters barriers that once separated us. This portion of the book picks up the same theme from a different angle. The goal of this chapter is to consider how this truth can be applied to places. The broken body of Jesus has already shattered the barriers standing between his people. But how can churches and pastors work out this truth practically in their own communities?

Just as we do week by week when preaching, we'll first explore what's broken in the places where God has planted us. After we glimpse our brokenness clearly, we'll be able to consider how the gospel of Jesus Christ can reshape neighborhoods and nations for his glory through his people.

PAYING ATTENTION TO THE PLACE WHERE YOU ARE

In 2015, I (Jamaal) preached a sermon from the second chapter of Ephesians in an all-White church in Columbus, Ohio. I was the first African American preacher ever to stand behind the pulpit of this historic church nestled in an affluent part of town. My purpose was to awaken the church to the realities of systemic racism and to display the beautiful ways the sacrifice of Christ has decimated the barriers that keep his people apart.

The sermon was well received, so I thought I would preach the same text in the historic African American church I served at the time. Of course, I made a few adjustments in the sermon to fit each context. In the church where I was a guest, I wanted to move people toward gospel unity by opening their eyes to the pain many of their African American brothers and sisters faced. In my home church, I wanted to cultivate a posture of forgiveness and grace toward White Christians and non-Christians. I didn't intend to ignore the historical realities, but my goal was to encourage my people to demonstrate gospel-driven love even as they pursued justice.

As I look back, I recognize that I wasn't as curious as I should have been about the collective hurt many of my members had endured. It wasn't that I didn't care. It wasn't even that I didn't ask. But I didn't persevere long enough in the asking.

I faced the same difficulty with the members of Forest Baptist Church as I did when I talked with my octogenarian grandparents about their experiences growing up in Sontag and Starkville, Mississippi. If you recall from a previous chapter, Starkville was the town where two men were lynched while vendors sold sodas and a crowd of White church members picnicked and sang a hymn. For my grandparents, these lynchings didn't originate in history textbooks. They were realities my ancestors knew firsthand. And yet, it was difficult and painful for them to speak to the next generation about what they had seen.

After I preached that sermon from Ephesians in the historic Black church where I served, I vividly remember a conversation with an older Christian gentleman whom I deeply respect. He approached me after the sermon and spoke to me with a tone of utmost kindness: "Pastor, I agree with you that we should forgive and not carry resentment—but do have compassion, because if you knew what some of us had been through, if you knew what they did to us, if you only knew what they did . . ."

What he shared still shakes me today.

The man described how Walnut Street in downtown Louisville was once a thriving center of Black culture and Black-owned businesses. Then, the city claimed the area in the name of "urban renewal," stripping the Black community of hard-earned resources and forcing many families to start over again. For this man, the destruction of Walnut Street was a story with faces and names he had known well. During this era, his brother—a college student at the time—had been arrested multiple times for participating in peaceful sit-ins, and the loss of wealth was something he had seen with his own eyes. People he knew and loved lost the businesses they built, and he had watched as families who once earned a middle-class way of life were reduced to destitution and poverty.

Was I wrong to preach this sermon from Ephesians to my congregation in a historic African American church? Certainly not. It was a message they needed to hear. And yet, I should have framed and applied the sermon in a way that acknowledged the specific pain they had experienced in this city. They needed to understand not only how the blood of Jesus can bring together Gentiles and Jews—which was Paul's primary point in the text—but also how the gospel can heal the pain that separates White and Black Gentiles.

I was faithful in my vocation, but I wasn't sensitive to my location.

In the modern era, people and places have become separated from one another, and it's easy for us to forget that we are embodied beings, embedded in particular places with particular stories.[3] No matter where you live, there is a story—a narrative—woven into your location. That Sunday, I needed to be more curious about the story of my people and their location so I could apply the gospel more effectively to their experiences.

So do you.

Think about your place. It might be a trailer park on the edge of town, a century-old home in the inner city, a rental house along a graveled road, or an apartment in the suburbs. Get curious, and ask some questions about your location: What habits shape you in this place? What do you sense and see when you step outside into your community? Is it fear or frustration, comfort or joy? Why do wealth and poverty mingle in your neighborhood in the way they do? What's the ethnic makeup of your location? Do you know why?

To help you as you consider these questions in your location, take a walk with us as we answer this question in ours.

THE PAIN OF OUR PLACE

If you meander with the two of us a couple of miles north of the renovated cathedral where Sojourn Church Midtown gathers, you'll find yourself on the east end of Main Street. Head west, and we're engulfed in the downtown business district. Here, distilleries and factories quickly give way to restaurants, office buildings, and urban bourbon tours. Mid-nineteenth-century structures with elegant cast-iron facades stand alongside modernist glass and steel. Near the corner of First and Main, the memorial for Breonna Taylor that took shape in a park in the summer of 2020 is preserved in a museum. Once we've passed First Street, we see hotels, more museums, and a producer of fine pecan liqueurs. The intersection at Seventh Street is punctuated by a gilded statue of a young King David—thirty feet tall and wearing nothing but his slingshot—followed a block later by a massive Louisville Slugger baseball bat that towers more than a hundred feet into the sky.

Then, everything changes.

An abrupt snarl of interstate ramps unexpectedly terminates the downtown business district. Nearly all the bourbon industries that draw millions of dollars each year into the downtown district are suddenly left behind. No eccentric pieces of public art protrude over the asphalt here.

Even if you've never visited Louisville before, you can't escape the jarring reality of the spatial metamorphosis that happens when you reach Ninth Street. Yes, there is much beauty west of Ninth Street—but this beauty mingles with limited opportunities. The income of a typical family here in the West End is less than one-third of the median income in the rest of Louisville. Nearly half the households have no access to an automobile. Sidewalks are broken, houses are rundown, and life expectancy drops by at least a decade compared to the east side of the city.[4]

Eighty-nine percent of residents are African American.

This is not a coincidence.

What you see here was crafted by more than a century of federal policies and municipal statutes. In the early twentieth century, cities throughout the United States passed laws preventing African Americans from freely choosing where they could reside.[5] Louisville was no different. The city council first confined African Americans to a handful of lower-quality neighborhoods in 1914. The Supreme Court struck down that statute, but segregation never stopped. One White resident urged his neighbors, "Let's make a Negro living on the West End . . . as comfortable as if he were living in Hell"—and they certainly tried.[6] Since African American families were limited to so few neighborhoods, landlords could—and did—inflate prices without improving or repairing properties. As a result, African Americans paid more money for lesser housing while being restricted to jobs with fewer chances for advancement.

And that's why Walnut Street was such a bright spot in Louisville.

Around three hundred Black-owned businesses flourished for decades in a strong and vibrant community along Walnut Street. This mecca of Black entrepreneurship was founded before the Civil War by a free woman of color. By the mid-twentieth century, there were flower shops, grocery stores, doctors, lawyers, and more.

For African Americans in Harlem, there was the famous 125th Street. For African Americans in Tulsa, there was Black Wall Street in the Greenwood District. For African Americans in Louisville, there was Walnut Street. "You could find everything you wanted on that street," one resident later recalled. "You could make some fast money and you could go broke. You could get entertained, get embalmed, and get fed." But then came urban renewal, which people at the time referred to as "Negro removal." By 1968, around one hundred and fifty Black-owned businesses had been obliterated. In the words of one business owner, "The clearing of Walnut Street vandalized the social fabric of the black community"—but it wasn't only businesses that were displaced. Homes were eradicated too, all in the name of eliminating urban blight. In one redevelopment area, more than three hundred African American families were displaced while only one White family was forced to move. All in all, African Americans represented more than 85 percent of the people removed from their homes, and the city assisted less than 30 percent of displaced families in finding new locations to live.[7] And African Americans still couldn't rent or purchase residences outside a narrow range of poorly resourced neighborhoods.

The dilapidation of neighborhoods like the West End didn't happen because African Americans moved in. It happened because these were the only places where African Americans *could* move. Limited to segregated neighborhoods, Black households struggled to maintain properties that had been purchased or rented at grossly inflated prices. Unequal lending practices, segregated neighborhoods, and limits on job opportunities forced families into circumstances that virtually guaranteed their communities would deteriorate.[8]

Even worse, informal housing discrimination in Louisville lasted long past the Fair Housing Act of 1968. As recently as 1985, an African American family moved into a neighborhood about ten miles southwest of Sojourn Church Midtown. A gathering of White supremacists, more than half of whom were also local police officers, vowed that no Black person would ever live in their community. The night that Robert and Martha Marshall took up residence in their new neighborhood, their residence was firebombed. Arsonists later returned and burned their home to the ground.[9]

HOW KNOWING YOUR PLACE HELPS YOU
CULTIVATE MULTIETHNIC KINGDOM CULTURE

That's the story of our place.

Now, imagine being that older gentleman in my congregation, hearing a faithful sermon from his pastor. What I said about forgiveness was completely true, but I brushed past his trauma without acknowledging his burdens. Then again, imagine the hundreds of thousands of African American Christians who have been beaten down by prejudice and who sit in the pews in majority White churches week after week, hearing platitudes that never take their sorrows seriously. What they hear in many cases is not a gospel-driven engagement with their pain. Instead, they hear statements such as, "Why can't you all just move on?" or "You should just be happy you're here—America is the greatest country on earth." Statements like these sidestep the ongoing impact of past and present prejudices.

But it isn't only African American believers who are hurting. There are White brothers and sisters who shut down when they hear this conversation because they've been wounded by people who didn't display the fruit of the Spirit when they spoke. There are Asian brothers and sisters who are hurting because of the pain they've experienced at the hands of African Americans. This past week, an immigrant family in my own neighborhood became a target of anti-Asian violence. A family member was robbed at gunpoint by an African American suspect and then shot. To make matters worse, I found out this precious Asian family had been regularly harassed by African American neighbors. Black brothers and sisters, it's not enough to speak against the racism that we may have experienced; we must condemn expressions of racism against other ethnicities too. What's more, there are Latino immigrants who long to be a part of this conversation, but they are rightly concerned by the fact that some Christians seem to think the answer to these problems is a communist or socialist society like the ones their families escaped. We don't have to agree with one another on every political detail, but we do need to listen seriously to these concerns.

Don't brush over the stories of the people in your location. Listen and use what you learn to show greater love to the people in your place. Reconciliation is painful and difficult. In some ways, it's like "holding on to each other, not letting go, and doing surgery on each other." And yet, "when we build trust and stay on the table to the end of the surgery, there is hope for healing in the most delicate and vital places."[10]

These are realities that we've had to learn the hard way, but we've also witnessed the beauty of what God can do when we acknowledge the pain that's woven into people's stories. Through the power of the gospel, he can transform bitterness into forgiveness, woundedness into fellowship, and prejudice into communion.

14

BUILDING UP WALLS THAT JESUS ALREADY BROKE DOWN

In many churches in the nineteenth-century American South, enslaved African Americans were chained along back walls, placed in back pews, or consigned to balconies. When it came time for Communion, they weren't allowed to receive the same cup or bread as their captors. Instead, they received the elements from an African American assistant who served only their part of the sanctuary.[1] But that's not the most shocking aspect of these arrangements, theologically speaking. What's worse is in some congregations, dividers were built across the sanctuaries several feet high to ensure that Black and White communicants never physically mingled.[2]

Meditate on this reality for a moment: The sacrifice of Jesus shattered every barrier that separates his followers, yet churches literally constructed barriers to separate people who confessed his name.

We still do, at times—and so did Christians in the first century. We may not construct physical walls, but we pile up relational barriers that keep our lives separated. And that brings us to the text in Paul's letter to the Ephesians that I preached to two different audiences.

HOW THE BLOOD BROUGHT THE CHURCH TOGETHER

In Ephesians, Paul addresses "faithful saints" in the metropolis of Ephesus (1:1). Throughout his letter, he addressed both Jewish and Gentile—non-Jewish—Christians, though it seems the majority of Christians in Ephesus may have been Gentiles. After richly encouraging his readers by pointing them to their shared adoption in Christ, Paul builds up Gentile believers (2:11-14). Throughout this letter, Paul takes on the tone of a father lavishing encouragement on a younger child who feels like he lacks a place in the family because of his older sibling's success. It's as if Paul is a father saying to his younger son, "Your place in the family doesn't depend on your past failures or present performance. You are who you are because I have chosen you as my child, and nothing can ever change that."

Both Jews and Gentiles had been chosen before the foundation of the world to receive every spiritual blessing (1:3-4). Both had been made alive when they were dead in trespasses and sins (2:1-8). Both were equally God's workmanship (2:10). This was no small thing for first-century Gentile Christians to hear! Paul knows that, and he reminds the Gentiles about what and where they were before God saved them. They had been "excluded from the citizenship of Israel." As a result, they were utterly "without hope and without God in the world" (2:12).

Then, Paul interrupts this litany of despair with a *but*: "But now in Christ Jesus, you who were far away have been brought near by the blood of Christ" (Ephesians 2:13). The simplicity and beauty of the clause "brought near by the blood of Christ" reminds me of an old hymn from the African American church, written by Evelyn Simpson-Curenton:

> I know it was the blood for me.
> One day when I was lost
> he died upon the cross.
> I know it was the blood for me.[3]

Nothing but this "blood for me" was able to tear down the walls that kept Jews and Gentiles apart in the first century. And this same blood represents the only power able to accomplish reconciliation in churches today.

HOW THE SACRIFICE OF CHRIST ENDS SOCIAL ALIENATION

The keys to ethnic reconciliation and multiethnic kingdom culture have been handed to the church through the nail-pierced palms of our Savior. Paul makes this point by emphasizing that peace among God's people comes only through the broken body and blood of Christ: "He is our peace, who made both groups one and tore down the dividing wall of hostility" (Ephesians 2:14).

In the Jerusalem temple, there was a literal barrier that stopped Gentiles from entering the inner courts where Israel worshiped, much like the ones separating Black and White believers in certain nineteenth-century churches. Jewish Christians would have readily recognized this aspect of Paul's imagery. The Gentile believers probably understood this barrier as the law that had brought about social alienation between Jews and Gentiles—and this social alienation seems to be Paul's main point in this section of his epistle (2:15).[4] Christ's death overcame the social alienation that separated Jews and Gentiles by ending the alienation between God and humanity.[5] This vision of bringing together God's chosen people from every nation combined far more than these two groups, for neither Jews nor Gentiles were monolithic.[6]

Now, consider this: If the death of Jesus tore down a division between Jews and Gentiles that had stood unmoved for more than a millennium, doesn't it make sense that this same death is able to bring communion between different ethnicities in the same church today?

The cross of Christ equips us to live lives that look more like heaven by allowing us to be honest with ourselves and with each other. Because of Christ, we can admit our sins, our faulty thinking, our intentional ignorance, and our unintended biases without being surprised or shocked by them. The gospel tells us that God knows the very worst about us and yet still sees us as if we are perfect in Christ. This truth allows us to own up to our own spiritual ugliness and to acknowledge with godly sorrow the sins of the generations before us and around us. The gospel empowers us to do all of this without shame or guilt.

What's more, the finished work of Christ enables Christians to come to these conversations with a sense of personal security and peace. We can come to conversations as active listeners, as people who don't feel the need to force someone else to see what we see.[7] Having this perspective doesn't mean we ignore sins and shortcomings. Sometimes, love looks like rebuking a brother or sister (Galatians 2:11-14). And yet, even in moments of rebuke, God calls us to treat one another in ways that are rich with beauty and grace (Galatians 6:1-5). "If we do not show beauty in the way we treat each other," Francis Schaeffer once observed, "then in the eyes of the world and in the eyes of our own children, we are destroying the truth we proclaim."[8]

HOW WE TRY TO REBUILD WALLS THAT JESUS ALREADY TORE DOWN

"People, I just want to say," a bruised and battered Rodney King once pled, "can we all just get along?"[9] For those of us who are in Christ, the answer should be an emphatic "yes."

At the same time, many of us cry out with the father in the Gospels whose child was afflicted, "Lord, I do believe, help my unbelief" (Mark 9:24).

So, why is this father's prayer our prayer as well? It's because the polarization among Christians—coupled in many cases with the painful racialized experiences of Black Christians—has worn us down. The father's prayer is appropriate because the data suggest there is a wide gap—a "wall of hostility," one might say—that still exists between how Black and White Christians see each other. It's as if Christians keep trying to rebuild walls Jesus has already torn down.

One of the reasons it seems these walls are continually being rebuilt is because some Christians still refuse to recognize the persistent impact of racism. In the words of Juan Sanchez, "Americans have been discipled in a vision of racial discrimination," and this vision has distorted what Christians see when they look at the world.[10]

Christina Edmondson and Chad Brennan recently completed an extensive commentary on national surveys that researched the attitudes of Christian and non-Christians toward issues related to racism. Here are two key takeaways from their research: First, Christians frequently have less accurate racial perspectives than the world. Second, Christians are often less motivated to address racial injustice than the world. These skewed views on racial issues are not simply the result of being uninformed. The reasons are more complex. They have to do with political allegiances that have taken precedence over Scripture, a lack of interest in addressing racial injustice, and more.

For example, when Edmondson and Brennan asked whether African Americans have been treated less fairly than Whites in certain situations, only four out of every ten White Christians recognized disparities in the treatment of African Americans.[11] When other researchers asked, "How motivated are you to address racial injustice in our society?" only 9 percent of White Christians were motivated to address racial injustice, whereas 19 percent of White non-Christians and nearly half of all African American Christians were motivated to do something about racial injustice.[12]

So how can our lives reflect the heart of Jesus regarding unity when African American Christians find themselves at a very different place on these issues than many of our White brothers and sisters? How can we move toward multiethnic churches when so many Christians seem so unmotivated to address the realities of racism? How can we talk about our pain with fellow believers who may not see the toll that racial injustice has taken on our lives?

"Lord, I do believe, help my unbelief."

YOUR INVITATION TO MULTIETHNIC KINGDOM CULTURE

Growing up, each of the churches I (Jamaal) attended designated a time during the worship service when the altar was open. The preacher would "open the doors," so to speak, and extend the offer of the gospel to non-Christians. Then, the preacher might also summarize the sermon for Christians and call believers to pray or take specific steps of repentance based on the sermon. Finally, he would call those who were not yet members of the church to join the church.

Right now, I want to follow those preachers' example. I want to close this chapter with an invitation of sorts. Because the gap between us is a gap in our love, I want to invite all of us to stop retreating behind walls of hostility and to move toward one another in love.

To my White brothers and sisters in Christ, my invitation for you is to love your African American brothers and sisters with thoughtfulness and intentionality. These patterns of intentionality may require slowing down and recognizing Black coworkers, neighbors, friends, and pastors may be carrying trauma you never see. Sometimes, loving intentionality simply looks like getting to know others and coming alongside them in the same ways Jesus would—with curiosity, care, and gospel hope. Having White brothers and sisters commit themselves to getting to know me in a natural yet intentional way—not forcing a relationship because I'm Black—while learning and sharing their own experiences continues to be a healing experience for me. As a Black man, given our country's history and my personal experiences, I can find myself bracing for mistreatment in unfamiliar White spaces. This emotional bracing is not something that makes me proud. I don't want to exploit it to put others at a relational disadvantage, but what I share is real and I hope you're able to receive this revelation considering the experiences I've described throughout this book. I have left out so many painful recollections as I wrote these chapters either because the hurt still runs too deep or because recounting these details would tarnish others' reputations.

The principles of thoughtfulness and intentionality apply to Black and Brown Christians as well. Take intentional steps toward your White brothers and sisters. Because of my sinful nature and past experiences, I can sometimes approach White Christians with a skepticism that they don't deserve. Perhaps your heart is tempted to do the same thing. What would it look like for you to remind yourself that because Christ has torn down the wall of hostility, you can give your brothers and sisters the benefit of the doubt? I know this is hard. Yet each person you meet is an individual, and they may be eager to pursue ethnic reconciliation or at least to join in a respectful conversation. Approach each fellow believer with the hope of Jesus.

My invitation for each of us—regardless of ethnicity or socioeconomic status—is to learn to hold our own stories and the stories of others before the Lord with humility, knowing we see only dimly and partially in this life (1 Corinthians 13:9, 12). Embrace the attitude of the apostle Paul in his letter to the Ephesians who—even as a Jewish man who had been unjustly imprisoned—took the time to encourage Gentile believers from a variety of backgrounds. He did this by acknowledging their struggles and lovingly applying the gospel to their story.

Could we work together to do the same?

"Lord, I do believe, help my unbelief."

15

LITURGIES OF COMMUNION

The room was dark, and the lights were dim. Between the lobby and the sanctuary, I (Jamaal) was reminded by five people that there was no need for me to dress up to come to church. One member even said, "Dude, you can relax here."

Okay, I thought. They didn't realize I had come straight from preaching at a local Black church. I had rushed to this service because a friend had been inviting me for months to check out his church. After putting it off, I thought I might as well go and surprise my friend. Once I found my friend and my seat, I felt weird but excited. The weirdness was because I was the only person of color there and the only one dressed up for church. But there was also excitement. The excitement came from the energy in the room. You could tell people knew they were about to experience something thoughtful and beneficial. I came with this sort of excitement too, because the church had an excellent reputation not only for faithfulness to Scripture but also for its contributions to the community.

The time of worship and the sermon were spiritually uplifting. I was spiritually fed, and I could see why people spoke highly of the church. They were reaching a certain demographic of people, and they were trying to reach the rest of the community as well.

Then, after the sermon, something strange happened.

People started walking to the front of the sanctuary, just like the congregants in my historically Black church did during the time of offering. But this wasn't time to tithe, and there wasn't any upbeat music playing. They were going to the front to take and eat because it was time for Communion.

Those who participated in Communion tore off a piece of bread from a common loaf. They then dipped the bread in wine or juice, depending on what their consciences allowed. Finally, they ate as they returned to their seats. This was a bit disconcerting to me because I don't even drink after my own wife. Why would I eat a piece of bread torn from a loaf five hundred other people have touched?

And yet, that's what they did in this church.

Years later, we still do.

HOW I LEARNED TO LOVE COMMUNION

That was the first service I ever attended at Sojourn Church Midtown. Nearly a decade after that first awkward encounter, I would become a lead pastor here. At first, my germophobic tendencies kept me from appreciating how Communion happened at Sojourn, but it eventually grew on me. There is something powerful about watching everyone come forward and partake from the same bread. And now, years later, there's something even more powerful when you see a multiethnic, multi-socioeconomic, multi-generational congregation take Communion together.

This holy meal was instituted by Jesus nearly two thousand years ago. During a Passover celebration with his disciples, Jesus transformed the exodus meal into a banquet that signified the tearing of his flesh and the shedding of his blood for his people just hours before his crucifixion. Isn't it amazing that the Lord left us with two sacraments that engage our physical selves and multiple senses? Both Communion and baptism are intimate Christian practices that form people through elements in which Christ himself is spiritually present. We—along with millions of Christians around the world—believe that when we participate in the liturgy of partaking in the body and blood of Christ, God is at work among us transforming our lives by forming our loves.

WHAT HAPPENED WHEN THE CORINTHIANS
LOST SIGHT OF GOD'S DESIGN

When Jesus ate the Last Supper with his disciples, he required only that the persons at the table weren't the one who would betray him. Reclining next to Jesus were people from different walks of life. They didn't share the same socioeconomic backgrounds, careers, skill sets, or family situa-tions. None were Gentile, but that's okay—that was coming soon, and it was already part of God's design.

Two decades later, an opposite approach to the Lord's Supper was taking place in the province of Achaia, and that's why Paul sends such a stern warning in his first epistle to the church in Corinth. Paul's goal in this letter isn't to lay out a theology of the Lord's Supper. It's to rebuke the church about what taking this meal in vain would do and had already done (1 Corinthians 11:29-30). The main issue in Paul's letter is that people were taking the holy sacrament in a way that separated people into social classes instead of uniting them as one body.

When first-century Christians gathered to eat, bread and wine weren't the only items on the menu. They shared an *agape* meal or "love feast"—an entire meal meant to be a time of fellowship and encouragement. The Lord's Supper happened in the context of this *agape* meal. The problem in Corinth was that those in higher social classes were treating the Christian love feast like a pagan banquet, during which the wealthy ate first and consumed the finest parts of the meal, then those who were socially and economically disadvantaged scraped a meal together from the leftovers.[1] Some celebrated the Lord's Supper as if it were the Great Messianic Banquet reserved for the end of time. In their enthusiasm, they stuffed themselves, saving nothing for Christian slaves whose arrival was delayed by assigned tasks. Some were gorged and drunken; not a crumb remained for others.[2]

Paul regarded this as a humiliation of the community and an abuse of the Supper of the Lord, whose own example contradicts such status divisions.[3]

In response, Paul tells the people they are despising the church and distorting the gospel. How might such practices undermine Christ's message? Let's listen to Christ's own words: "This is my body, which is for you. Do this in remembrance of me. . . . This cup is the new covenant in my blood. Do this, as often as you drink it, in remembrance of me" (1 Corinthians 11:24-25). This "remembrance" included Christ's sufferings, but it wasn't limited to Christ's sufferings. It was also a recollection of what he taught and how he lived. Jesus spent his life serving the mar-ginalized, the overlooked, and the diseased (Mark 1:32-34; 2:15-17;

7:26-30). He lived sharing freely and feeding the hungry (Mark 6:30-34; 8:1-9). And so, to celebrate the Lord's Supper in a way that reinforces classism or segregation is to reject the very meaning of this meal. In the Corinthian church,

> it was precisely because of a self-centered concern for honor, status, or peer group society and because of disregard for "the weak," the despised, or "the other," that the Lord's Supper had come to defeat its very purpose (11:17). For "remembrance" of Christ and of Christ's death "for others" entailed *identification* with the *Christ who denied himself for others.*[4]

That's why Paul informs the Corinthian church that they are sinning against the very "body and blood of the Lord" (1 Corinthians 11:27). Paul then goes on to give this command: "When you come together to eat, welcome one another" (1 Corinthians 11:33). What Paul intends here is for Christians to honor one another by eating together, making sure the haves and the have-nots enjoy the same meal.

Then and now, Communion is a reminder that Christ has broken down the barriers between us in his body and through his blood. I often wonder what Paul would say if he toured our city and stopped in a few churches on Sunday. Would his heart be broken by the ways one congregation seems to consist entirely of one ethnicity and social class while another is limited to a different class or ethnicity? Would he be disturbed by the lack of diversity resulting in some Christians never participating in Communion with anyone unlike themselves? Do our Communion tables bring together the tax collector and the zealot, the hip-hop culture kid and the Latino immigrant, the bank president and the hotel maid? "In this loaf of bread," Augustine said to a group of new Christians before they participated in the Lord's Supper, "you are given clearly to understand how much you should love unity."[5] Surely this unity should reach beyond people who look like ourselves.

Yes, there are separations in many of our contexts that stand outside our control. But what are we doing to bring together different social classes to the full degree that's possible in the places where we are?

HOW COMMUNION CAN CULTIVATE
MULTIETHNIC KINGDOM CULTURE

Communion is a holy ordinance for baptized believers in Jesus. No habit that we describe here can compare to a sacrament given to the church by Jesus himself in which our Savior is spiritually present. At the same time, there are other liturgies of life we can repeat to reinforce what God does among us through the Lord's Supper. These habits can help us to remember that we're a part of Christ's universal church and that he died to purchase a people from every nation, tribe, and tongue.

Share a monthly agape meal with family and friends whose back-grounds are different from your own. Intentionally pursue relationships with people who aren't like you. Don't make your discussions about superficial differences. Instead, seek to be learners. Approach the feast with joy and curiosity. People are amazing, like galaxies waiting to be explored. Listen to one another's stories. Laugh at yourselves when questions turn out to be more awkward than you intended. One church has pursued this pattern of life by launching "Dinners of 8" as an organized way to encourage the development of cross-ethnic friendships. Assigned to a diverse group of eight people, members meet once a month for dinner at the home of someone in the group. They talk about their stories, their families, church, faith, work, and a host of other topics. They meet each month for four to six months, then they form new groups. The result is an increasing network of crosscultural connections in which people know one another's stories.[6]

Learn the story of your place through weekly reading, walking, and praying. Sometimes, we don't know the story of the location where God has placed us. As a result, we don't recognize the pain people around us may have faced. Are you aware of how the ethnic and socioeconomic demographics of your state developed, or how segregation shaped the neighborhoods in your city? Choose a book that will help you to understand the history of racial and ethnic issues in your area. Gather a reading group and meet weekly as you work through this book together—but don't meet in a cozy, comfortable spot to talk about these issues from a distance. Go together to places mentioned in the book you've chosen. Develop habits of walking and praying together in these locations. As you get to know your place, you may learn you live in a region where lynchings took place. If so, do some research and learn as much as you can about the persons who were murdered in your city or county. Take your group to the locations where these atrocities happened. Spend time lamenting, repenting of any personal sins, and praying together for ethnic reconciliation.

When you partake in the Lord's Supper, consider the future culmination of God's story. In the book of Revelation, John depicts a future meal sometimes known as the marriage supper of the Lamb (Revelation 19:7-10). Among the Jews, a feast with family and friends followed the initial wedding ceremony. The Lord's Supper points to a greater and better marriage banquet when all of God's people throughout all time will gather with Jesus to celebrate the marriage covenant he has made with us—the church—as his bride. When that happens, we will be stunned first and foremost by the beauty of Jesus, but I suspect we will also be surprised by the unity and beauty of Christ's multiethnic bride. With this in mind, write a prayer that goes something like this and place it in your Bible: "Lord, one day I will be with you and your multiethnic bride forever. Help me to yearn for that day and rejoice that I am part of this bride even now. Give me opportunities to love brothers and sisters from every culture, color, and language. Amen." Each time your church partakes in the Lord's Supper, pull this paper from your Bible and silently raise this plea to God.

By God's grace at Sojourn Church Midtown, we have grown to see multiethnic gatherings in which Communion points us toward the marriage supper of the Lamb. Little by little, God is filling our church with every shade of melanin, and we are thankful.

We've come a long way, but Lord knows we still have a long way to go.

HOW COMMUNION CAN REINFORCE THE
REALITY OF THE SUPERNATURAL

Neighborhoods in our city are racially divided. These divisions shape people's habits, which in turn shape their lives. White lives don't readily intersect with Black lives, and we don't naturally develop diverse networks of relationships. And that's why, whenever a church is filled with a multiplicity of ethnicities, the world around us is glimpsing something supernatural at work, regardless of whether they admit what they are seeing.

This doesn't prove the full truth of the gospel, but it does call into question the most popular secular explanations of how such a community can be formed and sustained.

According to Jesus, the oneness of his people provides proof to the world that God the Father sent him. "I am in them and you are in me," Jesus prayed on the night he was betrayed, "so that they may be made completely one, that the world may know you have sent me and have loved them as you have loved me" (John 17:23). The implications of this plea reach far beyond diversity in the church. And yet, multiethnic, multi-generational, and multi-socioeconomic communities are at least one of the ways this oneness provides evidence of the power of Jesus at work among us. Because of the ethnic divisions fragmenting our world, a multi-ethnic community of faith participating in Communion together pictures this power in a particularly visible way, and the formation of a multi-ethnic kingdom culture in your church can help move this vision from hope to reality.

Multiethnic kingdom culture won't make us loved and approved by the world. But then again, that's never been our goal. The world will never approve of what we have to offer because what we offer first and foremost is a King who died and rose again and who now demands rebellious human beings everywhere to recognize his rightful glory. Our goal is not to witness the world's love for us; it is to be witnesses of God's love for the world.

One result of such a witness is—in the words of our friend Russell Moore—"*engaged alienation*, a Christianity that preserves the distinc-tiveness of our gospel while not retreating from our callings as neighbors, and friends, and citizens."[7] That's our hope for our church and yours as we work together to cultivate multiethnic kingdom cultures that reach from our neighborhoods to the nations.

A CORPORATE HYMN OF COMMUNION

Lost in darkness, in selfishness and pride,
All rebellious and blinded from the light.
We made idols in hopes that they would save
All while running far away from grace.

Then he called us out of darkness
Into his wondrous light;
Yes, he called us out of darkness
Into his wondrous light.
Come and see, come and see,
Come and see what that Lord has done for us.
Oh, proclaim, all you saints,
Oh, proclaim all the wonders of his love.
Though once strangers now we are made his own;
Founded solely on Christ the Cornerstone.
Now the church stands as a chosen race,
A holy people called to bear his name.
And he called us out of darkness
Into his wondrous light;
Yes, he called us out of darkness
Into his wondrous light.
Come and see, come and see,
Come and see what that Lord has done for us.
Oh, proclaim, all you saints,
Oh, proclaim all the wonders of his love.[8]

BENEDICTION:
A BLESSING
FOR THE ROAD

"Now unto him that is able to keep you from falling, and to present you faultless before the presence of his glory with exceeding joy, / To the only wise God our Saviour, be glory and majesty, dominion and power, both now and ever. Amen" (Jude 24-25 KJV).

As a very young child at New Macedonia Missionary Baptist Church on Chicago's South Side, I (Jamaal) was often filled with hope when I heard my pastor say these words. At that age, I had no idea they were the words of Jesus' half brother Jude or that it was the benediction concluding his epistle.

In fact, the hope I was experiencing had nothing to do with Jude's message of assurance regarding the keeping power of Jesus.

No, my hope lay in knowing I was less than an hour away from eating the best food in the world. After those services, my family frequently gathered at my grandmother's house for a meal, and the spread my grandmother laid out perfectly engaged all five senses.

Years later, during another Sunday morning service, I heard the voice of another Black pastor—this time in Lansing, Michigan—conclude the service with these same words from Jude. At this time in my life, hearing Jude's benediction didn't signal my stomach to crave my grandmother's cooking. Instead, the Spirit worked through these words to cause a craving in me for abundant life in Christ. That Sunday, I received the benediction as a blessing for the road instead of a starting gun for a race to the local buffet. The pastor's words encouraged my soul because I stood in need of reassurance that the Lord who saved me would also sustain me. I needed to be reminded that the triune God would empower me to apply the sermon I just heard.

Benedictions are powerful because, if you genuinely receive them, they remind you that "what is true of Jesus Christ is true of you," as my dear friend John Starke regularly says at Apostles Church Uptown. You are, after all, already seated in heavenly places with Christ (Ephesians 2:6). A well-spoken benediction helps us not to leave corporate worship anxiously, striving to live up to something we must accomplish in our own power. Instead, it equips us to leave the worship service ready to lean into something—into the person and work of Jesus.

As we conclude our time together in this book, our hope is that you now see how the life of the church can provide an argument for the power of the gospel and the truthfulness of God's Word. We pray that you yearn to see God's glory multiplied in your life as you pursue a multiethnic kingdom culture where you are.

But this is a church service. And so, before we send you out with a blessing for the road, it's time for the announcements.

TIME FOR THE ANNOUNCEMENTS

I think every pastor has mixed feelings about announcements and where to place them in a worship service. At Sojourn Church Midtown, they happen right after the last song, immediately before the benediction. Since this book has followed the liturgy of a typical service at Sojourn, this is where I'll leave you with a couple of announcements.

The first announcement is a clarification. Pursuing diversity in the way we're doing at Sojourn isn't the only model for living out a vision of multiethnic kingdom culture. Some congregations probably shouldn't divest themselves of their unique ethnic and cultural expressions, given their history and place in American society. And yet, even if that's your context, don't give up on multiethnic kingdom culture. Preach the gospel in ways that reach across ethnic barriers. Equip your members to understand the history of the global church so the next generation grows up appreciating the contributions of a multitude of ethnicities. Educate members about the injustices others have experienced and consider ways you can help to alleviate their long-term impact. Look for opportunities to partner with churches that are different from your own.

The second announcement is a plea for volunteers. It's for those of you in homogeneous communities in regions where it's virtually impossible to pursue an ethnically diverse life. Can I ask you to serve as a volunteer in the ministry of multiethnic kingdom culture in your location? Could you be someone who helps your fellow church members recognize the difference between Christian discipleship and American cultural values? Would it be possible for you to talk from time to time about the struggles ethnic minorities still face? Could you raise a generation of children who rejoice in a diversity of ethnicities? Your contributions in the place where you are can play a crucial role in the development of multiethnic kingdom culture.

WHY YOU NEED A BENEDICTION

Now, it's time for the benediction.

Pastor and author Jon Tyson has argued that because God created us for blessings, we can't flourish without them. After describing the beauty of Jesus' final blessing in the Gospels (Luke 24:50-51), Jon shares these words:

> It's because of this moment that we see the disciples of Christ in Acts operating from Jesus's blessing and not for Jesus's blessing. They were distributing what they already had, not out there working to earn something new. The same could be said of Jesus's life—he knew he had his Father's blessing from the very beginning, which meant he was free from the tyranny of seeking applause. . . . Working from a place of blessing leads to a completely different life than working for a blessing.[1]

When you pursue God's vision for diversity as a follower of Jesus, you aren't gaining God's blessing; you already have it in Christ. Your unity with Christians of every color and culture is not a goal you must achieve; it's a gift you've already received because of the finished work of Jesus. And so, as you go, our prayer is that the Lord would give you strength to move toward multiethnic kingdom culture not because you have to but because you get to, and you're blessed to. We pray you will never forget that this work is not something you live up to; it's something you lean into.

Imagine what your life would be like five years from now if you simply implemented a handful of the liturgies we've described. How would your friendships, family, church, and community be different? How might you be different? How much could your joy be multiplied if you fully embraced God's vision for his many-colored, multifaceted people?

May the Lord give you the grace to pursue this calling by abiding in him, for without him you can do nothing (John 15:5).

Thank you for journeying with us.

Now, receive this benediction from one of our pastors . . .

THE BENEDICTION

We began this expedition with a call to worship

And we'll end with a benediction

Which is simply a blessing for the road—

A plea for God's favor on mission,

To mobilize the whole body, no omissions.

Even across roads positioned between neighborhoods forbidden.

A plea to turn roadblocks into crossroads,

The path to inroads is often the road less traveled . . .

So this blessing is contingent upon the decision

to allow our backs to be places where crosses rode.

So, let's call this benediction

the via dolorosa commission . . .

We don't ride alone, but we'll ride or die in our commitment.

Because the destination is one in which we must close our eyes to see . . .

And prayerfully our eyes have been opened, so you know why we should plead

For God to give us a glimpse of the promised people pictured at the end of time, we read:

Behold, a great multitude that no one could number, from every nation, from all tribes and peoples and languages, standing before the King . . .

clothed in white robes, with palm branches in their hands,

and together they will sing . . .

"Salvation belongs to our God who sits on the throne, and to the Lamb!"
And if this is how a glorified people give glorious worship to a glorious God in his presence,

"Your will in heaven,

down to earth, will you bring?

To us! O let it be.

Through us! O let it be.

Even now, God, let us see."

And if there are any other witnesses here, who would agree . . .

Turn your palms and your hearts to the sky—

In a posture to receive . . .

May grace, mercy, and peace

Be to you

from God the Father and from our Lord Jesus Christ!

Grace to learn, give, and grieve . . .

To love, strive, believe . . .

To overcome the Divisive One

And everyone he's deceived.

Mercy to know you're loved

Mercy for times you've faltered . . .

Mercy for future stumbles,

Mercy that you will offer . . .

Peace for troubled souls,

Peace that perseveres,

Peace that binds pieces together,

finding its heart in the bosom of the Father who is near . . .

In the name of the Holy One,

Let this *peace*,

Let *this* peace,

Let this peace,

Be with you.

—Jason Stephens

AFTERWORD

JARVIS J. WILLIAMS

The Bible teaches that God has created every human being in his image and bestowed on humanity worth and dignity (Genesis 1–2). The Bible also teaches that because of the transgression of Adam and Eve, sin entered creation and brought a vertical, horizontal, and cosmic curse on the entire creation (Genesis 2–3; Romans 5:12). Because of sin, humanity's relationship with God is broken (vertical); humanity's relationship with one another is broken (horizontal); and humanity's relationship with the creation is broken (cosmic).[1] God's redemptive plan from the very beginning has been to redeem through Christ everything that Adam and Eve lost in the garden because of sin (Romans 8:19-39; Galatians 3–4). This means that God through Christ has in fact begun the process of vertical, horizontal, and cosmic restoration right now in this present evil age for those who are justified by faith in Christ because of Jesus' wrath-bearing death for sin and because of his victorious resurrection from the dead (Galatians 2:16; 6:15; Ephesians 1–5). The culmination of this great salvation will be realized in the new heavens and the new earth when Jesus returns a second time from heaven to earth to judge the living and the dead, to transform creation, to deliver his people from God's wrath, and to be worshiped by those whom God purchased by Jesus' blood from every tongue and tribe and people and nation (Revelation 5:9; 19–22).

Sadly, in the meantime until Jesus returns to make all wrongs right forever on earth as they are in heaven, sin continues to rule and reign over the entire creation like an evil tyrant in a variety of ways (Romans 6). One way in which sin reigns individually and cosmically is through churches that are alienated because of race and racism. Thankfully, because of the gospel of Jesus Christ, neither sin nor racism or any form of ethnic division has the final word (Romans 5–8). Spirit-empowered churches in all their multiethnic beauty and diversity serve as an apologetic that God is restoring through Jesus everything that Adam and Eve lost in the garden (Ephesians 2:1–3:8).

In Church as It Is in Heaven enters into the current conversation about racial and ethnic division in churches and society, and into this already-but-not-yet reality of brokenness and redemption, to offer hope to the people of God in a world that is increasingly polarized because of the universal curse of sin. Doctors (and pastors!) Jones and Williams have argued that an ethnically diverse church living in pursuit of redemptive kingdom diversity and Spirit-empowered love is one apologetic for the truthfulness of the gospel of Jesus Christ to the world. Yet they also recognize the stakes are high and the work is hard.

In the current climate, too many approach racial discourse minimizing or ignoring either the truth about the sin of racism or the hope of redemption in Jesus. *In Church as It Is in Heaven* has spoken about the sin of racism, but it hasn't stopped there. It has offered hope and redemption in Jesus. It discusses with clear prose and illuminating (and heartbreaking!) personal stories ways that sin continues to manifest itself through racism. As it discusses the brokenness of sin, *In Church as It Is in Heaven* has pointed the reader to the hope of redemption in Jesus Christ with the intent of helping Christians see that God's great salvation plan in Jesus can in fact bring racial healing in the church, in homes, and in communities.

You may have not agreed with everything in *In Church as It Is in Heaven*. Nevertheless, you have been challenged to consider your place and role in God's redemptive plan for the entire creation to restore everything that Adam and Eve lost in the garden and a few ways that this redemption can be worked out in pursuit of living a life like heaven in your church with respect to the unification of all things and all people in Christ.

ACKNOWLEDGMENTS

Jamaal: Our heavenly Father is gracious and has quite a sense of humor. About ten years ago, I provided training at a church in town. We looked together at what this church could do to bridge the ethnic gaps between the congregation and its surrounding neighborhood. One of the pastors said to me afterward, "You should take your notes and turn them into a book. All the content is there." To think that a decade later I am pastoring that church and writing a book that builds on those same principles truly humbles me. Since 2013, I have grown, suffered, and have had my thoughts sharpened on this subject by many family members, friends, and colleagues. Their voices whisper and echo throughout these pages. Indeed, one of the voices I have grown to appreciate the most is Timothy Paul Jones. It has been an enriching and genuine joy to craft this book with him.

I have been on quite a journey since joining Sojourn Church Midtown as a lead pastor. Now, I appreciate that journey and look forward more than ever to cultivating beauty with this church where I am blessed to be an under-shepherd of the Great Shepherd. The elders of Sojourn Church Midtown have given permission and space for me to write, dream, attempt, and even fail. Without their kindness, this book would not exist. To Michael Hall, Josh Hughes, Lindsay Eubanks, Lily McReynolds, Andy Norris, L. B. Onan, Luke Skeen, Jarvis Williams, thank you for reading this work and providing valuable feedback and support. Thanks also to Jonam Wang, my executive assistant, who consistently models what it means to "work as unto the Lord." Thank you all for your editorial eye, for believing in this project, and for being a life-giving presence. I extend my gratitude to Forest Baptist Church. It was in the rich soil of this church that these seeds first began to sprout. With this project being my first book, I would be remiss not to thank my pastor Dr. Stan Parker, who has journeyed with me for more than twenty years, as well as my late mentor and doctoral adviser Dr. T. Vaughn Walker. Words cannot express my gratitude to Dr. Walker as a friend in ministry and as a constant source of encouragement. Also, I am grateful for my parents, John and Pamela, whose faithful walk with Jesus while planting and leading churches shaped my love for Jesus and his church; my children, the Williams five, each one of them a little galaxy that Amber and I enjoy exploring, I am proud to be your father; and Amber, my wife and my love. In the words of Johnnyswim, "The last word that I'll say . . . a name so sweet, it sings like a melody, brings me peace, it brings me peace."

Timothy: In some sense, this book began more than two decades ago when two men in the church where I served as the pastor told an African American couple they weren't welcome in our congregation. That moment drove me to begin paying attention to issues of ethnic diversity and racism in ways I never had before. In the years that followed, a passion grew within me for multi-socioeconomic, multigenerational, and multiethnic ministry. Much of the direction of my thinking on multiethnic ministry took shape among the Lakota people, near the Standing Rock Reservation in South Dakota in 2005. The specific concepts in this book—seeing diversity as an apologetic, seeking to multiply multiethnic ministry through liturgical disciplines, and applying Philip Esler's use of social-identity theory to the life of the church—emerged in 2018 as I prepared a lecture for the Sojourn Network Leaders' Summit. It quickly became clear to me that there is no one with whom I would rather share this journey than Jamaal Williams, and I am glad to have walked this path together.

The sentences I contributed to this project were penned at Crescent Hill Coffee and at the Starbucks on Frankfort Avenue in Louisville, as well as on a ship in the inner passage of Alaska. Most of my contributions were written during a sabbatical from teaching duties, and I am grateful beyond words for the support of Matthew Hall, Paul Akin, Hershael York, and the trustees of the seminary. Many thanks are also due to my agent Mike Nappa, Love Thy Neighborhood intern Elisabeth Carlsen, administrative assistant Katie Williamson, teaching colleagues Jarvis Williams and Ayman

Ibrahim, and fellow Sojourn pastors Jason Stephens, Josh Rothschild, and Andy Norris, all of whom have provided invaluable feedback along the way. I am so grateful to serve with you all here at Sojourn. Hardly a Sunday goes by that I do not find myself with a lump in my throat as I watch our congregation move toward diversity that is increasingly reflective of John's vision of a multitude from every nation, tribe, people, and language. Throughout every step of this project, my wife, Rayann, and our four daughters have remained a steadfast encouragement. I rejoice in the work that God has given me to do, but I am always eager to return to the place where we have made our home. There, each day, a family formed by a crazy complex of unexpected adoptions awaits me. None of these children match when it comes to the color of their skin or the places from which they came, but God has brought us together by his grace, and I stand in awe of the blessings he has spun into my life through them all.

NOTES

INTRODUCTION: BROKEN CITY, BROKEN WORLD

[1] Darcy Costello, "LMPD Supplied 'False Information' on 'No-Knock' Warrant," *Louisville Courier-Journal*, May 16, 2020, www.courier-journal.com/story /news/local/2020/05/16/breonna-taylor-attorneys-say-police-supplied -false-information/5205334002/.

[2] Alex Acquisto, "National Guard Fired Shot That Killed Louisville Res- taurant Owner," *Lexington Herald-Leader*, June 9, 2020; Rose McBride, "Sojourn Church Members Work to Clean Up City and Help Community," WHAS 11, September 26, 2020, www.whas11.com/article/news/local /louisville-church-members-clean-up-streets-following-protest/417-1eb7 656d-d311-43c7-9327-548596740e36; John Wise, "'Please Keep Saying Her Name'—Breonna Taylor's Family Urges Peace," Wave 3 News, May 29, 2020, www.wave3.com/2020/05/29/please-keep-saying-her-name-breonna -taylors-family-urges-peace/; N'dea Yancey-Bragg, "Breonna Taylor Over- night Updates," *USA Today*, September 23, 2020, www.usatoday.com /story/news/nation/2020/09/23/breonna-taylor-announcement-grand -jury-louisville-police-case-updates/5814876002/.

[3] Jess Clark, "Police, FBI Investigating Shooting of Black Louisville Church," WFPL, June 5, 2020, https://wfpl.org/police-fbi-investigating-shooting-of -black-louisville-church/.

[4] "Victims of Kentucky Supermarket Shooting Identified by Police," Reuters, October 25, 2018, www.reuters.com/article/us-kentucky-shooting/victims -of-kentucky-supermarket-shooting-identified-by-police-idUSKCN1MZ38K.

[5] Jarvis Williams, *Redemptive Kingdom Diversity* (Grand Rapids, MI: Baker, 2021).

[6] "The Gospel, Race, and Justice," Sojourn Church Midtown, August–September 2020, www.sojournchurch.com/midtown/justice.

[7] *Race* functions in two ways in this book: (1) predominantly, "the whole of the human species," and (2) occasionally, due to historical functions of the term, "a classification of human beings according to phenotypical qualities and degrees of difference, with a socially structured ideal or norm by which these classifications are ranked." The process by which humans are classified into "races" in the second sense of the term is known as *racialization*. For an introduction to the conditions and causes of the racialization of sub-Saharan Africans, see James Buckwalter, "The Transatlantic Slave Trade and the Creation of the English *Weltanschauung*, 1685–1710," (independent study paper, Eastern Illinois University, 2009) www.eiu.edu/historia/Historia2009Buckwalter.pdf. The differences considered to be salient in racialization of sub-Saharan Africans have been demonstrated to be biologically meaningless. See Steve Jones, *The Language of the Genes*, rev. ed. (New York: HarperCollins, 2000), 62-65, 255-66; Colin Kidd, *The Forging of Races* (New York: Cambridge University Press, 2006), 3. Though race may be biologically meaningless, the social and societal impact of racialization is real. See Ashley Montagu, *Man's Most Dangerous Myth* (New York: Columbia University Press, 1945); Audrey and Brian Smedley, "Race as Biology Is Fiction, Racism as a Social Problem Is Real: Anthropological and Historical Perspectives on the Social Construction of Race," *American Psychologist* 60, no. 1 (January 2005): 16-26; Audrey and Brian Smedley, *Race in North America*, 4th ed. (Milton Park, UK: Routledge, 2011). See also Michael Dyson, *Race Rules* (New York: Vintage, 1997), 33. *Multiracial*, as used in this book, refers specifically to "the presence and inclusion of persons of African descent as equal partners in social contexts that have been shaped by racialization."

[8] Without a historical Adam and Eve who were the parents of all humanity and whose voluntary rebellion against God introduced a lust for dominance into a cosmos previously untainted by human sin, the nature of racial injustice and ethnic prejudice *as sin* is diluted. For the theological necessity of a historical Adam and Eve, see C. John Collins, *Did Adam and Eve Really Exist?* (Wheaton, IL: Crossway, 2011) 135.

[9]In creation, God designed humanity to develop around the globe in diverse ways. Due to the fall, human beings at first refused to extend throughout the earth and then began to love their own cultures wrongly, viewing their own cultures, ethnicities, and nations as superior to others. Thus, rather than displaying divine glory, the distinctions among humanity declined into tribalism, isolation, and confusion. See Herman Bavinck, *Reformed Dogmatics: God and Creation*, trans. John Vriend (Grand Rapids, MI: Baker, 2004), 523-26. The gospel brings about a new principle of human relations by which Christians can rejoice in their own culture, ethnicity, and nation while simultaneously embracing others, refusing to treat any culture, ethnicity, or nation—including their own—with partiality.

[10]This book rejects the homogeneous unit principle as described, e.g., in Donald McGavran, *Understanding Church Growth*, rev. and ed. C. Peter Wagner (Grand Rapids, MI: Eerdmans, 1990), x, 61, 85, 89, 163. According to Wagner, the segregation of churches by ethnicity should be celebrated rather than lamented. C. Peter Wagner, "How Ethical Is the Homogeneous Unit Principle?," *Occasional Bulletin of Missionary Research* 2, no. 1 (January 1, 1978): 12. For ethnic biases inherent in these strategies, see Jesse Curtis, "White Evangelicals as a 'People': The Church Growth Movement from India to the United States," *Religion and American Culture* 30, no. 1 (March 2020): 108-46.

[11]The term translated "rich variety" (NRSV, NLT) or "multi-faceted" (CSB, NET) "is pregnant with meaning. It is πολυποίκιλος . . . , a word that means 'variegated' and that was used in classical Greek writers with reference to cloth or flowers." Francis Foulkes, *Ephesians* (Grand Rapids, MI: Eerdmans, 1989), 106. Given the context in Ephesians 2:11–3:13 of the inclusion of Gentiles with Jews in the church, Paul seems to have seen this union of different cultures and ethnicities in the Ephesian church as one tangible expression of God's beautiful and multifaceted wisdom, for which God was and is supremely worthy of praise. For "manifold" as reference to creation of one new humanity from Jews and Gentiles, see Frank Thielman, *Ephesians* (Grand Rapids, MI: Baker, 2020), 216.

[12]D. A. Horton, *Intensional* (Colorado Springs, CO: NavPress, 2019), 97. See also J. Daniel Hays, *From Every People and Nation* (Downers Grove, IL: InterVarsity Press, 2003), 204.

[13]Esau McCaulley, *Reading While Black* (Downers Grove, IL: InterVarsity Press, 2020), 115-16.

[14]Except when referring to dynamics related to early modern racialization and the resultant racism, we have chosen to use the term *ethnicity* in place of *race*. For further discussion and rationale, see Love Sechrest, *A Former Jew* (London: T&T Clark, 2009), 57, 91-106.

[15]That which is true of the church universally and eschatologically should also characterize the church locally and existentially. Christ's presence in the church through his Spirit is "a proleptic experience of the eschatological gathering of the entire people of God." Miroslav Volf, *After Our Likeness* (Grand Rapids, MI: Eerdmans, 1997), 145. See also Jonathan Pennington, *Heaven and Earth in the Gospel of Matthew*, (Leiden, Netherlands: Brill, 2007), 155. An overemphasis on the universal and eschatological aspects of the church can result in an idealization of the church and an underemphasis on the call to testify to the power of the resurrection in the present and local church, Karl Barth, *Dogmatics in Outline* (New York: Harper, 1959), 142. The positional and universal oneness of all believers in Christ cosmically calls Christians to strive for practical and personal pursuits of multiethnicity in their lives here and now. See also Irwyn Ince, *The Beautiful Community* (Downers Grove, IL: InterVarsity Press, 2020), 11; and Daniel T. Slavich, "In Church as It Is in Heaven: An Argument for Regenerate and Ethnically Diverse Local Church Membership," *Midwestern Journal of Theology* 16, no. 1 (2017): 38-60.

1. THE EVIDENCE THAT OUR WORLD HAS YET TO SEE

[1]See Frank R. Baumgartner, Derek A. Epp, and Kelsey Shoub, *Suspect Citizens* (New York: Cambridge University Press, 2018), 2-16, 36-38; John Lamberth, "Driving While Black," *Washington Post*, August 16, 1998, www.washingtonpost.com/archive/opinions/1998/08/16/driving-while -black/23ecdf90-7317-44b5-ac43-4c9d7b874e3d/; Katheryn K. Russell, "'Driving While Black': Corollary Phenomena and Collateral Consequences," *Boston College Law Review* 40, no. 3 (May 1999): 718-21; Patricia

Warren et al., "Driving While Black: Bias Processes and Racial Disparity in Police Stops," *Criminology* 44, no. 3 (August 2006): 731. For a theological perspective on this phenomenon, see Mark Liederbach and Evan Lenow, *Ethics as Worship* (Phillipsburg, NJ: P&R, 2021), 330-31.

[2] In Scripture, justice enacted by humans toward humans entails treating one another in genuinely human ways, as articulated in God's covenant, by which God reveals how to live in right relationship with him, how to engage with one another as fellow bearers of God's image, and how to be good stewards of the earth's resources. See Peter Gentry, "Isaiah and Social Justice," *Midwestern Journal of Theology* 12, no. 1 (Spring 2013): 12-13. This understanding is not incompatible with Luigi Taparelli d'Azeglio's presentation of *giustizia sociale* as the constant and perpetual will to render to each his right. See Thomas Behr, *Social Justice and Subsidiarity* (Washington, DC: Catholic University of America Press), 86. For the purposes of this book, *social justice* refers to "the treatment of every human being in a genuinely human way by perpetually willing to render to every person his or her right."

[3] Zoltan Hajnal, *Divided* (New York: Cambridge University Press, 2020), 248.

[4] John R. W. Stott, *Our Guilty Silence* (Grand Rapids, MI: Eerdmans, 1967), 71. For similar sentiments from other eras, see, e.g., T. B. Maston, *The Bible and Race* (Nashville, TN: Broadman, 1959), 95; and Mark DeYmaz, *Leading a Healthy Multiethnic Church*, rev. ed. (Grand Rapids, MI: Zondervan, 2020), 36.

[5] For early Christians, the church was central not only as a relational community but also as evidence of the gospel and as a context for the formation of a new identity. The church was "the place where the captives [were] released." C. Kavin Rowe, *One True Life* (New Haven, CT: Yale University Press, 2016), 134.

[6] Aristides of Athens, *Aristide: Apologie*, ed. and trans. Marie-Joseph Pierre et al., *Sources Chrétiennes* 470 (Paris: Cerf, 2003), chaps. 15-16. Similar emphases on ecclesial ethics as one aspect of a comprehensive apologetic for the truth of Christianity may also be found in Athenagoras of Athens, *Legatio pro Christianis*, ed. Miroslav Marcovich (Berlin, Germany: De Gruyter, 1990).

[7] Aristides, *Apologie*, 16.

[8]Justin Martyr, *Justin, Apologie pour les Chrétiens*, ed. and trans. Charles Munier, *Sources Chrétiennes* 507 (Paris: Cerf, 2006), chap. 14. Although ancient conceptions of ethnicity were not identical to modern conceptions, τοὺς οὐχ ὁμοφύλους and τὰ ἔθη suggest that Justin was describing people previously separated by ethnic and cultural differences who now lived in fellowship with one another.

[9]The beauty of the overall Christian lifestyle was one aspect of what drew "strangers to join the ranks." Minucius Felix, *Octavius*, 31:7, in *Tertullian: Apology. De Spectaculis. Minucius Felix: Octavius*, Loeb Classical Library 250, trans. T. R. Glover and Gerald Rendall (Cambridge, MA: Harvard University Press, 1931). Christ makes his "defense in the lives of genuine disciples, for their lives cry out the real facts." Origen of Alexandria, preface to *Origen: Contra Celsum*, trans. Henry Chadwick (New York: Cambridge University Press, 1965), 2.

[10]Myron Bradley Penner, *The End of Apologetics* (Grand Rapids, MI: Baker, 2013), 139; see also 165.

[11]See Richard Twiss, *Rescuing the Gospel From the Cowboys* (Downers Grove, IL: InterVarsity Press, 2015), 15; and Sarah Shin, *Beyond Colorblind* (Downers Grove, IL: InterVarsity Press, 2017), 22.

[12]According to Philip Esler, early Christians formed a distinctive, superordinate Christian identity that bound their communities together and transformed other aspects of identity without eliminating these other aspects. Membership in the Christian community comprised a central and transforming part of one's identity but not to the exclusion of ethnicity, in part because the church was perceived as a voluntary association, which provided a different type of group identity. For a summary of this application of Henri Tajfel's social-identity theory to early Christianity, which has shaped much of our work in the area of ethnic reconciliation, see Philip Esler, "Jesus and the Reduction of Intergroup Conflict: The Parable of the Good Samaritan in Light of Social Identity Theory," *Biblical Interpretation* 8, no. 4 (2000): 327; and Steve Mason and Philip F. Esler, "Judaean and Christ-Follower Identities: Grounds for a Distinction," *New Testament Studies* 63, no. 4 (October 2007): 493-515.

[13]Augustine of Hippo, *De Vera Religione*, in *De magistro, De Vera Religione*, ed. Domenico Bassi (Rome: Edizioni Testi Christiani, 1930), chap. 4.

[14]The author of Acts highlighted the multiethnicity of the Antiochene church's prophets and teachers to the point that the ethnic diversity of the leadership becomes one of the dominant emphases in Acts 13:1. See David Peterson, *The Acts of the Apostles* (Grand Rapids, MI: Eerdmans, 2009), 374.

[15]Paul's concern in Galatians was not merely ethnic or cultural; it was also covenantal and had to do with the addition of Jewish practices and signs to the gospel. However, simply because the issue was *more than* ethnic or cultural doesn't mean it was *less than* ethnic or cultural. See Craig Keener, *Galatians* (Grand Rapids, MI: Baker, 2019), 166-67. Paul's words should *not* be taken to suggest that Peter was no longer a believer when he committed this sin; Paul referred to Peter as a hypocrite not as a heretic or an unbeliever (Galatians 2:13). For further discussion, see Todd Scacewater, "Galatians 2:11-21 and the Interpretive Context of 'Works of the Law,'" *Journal of the Evangelical Theological Society* 56, no. 2 (June 2013): 310-17.

[16]Scot McKnight, *A Fellowship of Differents* (Grand Rapids, MI: Zondervan, 2014), 76.

[17]G. Walter Hansen, *Galatians* (Downers Grove, IL: InterVarsity Press, 1994), 67-68. Seeking to overcome ethnic divisions is not optional for those who believe the gospel; it's "intrinsic to discipleship." Derwin Gray, *How to Heal Our Racial Divide* (Carol Stream, IL: Tyndale, 2022), 16.

[18]One evidence for the truth of Christianity that Augustine of Hippo presented to Romanianus was the consistency between Christians' liturgies and their lives. The Greek philosophers had, according to Augustine, participated in pagan worship, yet these same philosophers taught in their schools that the gods were not real. Christians, however, lived consistently the truths that they professed through their confessions and liturgies, *De Vera Religione*, 3-7. Today, there is inconsistency between what Christians profess about multiethnic congregations and what is practiced. One of the goals of this book is to bring Christian practices into conformity with outward professions so that these new practices present the world around us with a renewed defense of the gospel.

[19]Bob Smietana, "Racial Diversity at Church More a Dream than Reality," LifeWay Research, January 17, 2014, https://research.lifeway.com/2014/01/17/research-racial-diversity-at-church-more-dream-than-reality/.

20 Jenell Paris, "Race: Critical Thinking and Transformative Possibilities," in *This Side of Heaven*, ed. Robert Priest and Alvaro Nieves (New York: Oxford University Press, 2007), 26.

21 Michael Emerson with Rodney Woo, *People of the Dream* (Princeton, NJ: Princeton University Press, 2006), 160.

22 Emerson, *People of the Dream*, 39-44; Kevin Dougherty, Mark Chaves, and Michael O. Emerson, "Racial Diversity in U.S. Congregations 1998–2019," *Journal for the Scientific Study of Religion* 59, no. 4 (December 2020): 651-58.

23 Martin Luther King Jr., interview on *Meet the Press*, April 17, 1960, https:// kinginstitute.stanford.edu/king-papers/documents/interview-meet -press. The statement began to circulate around 1953 and was attributed to Kenneth Dexter Miller, president of the New York City Mission Society, and to Marie Johnson, whose husband served as the president of Fisk University. See *Huntingdon Daily News*, April 24, 1953, 2; *Pottsville Republican and Herald*, April 24, 1953, 5; "The Press: The U. S. Negro, 1953," *Time*, May 11, 1953, https://content.time.com/time/subscriber/article/0,33009 ,935334,00.html. King's statement came in response to a question about how many White individuals attended Ebenezer Baptist Church in Atlanta.

2. THE GAP IN OUR LOVE

1 Increased education of parents does not necessarily lead to greater openness to racial integration in their children's schools, suggesting that increased knowledge may not necessarily translate into a transformation of perceptions or practices. See David Sikkink and Michael Emerson, "School Choice and Racial Segregation in US Schools: The Role of Parents' Education," *Ethnic and Racial Studies* 31, no. 2 (February 2008): 267-93.

2 Augustine of Hippo, *Confessions, Volume I: Books 1–8*, Loeb Classical Library 26, ed. Carolyn J.-B. Hammond (Cambridge: MA: Harvard University Press, 2014), 7:21 (27).

3 This line of thinking has been shaped by the work of James K. A. Smith. See, e.g., *Desiring the Kingdom* (Grand Rapids, MI: Baker, 2009), 25; and *You Are What You Love* (Grand Rapids, MI: Brazos, 2016), 2, 29.

[4]The English word *liturgy* derives from the Greek λειτουργία. Outside biblical texts, λειτουργία and λειτουργικός could refer to any public service, including but not limited to service in temples. See "λειτουργία," "λειτουργικός," *A Greek-English Lexicon,* comp. H. G. Liddell and Robert Scott, rev. H. S. Jones and Roderick McKenzie (New York: Oxford University Press, 1996). In the Septuagint, λειτουργία generally referred to the ministry of the priests in the Jewish tabernacle and temple. In the New Testament, everyone who is united with Christ becomes a participant in the fulfillment of this priesthood. Christians enact their priestly identity in Christ through habits by which they are conformed to his image as a holy and devoted community; λειτουργία in the new covenant thus encompasses habits such as personal and corporate worship, prayer, and giving (see, e.g., Acts 13:2; Romans 15:27; 2 Corinthians 9:12).

[5]According to Augustine, the customs of a non-Christian's life result in dispositions which so thoroughly misdirect his or her loves that he or she is unwilling to receive the gospel. Augustine of Hippo, *De Vera Religione,* in *De magistro, De Vera Religione,* ed. Domenico Bassi (Rome: Edizioni Testi Christiani, 1930), chaps. 3-4, 6, 22, 64, 65, 67, 88. True repentance requires the formation of different habits and customs which non-Christians are unwilling to pursue. Those who repent in response to God's revelation submit to this divine authority and receive renewed rationality to guide them through the reformation of their souls in seven "spiritual ages" (*spirituals aetates*). Particularly in the fourth stage, Christians develop virtue through new liturgies of life that reshape their loves (*De Vera Religione,* chap. 49). For further discussion, see John G. Prendiville, "The Development of the Idea of Habit in the Thought of Saint Augustine," *Traditio* 28 (1972): 29-99. Thomas Aquinas also recognized how wrongdoing can arise from the context of habits. For a helpful application of Thomistic moral theory to habits that sustain racism, see Colleen McCluskey, *Thomas Aquinas on Moral Wrongdoing* (New York: Cambridge University Press, 2019), 175-77.

[6]Unbeknownst to me (Timothy) when I first applied this understanding of liturgy to our work at Sojourn Church Midtown in 2018, a pastor named David Swanson was already engaging in a similar process in his church in Chicago. I was not aware of this until Jamaal Williams and I were

working on this book, and Jamaal introduced me to David Swanson, *Rediscipling the White Church* (Downers Grove, IL: InterVarsity Press, 2020). Although some similarities may be observed between this book and *Rediscipling the White Church*, what we are doing emerged separately and differs significantly from the approach Swanson has taken.

[7]Ungodly habits develop from a distortion of the will followed by a desire that is repeatedly indulged. When such habits develop, the mind can eventually be "drawn and held, even against its will" by these habits. Augustine of Hippo, *Confessions, Volume I: Books 1–8*, Loeb Classical Library 26, ed. Carolyn Hammond (Cambridge, MA: Harvard University Press, 2014), 8:5 (11-12).

[8]Augustine saw this pattern as an expression of God's clemency toward humanity in the aftermath of the fall of Adam and Eve. *De Vera Religione*, chap. 29. As an aspect of sanctification, this "work toward righteousness" in partnership with the Spirit should not be confused with justification, which is enacted solely by God's resurrecting grace independent of any human work or effort. See Herman Bavinck, *Reformed Dogmatics*, ed. John Bolt and trans. John Vriend, vol. 4, *Holy Spirit, Church, and New Creation* (Grand Rapids, MI: Baker, 2008), 252-54.

[9]John Webster, *The Culture of Theology* (Grand Rapids, MI: Baker, 2019), 136.

[10]According to some psychologists, the embodied habits of our lives can train the cognitive system to which Keith Stanovich and Richard West refer as "System I" and which Daniel Kahneman has dubbed "fast thinking." System I or fast thinking is rapid and involuntary, in contrast to System II or slow thinking which is slower and more deliberate. See Keith Stanovich and Richard West, "Individual Differences in Reasoning: Implications for the Rationality Debate?," *Behavioral and Brain Sciences* 23, no. 5 (October 2000): 645-726; Daniel Kahneman, "A Perspective on Judgment and Choice: Mapping Bounded Rationality," *American Psychologist* 58, no. 9 (September 2003): 697-720; Daniel Kahneman, *Thinking, Fast and Slow* (New York: Farrar, Strauss, and Giroux, 2011), 89-96.

[11]"We strive by means of the fleshly forms that hold us back to arrive at knowledge deeper than any fleshly sense can know." Augustine of Hippo, *De Vera Religione*, chap. 45. Both similarities and differences between Augustine and Thomas Aquinas are evident in the way that Thomas

expresses the relationship between bodily habits and an arousal to
knowledge: "Experience shows that by acts of the body the soul is
aroused to a certain knowledge or affection. Wherefore it is evidently
reasonable that we should employ our bodies to raise our minds to God."
Thomas Aquinas, *Summa Contra Gentiles*: *Books III and IV: Latin-English
Opera Omnia* (Steubenville, OH: Emmaus, 2019), 3:119:5.

[12]*Culture* is "a socially structured entity in which artifacts are embedded
and values are preserved in groups and institutions, primarily through
shared narratives." Cultures include (1) visible artifacts, (2) stated values,
and (3) hidden values. Edgar Schein with Peter Schein, *Organizational
Culture and Leadership*, 5th ed. (Hoboken, NJ: Wiley, 2016), 18. When an
organization's stated values contradict actual practices—such as when
churches with a stated openness to diversity in diverse contexts remain
monocultural and monoethnic—the problem is typically due to an incon-
gruity between the organization's stated values and the hidden values of
which members may be unaware. New bodily liturgies can begin to dis-
lodge hidden values that have kept the community from movement
toward multiethnic kingdom culture, especially when members simultaneously are made aware of how these hidden values may have stalled
or prevented growth in diversity.

[13]The order of weekly worship at Sojourn Church Midtown follows the
order that John Calvin established for the churches in Geneva for
Sundays on which Communion was observed, with giving and passing
of the peace added prior to the sermon as the congregation's response to
confession, pardon, and absolution. For tables summarizing Calvin's
orders of worship, see John T. Dyck, "Calvin and Worship," *Western Reformed Seminary Journal* 16, no. 1 (February 2009): 36-39.

[14]Jasmine Holmes, *Mother to Son* (Downers Grove, IL: InterVarsity Press,
2020), 61.

[15]See conversation with Derwin Gray in Bob Smietana, "Racial Diversity at
Church More a Dream than Reality," LifeWay Research, January 17, 2014,
https://lifewayresearch.com/2014/01/17/research-racial-diversity-at-church
-more-dream-than-reality/.

[16]Sociologists have defined a multiethnic church as a congregation in
which no more than 80% of the congregation is representative of one

single ethnicity. See, e.g., Michael Emerson with Rodney Woo, *People of the Dream* (Princeton, NJ: Princeton University Press, 2006), appendix C. While this definition is statistically useful and necessary to sustain social-scientific research methods that involve statistical measures, it may not be ecclesiologically helpful. When church leaders utilize this number as a prescriptive goal for mission instead of a descriptive observation for sociological study, churches may find themselves focusing on increasing relative percentages of underrepresented groups; a better and more faithful focus for church leaders should be shepherding their congregations in ways that recognize barriers to multiethnic unity and that develop habits of life characterized by multiethnic, multigenerational, and multi-socioeconomic love of neighbors.

[17] Augustine of Hippo, *De Doctrina Christiana Libri Quatuor* (Ingolstadt, Germany: Attenkover, 1826), 2:9 (7); 2:18 (28).

[18] Charlie Dates, "What We Can Learn from the Black Church When We Are Pushed to the Margins," *The Exchange*, August 29, 2016; and Korie Edwards and Rebecca Kim, "Estranged Pioneers: The Case of African American and Asian American Multiracial Church Pastors," *Sociology of Religion* 80, no. 4 (January 2019): 456-77. See also Korie Edwards, *The Elusive Dream* (New York: Oxford University Press, 2008).

[19] Some scholars have chosen to use the term *ethnic conciliation* instead of *ethnic reconciliation*, recognizing that "*re*-conciliation" could imply that, "at one point, the various ethnicities within the United States were at a point of conciliation." D. A. Horton, *Intensional* (Colorado Springs, CO: NavPress, 2019), 17-18. Although we deeply respect individuals such as Horton who have opted for the term *conciliation*, we have retained *reconciliation*. This usage of *reconciliation* is not intended to suggest any past point of conciliation in any postlapsarian human culture; it is intended instead to point to a restoration of relationships through the power of Christ that reflects *God's original design* for his creation. Simply put, the *re-* in *reconciliation* does not imply a previous conciliation at any past moment in the history of human civilization after humanity's fall; it points instead to the perfect communion for which God crafted humanity in the Garden of Eden, which he will restore and surpass in the

future. This coheres with Paul's usage of ἀποκαταλλάσσω in Ephesians 2:16 and Colossians 1:20-22.

3. LITURGIES OF LOVE AND LONGING

[1]Mike Cosper, *Rhythms of Grace* (Wheaton, IL: Crossway, 2013), 125.

[2]"Nos autem omnis sexus, et generis, et aetatis," Lactantius, *L. Caelius Firmianus Lactantius: Divinarum Institutionum Libri Septem, Fascicle 3, Libri V et VI*, ed. Eberhard Heck and Antonie Wlosok (Berlin, Germany: De Gruyter, 2009), 6:3.

[3]John Perkins with Karen Waddles, *One Blood* (Chicago: Moody, 2020), 85.

[4]Dallas Willard, *The Allure of Gentleness* (New York: HarperOne, 2015), 168.

[5]Anthony O'Hear, *Beyond Evolution* (New York: Clarendon Press, 1997), 133.

[6]Carl F. H. Henry, *God, Revelation, and Authority*, vol. 4, *God Who Speaks and Shows* (Wheaton, IL: Crossway, 1999), 714, 719.

[7]Bobby Gilles and Jonaton Barahona, "Your House," Sojourn Music, 2021. Used by permission.

PART 2: LAMENT

[1]Words that diminish the lives of others are "set on fire by hell" and destroy the course of people's lives (James 3:6). Because racial supremacy destroys lives by treating some ethnicities as inferior to others, every expression of racial supremacy should be seen by Christians as a hellish lie. For discussion of the unique identification of hell as a source of evil inclinations in the epistle of James, see Peter Davids, *James* (Grand Rapids, MI: Eerdmans, 1982), 143.

4. LAMENTING THE WOUND

[1]Sarah Gardner, "What We Talk About When We Talk about Confederate Monuments," *Origins*, November 2017, https://origins.osu.edu/article /what-we-talk-about-when-we-talk-about-confederate-monuments; Justin Bey, "Woman Killed in Charlottesville, Virginia Car Attack Identified," CBS News, August 13, 2017, www.cbsnews.com/news/heather -heyer-charlottesville-virginia-car-attack/.

[2]For lynching statistics, see "Lynching, Whites and Negroes, 1882–1968," Tuskegee University, https://web.archive.org/web/20160313030351/http: //192.203.127.197/archive/bitstream/handle/123456789/511/Lyching%20 1882%201968.pdf. For the revival of the Ku Klux Klan in the 1920s, see

Linda Gordon, *The Second Coming of the KKK* (New York: Liveright, 2017), 11-18.

[3]Although very young children naturally notice physical differences, the salience assigned to these differences and any racialized hierarchicalizations perceived in them are learned. See Frances Aboud, "The Development of Prejudice in Childhood and Adolescence," in *On the Nature of Prejudice*, ed. John F. Dovidio, Peter Glick, and Laurie A. Rudman (Hoboken, NJ: Blackwell, 2005), 310-26; Frances Aboud, "A Social-Cognitive Developmental Theory of Prejudice," *Handbook of Race, Racism, and the Developing Child*, ed. Stephen Quintana and Clark McKown (Hoboken, NJ: Wiley, 2008), 58; Debra Van Ausdale and Joe Feagin, *The First R* (Lanham, MD: Rowman & Littlefield, 2001), 199; Phyllis Katz, "Racists or Tolerant Multiculturalists? How Do They Begin?," *American Psychologist* 58, no. 11 (November 2003): 897-909.

[4]Wendell Berry, *The Hidden Wound* (Berkeley, CA: Counterpoint, 2010), 3.

[5]William Faulkner, *Requiem for a Nun*, Vintage International Edition (New York: Random House, 2011), 73.

[6]*Racism*, as used in this book, is defined as "the formation or maintenance of racial group inequality and the justification of that inequality, particularly as it relates to the impact of the racialization of 'black' and 'white.'" This definition is adapted from Michael Emerson and George Yancey, *Transcending Racial Barriers* (New York: Oxford University Press, 2011), 18. Other common definitions of *racism* include "a system of advantage based on race" and "prejudice plus power." Beverly Tatum, "Defining Racism: 'Can We Talk?,'" *Race, Class, and Gender in the United States*, ed. Paula Rothenberg (New York: MacMillan, 2007); and Daniel Wellman, *Portraits of White Racism* (New York: Cambridge University Press, 1977). By defining *racism* as a disposition coupled with power, some authors assert that Black persons cannot be racist toward Whites, because the social structures of racism have excluded Black persons from the power structures necessary to leverage the prejudices they may hold. See, e.g., Beverly Tatum, *Why Are All the Black Kids Sitting Together in the Cafeteria? And Other Conversations about Race*, rev. ed. (New York: Basic Books, 2003), 7-10. We reject this assertion for the following reasons: (1) Simply because African American communities may

have diminished social and structural power, it does not follow that African American individuals lack every social or structural power that might enable racism to provide benefits. Even within the constraints of Tatum's definition, African American persons could still be capable of racism in proportion to the power they possess and perceived benefits they experience. Secular antiracists recognize this reality; see Ibram X. Kendi, *How to Be an Antiracist* (New York: Random House, 2019), 142. (2) For Christians, sin can be present not only in what we *do* but also in what we *would do* if we had the capacity and the opportunity (Matthew 5:20–30). Even if a particular African American person does not possess power to enact racism in a manner that results in social benefits, the mere incapacity to gain benefits by means of sinful acts does not mean that an individual is innocent of a particular sin, if this sin is what he or she desires to do or would do, given the opportunity. See W. Dwight McKissic Sr., "Why the Stain of Racism Remains in the Southern Baptist Convention," in *Removing the Stain of Racism from the Southern Baptist Convention*, ed. Jarvis Williams and Kevin Jones (Nashville, TN: B&H, 2017), 131-35; Jarvis Williams, *Redemptive Kingdom Diversity* (Grand Rapids, MI: Baker, 2021), 6-7, 152-63; George Yancey, *Beyond Racial Division* (Downers Grove, IL: InterVarsity Press, 2022), 10.

[7]Thomas Schreiner, *1, 2 Peter, Jude* (Nashville, TN: B&H, 2003), 491.

[8]Mark Vroegop, *Dark Clouds, Deep Mercy* (Wheaton, IL: Crossway, 2019), 26.

[9]Frederick Douglass, *Autobiographies: Narrative of the Life of Frederick Douglass, an American Slave; My Bondage and My Freedom; Life and Times of Frederick Douglass*, The Library of America, vol. 68 (New York: Penguin Putnam, 1994), 185.

[10]Mark Charles and Soong-Chan Rah, *Unsettling Truths* (Downers Grove, IL: InterVarsity Press, 2019).

[11]Quoted in Eric Saunders, "Show the Work," United? We Pray, November 5, 2019, https://uwepray.org/articles/united-we-pray-show-the-work.

[12]"So far as the Old Testament is concerned, it is not true that every lamenter *eo ipso* (since he or she appears before God with a lament) would have to confess sins." Claus Westermann, *Praise and Lament in the Psalms*, trans. Keith Crim and Richard Soulen (Louisville, KY: John Knox, 1981), 273-74. See also "Lament Psalms," *Dictionary of Biblical Imagery*,

ed. Leland Ryken, James C. Wilhoit, and Tremper Longman III (Downers Grove, IL: InterVarsity Press, 2010), 484.

[13]Bruce Waltke et al., *The Psalms as Christian Lament* (Grand Rapids, MI: Eerdmans, 2014), 1. See also Erich Zenger, *A God of Vengeance?*, trans. Linda Maloney (Louisville, KY: Westminster John Knox, 1996), 75.

[14]John Onwuchekwa, *Prayer* (Wheaton, IL: Crossway, 2018), 97.

[15]*The Economic Cost of Abortion*, June 15, 2022, 6, www.jec.senate.gov /public/index.cfm/republicans/2022/6/the-economic-cost-of-abortion.

[16]Jemar Tisby, *How to Fight Racism* (Grand Rapids, MI: Zondervan, 2021), 93.

[17]For Samaritans as social outgroup subjected to ethnic prejudices, see Philip Esler, "Jesus and the Reduction of Intergroup Conflict: The Parable of the Good Samaritan in Light of Social Identity Theory," *Biblical Interpretation* 8, no. 4 (2000): 329-31.

[18]Paula Fredriksen and Oded Irshai, "Christian Anti-Judaism: Polemics and Policies," *The Cambridge History of Judaism*, vol. 4, *The Late Roman-Rabbinic Period*, ed. Steven Katz (New York: Cambridge University Press, 2006), 977-98. For a different view of the relationship between Jews and Gentile Christians prior to the fourth century, see Jacob Neusner, *Judaism and Christianity in the Age of Constantine* (Chicago: University of Chicago Press, 1987), 61-85. Before the mid-second century, "nations" or "Gentiles" (ἔθνη) functioned as a designation used by Jews to describe non-Jews, broadly analogous to the Greek usage of βάρβαροι. According to Terence Donaldson, beginning no later than the time of Justin Martyr, Christians— now comprised primarily of Gentiles—began to describe themselves as a distinct "empire-like, transethnic people." Terence Donaldson, *Gentile Christian Identity from Cornelius to Constantine* (Grand Rapids, MI: Eerdmans, 2020), 471.

[19]For mockery of Christians due to their care of those in prison, notice the sarcasm in chapters 11 and 12 of "The Passing of Peregrinus," in Lucian, *The Passing of Peregrinus. The Runaways. Toxaris or Friendship. The Dance. Lexiphanes. The Eunuch. Astrology. The Mistaken Critic. The Parliament of the Gods. The Tyrannicide. Disowned*, Loeb Classical Library 302, trans. A. M. Harmon (Cambridge: MA, Harvard University Press, 1936). For barbarians, enslaved persons, women, and uneducated

persons in the churches, see the reply to Celsus in Origen of Alexandria, *Contra Celsum: Gegen Celsus*, vol. 5, *Fontes Christiani*, trans. Michael Fiedrowicz (Freiburg, Germany: Herder, 2012), 7:36, 41. See also Tertullian of Carthage, *Quintile Septimi Florentis Tertulliani Ad Nationes Libri Duo*, ed. Philip Borleffs (Leiden, Netherlands: Brill, 1929), 1:2. Tertullian was likely waxing rhetorical when he claimed that "omnem sexum, omnem aetatem, omnem denique dignitate" were becoming Christians, but the rhetorical flourish could not have been effective unless persons from a broad range of social strata really were joining the churches.

[20] The apostle Paul had already explicitly forbidden stealing persons for the purpose of selling or enslaving them (1 Timothy 1:10); see the verb form (ἠνδραπόδισαν) of this term in Herodotus, *The Persian Wars, Volume I: Books 1-2*, Loeb Classical Library 117, trans. A. D. Godley (Cambridge, MA: Harvard University Press, 1920), 1:151:2. See also "ἐχόντων πολιορκίᾳ εἷλον καὶ ἠνδραπόδισαν" in Thucydides, *History of the Peloponnesian War, Volume I: Books 1-2*, Loeb Classical Library 108, trans. C. F. Smith (Cambridge, MA: Harvard University Press, 1919), 1:98:1. Although Augustine of Hippo did not oppose enslavement per se, he agreed that no human being is constrained by nature to be a slave, and he contended that slavery harmed the spiritual health of masters, *Augustine: City of God: Books 18:36–20*, Loeb Classical Library 416, trans. W. C. Green (Cambridge, MA: Harvard University Press, 1960), 19:15-17. See also Peter Garnsey, *Ideas of Slavery from Aristotle to Augustine* (New York: Cambridge University Press, 1996), 219; Jennifer Glancy, *Corporal Knowledge* (New York: Oxford University Press, 2010); Jennifer Glancy, *Slavery in Early Christianity* (Minneapolis, MN: Fortress Press, 2006), 98-99; Kyle Harper, *Slavery in the Late Roman World, A.D. 275–425* (New York: Cambridge University Press, 2011), 92-94; Margaret Mary, "Slavery in the Writings of St. Augustine," *The Classical Journal* 49, no. 8 (May 1954): 363-69. Once, when Augustine was away from Hippo, his parishioners raided a slaving ship to set captives free; questions regarding the legal status of these captives arose due to a dilemma introduced in the Diocletianic tax reforms whereby a person could be legally both free and enslaved. See Augustine of Hippo, "Epistula 10*," in *Œuvres de saint Augustin 46B: Lettres 1*–29**, ed. Johannes Divjak (Paris Études Augustinienne,

1987), 166-83. For further discussion, see Susanna Elm, "Sold to Sin through *Origo*: Augustine of Hippo and the Late Roman Slave Trade," *Studia Patristica* 98 (2017): 19-21. Gregory the Great sided with Augustine's perspective that enslavement is not the natural state of any human being, although Gregory the Great did also see enslavement as an unavoidable aspect of a fallen social order and as an opportunity for evangelism. See *Gregorius Magnus: Registrum Epistularum: Libri I–VII*, Corpus Christianorum Series Latina 140, ed. Dag Norberg (Ghent, Belgium: Brepols, 1982), epistula 6:12; Adam Serfass, "Slavery and Pope Gregory the Great," *Journal of Early Christian Studies* 14, no. 1 (Spring 2006): 86-103. Basil of Caesarea likewise declared that no one is a slave by nature. Basile de Césarée, *Sur le Saint-Esprit, Sources Chrétiennes* 17, ed. Benoît Pruche (Paris: Cerf, 1968), chap. 20.

[21]Gregory of Nyssa, *Gregorii Nysseni Opera: Volume V: In Inscriptiones Psalmorum, In Sextum Psalmum, In Ecclesiasten Homiliae*, ed. Wernerus Jaeger (Leiden, Netherlands: Brill, 1962), 5:334-36. See also Clifton Huffmaster, "Slavery as a Foil: Gregory of Nyssa's *In Ecclesiasten Homilae IV*," *Berkeley Journal of Religion and Theology* 5, no. 1 (2019): 77-93.

[22]James H. Sweet, "Is History History?," *Perspectives on History*, August 17, 2022, www.historians.org/research-and-publications/perspectives-on -history/september-2022/is-history-history-identity-politics-and -teleologies-of-the-present.

5. THE LIES THAT BLIND US TO THE TIES THAT BIND US

[1]*Hidden Figures*, directed by Theodore Melfi (Los Angeles, 20th Century Fox, 2016).

[2]Charles Haddon Spurgeon, "The Monster Dragged to Light," *Sermons of Rev. C.H. Spurgeon of London*, vol. 10 (New York: Robert Carter and Brothers, 1883), 129-30. For similar sentiments from the perspective of a sociologist, see George Yancey, *Beyond Racial Gridlock* (Downers Grove, IL: InterVarsity Press, 2006), 25.

[3]Anthony G. Greenwald, Debbie E. McGhee, and Jordan L. K. Schwartz, "Measuring Individual Differences in Implicit Cognition: The Implicit Association Test," *Journal of Personality and Social Psychology* 74, no. 6 (June 1998): 1473-76. For applications of IAT, see Marianne Bertrand and Sendhil Mullainathan, "Are Emily and Greg More Employable than

Lakisha and Jamal? A Field Experiment on Labor Market Discrimination," *The American Economic Review* 94, no. 4 (September 2004): 991-1013; W. S. Gilliam et al., "Do Early Educators' Implicit Biases Regarding Sex and Race Relate to Behavior Expectations and Recommendations of Preschool Expulsions and Suspensions?," Yale University Child Study Center, September 28, 2016, 1-18, https://marylandfamiliesengage.org/wp-content/uploads/2019/07/Preschool-Implicit-Bias-Policy-Brief.pdf. Despite its widespread use, it is important to recognize the limits of the IAT. The test has been at times presented as a measure of unconscious racist attitudes which result in racist actions. However, at best, the IAT measures the presence of racial associations of which we are unaware, which may or may not be exhibited in behaviors; furthermore, the scale is a relative scale without any objective external criterion. For limitations and examples of the misuse of the IAT, see Gregory Mitchell and Philip Tetlock, "Popularity as a Poor Proxy for Utility: The Case of Implicit Prejudice," in *Psychological Science Under Scrutiny: Recent Challenges and Proposed Solutions*, ed. Scott Lilienfeld and Irwin Waldman (Hoboken, NJ: Wiley, 2017), 164-95; Klaus Fiedler, Claude Messner, and Matthias Bluemke, "Unresolved Problems with the 'I,' the 'A,' and the 'T': A Logical and Psychometric Critique of the Implicit Association Test (IAT)," *European Review of Social Psychology* 17, no. 1 (2006): 79-103; Hart Blanton and James Jaccard, "Unconscious Racism: A Concept in Pursuit of a Measure," *Annual Review of Sociology* 34, no. 1 (June 2008): 277-97. For possible solutions, see Franziska Meissner et al., "Predicting Behavior with Implicit Measures: Disillusioning Findings, Reasonable Explanations, and Sophisticated Solutions," *Frontiers in Psychology* (November 8, 2019), www.frontiersin.org/articles/10.3389/fpsyg.2019.02483/full. Nevertheless, Scripture and the Christian tradition do clearly recognize the possibility of sinful attitudes of which one may be unaware and which may or may not be exhibited in the form of behaviors. As such, the possibility of implicit biases as well as the importance of bringing such biases to light should be a point of interest for Christians, even if the current methods of measuring implicit biases are problematic at best and perhaps fundamentally flawed.

[4]Augustine of Hippo, *Confessions, Volume II: Books 9–13*, Loeb Classical Library 27, ed. and trans. Carolyn J.-B. Hammond (Cambridge, MA:

Harvard University Press, 2016), 10:37, 48. Augustine asserted early in his Christian life that an act was not sinful unless the individual willed that action. Scripture later compelled Augustine of Hippo to admit that a sinful act still entails sin, regardless of the individual's will or intent because it entails participation in the primal sin of Adam and Eve (*De libero arbitrio* 3:18:51; 3:19:54). See Malcolm Alflatt, "The Development of the Idea of Involuntary Sin in Saint Augustine," *Revue des Etudes Augustiniennes* 20 (1974): 114-15; Malcolm Alflatt, "The Responsibility for Involuntary Sin in Saint Augustine," *Recherches Augustiniennes et Patristiques* 10 (1975): 171-86; William Babcock, "Augustine on Sin and Moral Agency," *Journal of Religious Ethics* 16 (1988): 28-55; Robert O'Connell, "'Involuntary Sin' in the *De Libero Arbitrio*," *Revue des Etudes Augustiniennes* 37 (1991): 23-36; Wu Tianyue, "Augustine on Involuntary Sin," *Augustiniana* 59 (2009): 45–78. When a sin is committed involuntarily, the sinner is still responsible because the individual sinner, through this act, acts in personal solidarity with Adam and Eve. See Augustine of Hippo, *De Nuptiis Et Concupiscentia*, 1:23:25; 1:24:27; 1:27:30. "An involuntary sinful act is one which arises from the presence of concupiscence within man, with no sinful intention on the part of the individual, but arising from the fault of man-in-Adam." Alflatt, "Responsibility for Involuntary Sin," 182; see also Tianyue, "Augustine on Involuntary Sin," 48, summarizing O'Connell.

[5] Regarding self-deception and racial injustice, see Gregg Ten Elshof, *I Told Me So* (Grand Rapids, MI: Eerdmans, 2009), 32-38.

[6] The assertion that racial superiority is a heresy does not necessitate that every individual holding this heresy at death has been eternally condemned. Heresy "is not entirely incompatible with true faith and regeneration. Believers, too, can fall into a state of heresy, remain in it, and even die in it." See Herman Bavinck, "The Catholicity of Christianity and the Church," trans. John Bolt, *Calvin Theological Journal* 27 (1992): 240-41.

[7] For specific comparisons and contrasts between ancient slavery and chattel enslavement of Africans in the medieval and modern eras, see, e.g., Roy Brooks, "Ancient Slavery Versus American Slavery: A Distinction with a Difference," *University of Memphis Law Review* (2002–2003): 265-73; and Murray Harris, *Slave of Christ* (Downers Grove, IL: InterVarsity Press,

1999), 25-46. This is not to suggest that Greco-Roman slavery was somehow innocuous or desirable; Paul urged enslaved Christians to gain their freedom if possible, recognizing that their status of bondage could limit their capacity to flourish in faithfulness to Jesus (1 Corinthians 7:21). Nevertheless, the bases and practices of these two practices of enslavement were clearly distinct.

[8]Derek Kidner, *Genesis* (Downers Grove, IL: InterVarsity Press, 1967), 111. See also Augustine of Hippo, *Augustine: City of God: Books 16–18:35*, Loeb Classical Library 415, trans. Eva Stanford and William Green (Cambridge, MA: Harvard University Press, 1965), 16:1-3. Augustine of Hippo depicted Ham as the symbolic progenitor of heretics. At no time in this exposition, however, did Augustine link enslavement or the curse on Canaan with persons of any particular ethnicity. Darker flesh could function at times as a metaphor for human sinfulness (see, e.g., Augustine's commentary on Psalm 74:14), and the distance and difference of Ethiopians could highlight the full extent of God's salvation reaching all nations (see, e.g., "extremos videlicet et teterrimos hominem" in Augustine's commentary on Psalm 72:9). Augustine of Hippo, *Enarrationes in Psalmos LI—C*, in Corpus Christianorum Series Latina 39, ed. Eligius Dekkers and Johannes Fraipont (Ghent, Belgium: Brepols, 1956), 71:9 (72:9); 73:14 (74:14). In this, Augustine's views followed common approaches to allegorical interpretation and reflected perspectives of his own time, which are difficult for contemporary people to separate from modern expressions of racial prejudice. Nevertheless, no connection is made in these writings between darker flesh and bondage. For discussion of these texts in the writings of Augustine, see Jonathan K. Nelson, "Ethiopian Christians on the Margins: Symbolic Blackness in Filippino Lippi's *Adoration of the Magi*, and *Miracle of St Philip*," *Renaissance Studies* 35, no. 5 (November 2021): 871-72; and Cord Whitaker, *Black Metaphors* (Philadelphia: University of Pennsylvania Press, 2019), 186-87.

[9]The earliest surviving record of any link between bondage and blackness based on Noah's curse seems to be a sixth- or seventh-century Eastern text known as *Cave of Treasures*, translated into Arabic in the seventh or eighth century. By the eighth century, this connection was already being invoked in a variety of Muslim sources to justify enslavement of

Africans, perhaps after having spread through Muslim retellings of biblical stories in "tales of the prophets." Muslim historian Al-Tabari mentions at least six prophetic traditions that connected the curse of Ham with blackness and servitude. Slavery in Europe had declined throughout the Middle Ages before reemerging alongside colonial expansion, the rise of merchant capitalism, and the growing racialization of sub-Saharan Africans in Arabian and North African regions. During this time, the curse on Canaan did at times function in medieval Europe as an explanation of the origins of social hierarchies. With the rise of a European trade in African persons, negative characteristics ascribed to European serfs were transferred to Africans. By the end of the seventeenth century, the object of Noah's curse was commonly shifted from Canaan to Ham, contradicting the very words of the text. However, prior to the eighteenth century, the justification of the enslavement of Africans among Christians and Muslims alike seems to have been based primarily, though not exclusively, on the assumption that Africans were pagans and infidels, not on the curse of Ham. It was not until the eighteenth and nineteenth centuries that the Hamitic myth appears to have provided a key rationale among Christians for the denigration of Africans. See John Azumah, *The Legacy of Arab-Islam in Africa* (New York: Simon and Schuster, 2014), chap. 4; Charles Blackburn, *The Making of New World Slavery*, 2nd ed. (London: Verso, 2010); David Goldenberg, *Black and Slave* (Berlin: De Gruyter, 2017), 83-95; David Goldenberg, *The Curse of Ham* (Princeton, NJ: Princeton University Press, 2005), 131-35; Stephen Haynes, *Noah's Curse* (New York: Oxford University Press, 2002), 7; Charles Irons, *The Origins of Proslavery Christianity* (Chapel Hill: University of North Carolina Press, 2009), 25; Thomas Sowell, *Black Rednecks and White Liberals* (New York: Encounter, 2005), 111-14; David Whitford, *The Curse of Ham in the Early Modern Era* (Farnham, UK: Ashgate, 2009), 77-105; Andre Wink, *Al-Hind: The Making of the Indo-Islamic World*, 3rd ed. (Leiden, Netherlands: Brill, 1996), 30-33.

[10]Particularly after the Muslim advance into Europe slowed in the eighth century, the Muslim slave trade moved more aggressively southward, since Muslims could not enslave fellow Muslims. By the late medieval and early modern eras, although not all enslaved persons in Arabian

regions in northern Africa and southwest Asia were Black, virtually all Black persons in these regions were enslaved. However, blackness still did not necessarily imply enslavement in western European contexts at least as late as the fourteenth century. Contrary to claims of humane Muslim bondage, Muslim slavery was as cruel as any other slave system. The primary justification of slavery for Muslims was *kufr*, nonbelief in Islam. While enslavement had a long history in Africa before the spread of Islam, slave raiding and slave trading, virtually unknown in African non-Muslim societies, became common in the Muslim social order. The *hadiths* of Bukhari reveal that Muhammad himself owned slaves, though the ethnicity of these persons is unknown. See Robin Blackburn, "The Old World Background to European Colonial Slavery," *The William and Mary Quarterly* 54, no. 1 (January 1997): 74; David Brion Davis, *Inhuman Bondage: The Rise and Fall of Slavery in the New World* (New York: Oxford University Press, 2008), 58-61; David Brion Davis, *Slavery and Human Progress* (New York: Oxford University Press, 1984), 33; David Goldenberg, *Black and Slave* (Berlin: De Gruyter, 2017), 99-101; Ayman Ibrahim, *A Concise Guide to the Life of Muhammad* (Grand Rapids, MI: Baker, 2022), 167-68; Bernard Lewis, *Race and Color in Islam* (New York: Harper & Row, 1971), 5. Among Muslims, an enslaved person's conversion to Islam did not result in manumission, though it did likely result in improved status over time. "Slave-owners wanted slaves to become Muslims, but for themselves to be better Muslims." Frederick Cooper, "The Problem of Slavery in African Studies," *Journal of African History* 20, no. 1 (1979): 124.

[11]For examples of medieval church rulings that sustained slavery, see Frederik Pijpher, "The Christian Church and Slavery in the Middle Ages," *The American Historical Review* 14, no. 4 (July 1909): 692. Thomas Aquinas concluded that, although slavery had not been part of the original order of the world, some persons in a fallen world are fitted by nature for bondage. In this, Thomas followed Aristotle, *Politics*, Loeb Classical Library 264, trans. Harris Rackham (Cambridge, MA: Harvard University Press, 1932), 1:5:1-11 (1254a:18–1254b:36); on Aristotle, see Julie Ward, "*Ethnos* in the *Politics:* Aristotle and Race," *Philosophers on Race*, ed. Julie Ward and Tommy Lott (Hoboken, NJ: Blackwell, 2002), 25-27. Thomas

understood the defective rationality that indicated natural fittedness for slavery as more likely to characterize persons in other lands, due (in his mind) to intemperate climates or evil customs. Thomas Aquinas, "Sententia libri Politicorum," *Sancti Thomae de Aquino: Opera Omnia iussu Leonis XIII: P.M. edita Tomus XLVIII: Sententia libri Politicorum, Tabula Libri Ethicorum* (Rome: Ad Sanctae Sabinae, 1971), 1:1:9. The Muslim philosopher Avicenna made similar arguments. David Brion Davis, *Inhuman Bondage* (New York: Oxford University Press, 2008), 55. By the late seventeenth century, the terms "Negro and slave" had become "homogeneous and convertible" in the New World. See, e.g., Morgan Godwyn, *The Negro's and Indian's Advocate, Suing for Their Admission into the Church* (London: Godwyn, 1680), 36.

[12]Isabel Wilkerson rightly recognizes *caste* as an apt description of the ranking of races in the United States; however, her work seems to treat this use of *caste* as if it has previously been a historical rarity in reference to the social status of African Americans. See Isabel Wilkerson, *Caste* (New York: Random House, 2020), 23. The term *caste* was, however, commonly applied to the ranking of ethnicities in America throughout the nineteenth century. For a sampling of this function of *caste* in primary sources, see, e.g., William Alexander, *History of the Colored Race in America*, 8th rev. ed. (Kansas City, MO: Palmetto, 1890), 18; William Brown, *The Negro in the American Rebellion* (Boston: Lee and Shepard, 1867), 361; Harvey Newcomb, *The "Negro Pew"* (Boston: Knapp, 1837), 67-87; Norman Wood, *The White Side of a Black Subject* (Chicago: American, 1897), 400. Even those who promoted white supremacy referred to the hierarchicalization of races as a caste system; see, e.g., John Campbell, *Negromania: Being an Examination of the Falsely Assumed Equality of the Various Races of Men* (Philadelphia: Campbell and Power, 1851), 96.

[13]Today, Latinos with darker skin experience higher levels of ethnic discrimination than Latinos with lighter skin. See Nayeli Y. Chavez-Dueñas, Hector Y. Adames, and Kurt C. Organista, "Skin-Color Prejudice and Within-Group Racial Discrimination," *Hispanic Journal of Behavioral Sciences* 36, no. 1 (2014): 7; Pew Research Center, *Majority of Latinos Say Skin Color Impacts Opportunity in America and Shapes Daily Lives*, November

4, 2021, 21. Dissatisfaction with darker skin drives multibillion-dollar skin bleaching and cosmetic surgery industries. Evelyn Glenn, "Yearning for Lightness: Transnational Circuits in the Marketing and Consumption of Skin Lighteners," *Gender and Society* 22, no. 3 (June 2008): 281-302, www .jstor.org/stable/27821646; Margaret Hunter, "The Persistent Problem of Colorism: Skin Tone, Status, and Inequality," *Sociology Compass* 1, no. 1 (September 2007): https://compass.onlinelibrary.wiley.com/doi/abs/10 .1111/j.1751-9020.2007.00006.x.

[14] The racialized function of Noah's curse spread as the expanding Transatlantic Slave Trade was critiqued and questioned, David Whitford, "'Forgetting Hime Selfe after a Most Filthie and Shamefull Sorte': Martin Luther and John Calvin on Genesis 9," *Calvin and Luther*, ed. R. Ward Holder (Göttingen, Germany: Vandenhoeck and Ruprecht, 2013), 47. By 1862, this perspective was the "general, almost universal, opinion in the Christian world," according to African American Episcopal priest Alexander Crummell, quoted in David Brion Davis, *Inhuman Bondage* (New York: Oxford University Press, 2008), 66.

[15] The causes of this process of racialization were far more complex than the distortion of a single text. Precedents for racialization and racism already existed in the ancient world. Ancient Greek writers frequently identified physical characteristics that identified groups as uniformly good or bad, as well as hierarchicalizing coloration and connecting coloration with climate. See Benjamin Isaac, *The Invention of Racism in Classical Antiquity* (Princeton, NJ: Princeton University Press, 2002), 23-38, 55-65; and Colin Kidd, *The Forging of Races* (New York: Cambridge University Press, 2006) 76-77. The climatological explanation of differences in skin color was so widespread that some persons as late as the eighteenth century believed that, if Africans moved to Sweden, they and their descendants would gradually turn White. Nancy Isenberg, *White Trash* (London: Penguin Books, 2017), 99-100. The negative view of lighter and darker ethnicities among some ancient writers may have provided at least some of the background for later negative perceptions of Africans. At the same time, a distinct and unique process of racial hierarchicalization did take place in the seventeenth and eighteenth centuries. Although non-Africans experienced enslavement during the medieval and

early modern eras, most notably along the Barbary Coast, "the deci-mation inflicted on sub-Saharan Africa and on black Africans in the Americas hugely outweighed, in its scope if not in all its specific horrors, that which was imposed on white slaves in Barbary." Robert Davis, *Christian Slaves, Muslim Masters* (New York: MacMillan, 2004), 192.

[16] Jonathan Edwards, *The Injustice and Impolicy of the Slave Trade and of the Slavery of the Africans*, 3rd ed. (New Haven, CT: New Haven Anti-Slavery Society, 1833), 13-15. The elder Jonathan Edwards seems to have been uneasy about the morality of enslavement, yet his views were complex and sometimes seemingly contradictory. He defended the legitimacy of slavery as an institution and saw it in part as a divine judgment on Af-ricans. Yet he also condemned the cruelties of the Atlantic slave trade and called for an end to the practice. See Richard Bailey, *Race and Re-demption in Puritan New England* (New York: Oxford University Press, 2011), 119-23. For further examples of exegeses from this era of the curse on Canaan that made no connection between blackness and enslavement; see, e.g., John Bunyan, "An Exposition of the Ten First Chapters of Genesis," in *The Works of That Eminent Servant of Christ, Mr. John Bunyan*, vol. 6, 4th ed. (Edinburgh: Sands, Murray, and Cochran, 1769; orig. pub. 1691), 434; and Joseph Thompson, *Teachings of the New Tes-tament on Slavery* (New York: Joseph Ladd, 1856), 8-10. The rise of the heresy of a supposed Hamitic curse on Africans in English-speaking con-texts coincided with an increased separation between White and Black Christians. In North America, relations between White and Black Chris-tians seem to have been more porous in the eighteenth century than in the nineteenth century; see Curtiss Paul DeYoung et al., *United by Faith* (New York: Oxford University Press, 2003), 46-48.

[17] Alexander Stephens, "Speech Delivered on the 21st March 1861," in *Alex-ander H. Stephens, in Public and Private*, ed. Henry Cleveland (Phila-delphia: National Publishing Company, 1866), 723.

[18] Patrick Mell, *Slavery* (Penfield, GA: Brantly, 1844), 15.

[19] Paul Harvey, *Redeeming the South* (Chapel Hill: University of North Car-olina Press, 1997), 33-34; Daniel Stowell, *Rebuilding Zion* (New York: Oxford University Press, 1998), 83-84; Gregory Wills, *Democratic Religion* (New York: Oxford University Press, 2003), 68-75; C. Vann Woodward, *The*

Strange Career of Jim Crow, commemorative ed. (New York: Oxford University Press, 2002), 22.

[20]For the Coney Island variation of this perverse amusement, see Kevin Baker, "The Original Fantasy Island," in *Brooklyn*, ed. Michael Robbins and Wendy Palitz (New York: Workman, 2001), 52, where the game is described as "a standard carny attraction." The game was also known as "African Dodger." For a sampling of sources that reveal the ubiquity of the attraction in early twentieth-century America, see "Dodger Is an Expert but Sometimes He Is Hit," *Richland Shield and Banner*, October 31, 1907; "'Coon Hitting' Peril," *Philadelphia Record*, September 22, 1908; "The Black Dodger," *Wayne County Democrat*, September 19, 1913; "Threw Stone at African Dodger; Hit Him in Eye," *Youngstown Vindicator*, May 15, 1915. This game was eventually supplanted by an attraction with the racist ascription "Drop the Chocolate Drop" in which an African American man was plunged into a tank of water whenever the thrown baseball struck a trigger paddle. See "Successor to the 'African Dodger,'" *Popular Mechanics*, November 1910. A form of this attraction persists today as the "dunk tank."

[21]Howard Bridgman, "The Murderers of Frank," *The Congregationalist and Christian World* 34 (August 26, 1915): 271-72; and Amy Wood, *Lynching and Spectacle* (Chapel Hill: University of North Carolina Press, 2009), 39.

[22]Edwin Arnold, "Across the Road from the Barbecue House," *Mississippi Quarterly* 61 (Winter–Spring 2008): 267-92; Donald Mathews, *At the Altar of Lynching* (New York: Cambridge University Press, 2018), 268-70; Chad Seales, *The Secular Spectacle* (New York: Oxford University Press, 2013), 69. As far as I can determine, the lynching seems to have taken place near the northwest corner of the intersection of Jackson Street and Sprayberry Road in Newnan, Georgia.

[23]For examples of representatives of majority-White denominations and churches standing against lynching, see Robert Miller, "Protestant Churches and Lynching, 1919–1939," *Journal of Negro History* 42, no. 2 (April 1957): 118-31.

[24]For persistence of racial prejudices in the second half of the twentieth century, see Lawrence D. Bobo, "Racial Attitudes and Relations at the Close of the Twentieth Century," in *America Becoming: Racial Trends and*

Their Consequences, vol. 1, ed. Neil J. Smelser, William Julius Wilson, and Faith Mitchell (Washington, DC: National Academies Press, 2001), 264-301, https://nap.nationalacademies.org/read/9599/chapter/10#267. For examples from churches in the twentieth century as well as significant shifts away from prejudice and partiality, see Donald Collins, *When the Church Bell Rang Racist* (Macon, GA: Mercer University Press, 1998); and David Roach, *The Southern Baptist Convention and Civil Rights, 1954–1995* (Eugene, OR: Pickwick, 2021). Roach demonstrates that, while moderate Southern Baptists did champion certain aspects of the civil rights movement, Southern Baptists' most consequential movements away from racism coincided with a return to belief in the sufficiency and inerrancy of Scripture.

25 "We are not *personally* guilty of the sins that someone else did 300 years ago. . . . But we as a human race are together guilty of creating a society that includes injustice." Mark Liederbach and Evan Lenow, *Ethics as Worship* (Phillipsburg, NJ: P&R, 2021), 304. As such, a Christian rightly laments past and present injustices regardless of whether one is personally responsible for these injustices, particularly when those injustices are part of the story of one's own people or nation. The seventeenth-century Westminster Assembly eloquently acknowledged how individuals may be accessory to sins committed corporately by one's people or nation: "We acknowledge our great sinfulness, . . . by reason of Actual sins, our own sins, the sins of Magistrates, of Ministers, and of the whole Nation, unto which we are many ways accessary [sic]." *The Directory for the Publick Worship of God Agreed upon by the Assembly of Divines at Westminster* (Philadelphia: Benjamin Franklin, 1745), 12.

26 This textbook, originally published in 1977, does condemn the enslavement of Africans; nevertheless, the author explicitly linked persons of African descent with the curse of Ham and ascribed lesser capacities to these individuals based on Noah's foresight expressed in his curse. For the most recent edition of this textbook, see Henry Morris, *The Beginning of the World* (Green Forest, AR: New Leaf, 1991), 134. The supposed "curse of Ham" also provided one of the ideological bases for the massacre of 800,000 Tutsis and moderate Hutus in Rwanda in the mid-1990s.

Emmanuel Katongole, *Mirror to the Church* (Grand Rapids, MI: Zondervan, 2009), 56-60.

[27] George Yancey, *Beyond Racial Gridlock* (Downers Grove, IL: InterVarsity Press, 2006), 34.

[28] Luther Adams, *Way Up North in Louisville* (Chapel Hill: University of North Carolina Press, 2010), 30-33, 181-84; Dale Dannefer, Marissa Gilbert, and Chengming Han, "With the Wind at their Backs: Racism and the Amplification of Cumulative Dis/Advantage," *Annual Review of Gerontology and Geriatrics* 40 (October 2020): 115-19; Michael Emerson and Christian Smith, *Divided by Faith* (New York: Oxford University Press, 2000), 161-62; Ira Katznelson, *When Affirmative Action Was White* (New York: Norton, 2005), 113-25; Douglas Massey and Nancy Denton, *American Apartheid* (Cambridge, MA: Harvard University Press, 1993), 115-60; Richard Rothstein, *The Color of Law* (New York: Liveright, 2017), xii, 64, 75, 96, 110-13, 155-58, 182-85. In some regions, convict-leasing also stripped African American households of their primary providers and destroyed the health and the dignity of these providers. Douglas Blackmon, *Slavery by Another Name* (New York: Doubleday, 2008), 54-72. Presbyterian theologian B. B. Warfield noted the impact of these societal habits on the capacity of African Americans to advance socially and economically: "Become what he individually may, [the African American] cannot rise into the classes above him. It is probably impossible for any of us to realize the deadening burden of this hopelessness. It clips the wings of every soaring spirit." B. B. Warfield, "A Calm View of the Freedmen's Case," *The Church at Home and Abroad* 1 (January 1887): 64.

[29] O. S. Hawkins, "Race and Racism in the Southern Baptist Convention: The Lost Legacies of George W. Truett and W. A. Criswell," *Southwestern Journal of Theology* 63 (Spring 2021): 119-23; Rothstein, *The Color of Law*, 103-5; Herman Long and Charles Johnson, *People Versus Property* (Nashville, TN: Fisk University Press, 1947), 82-83.

[30] Rothstein, *The Color of Law*, 181-83. Other gains from which African Americans were largely excluded include the Homestead Act of 1862. Millions of Americans still benefit from the Homestead Act in which 270 million acres were seized from Native American tribes and redistributed to more than 1.6 million families. Fewer than six thousand families

approved to receive land—less than 1 percent of the total number—were African American. See Williams Darity and Kirsten Mullen, *From Here to Equality* (Chapel Hill: University of North Carolina Press, 2020), 37; Trina Shanks, "The Homestead Act: A Major Asset-Building Policy in American History," Center for Social Development Research (Center for Social Development Working Paper No. 00-9, Washington University, 2000), https://openscholarship.wustl.edu/csd_research/46/.

[31] Still today, when it comes to home loans, African American and Latino families continue to be rejected more often than equally qualified White families. See Stephen Ross and John Yinger, *The Color of Credit* (Cambridge, MA: MIT Press, 2002), 5, 273-368.

[32] Mary Jackman and Marie Crane, "'Some of My Best Friends Are Black': Interracial Friendship and Whites' Racial Attitudes," *Public Opinion Quarterly* 50, no. 4 (Winter 1986): 459-86; Daniel A. Powers and Christopher G. Ellison, "Interracial Contact and Black Racial Attitudes: The Contact Hypothesis and Selectivity Bias," *Social Forces* 74, no. 1 (September 1995): 205-26. Interracial friendships also diminish the extent to which African Americans rely on perceptions of discrimination when formulating intergroup attitudes. Linda R. Tropp, "Perceived Discrimination and Interracial Contact: Predicting Interracial Closeness among Black and White Americans," *Social Psychology Quarterly* 70, no. 1 (2007): 70-81.

[33] Even in the twenty-first century, African American families moving into majority-White neighborhoods may find they are not welcomed due to their ethnicity. See interview with an African American pastor in Minnesota in Jaison K. D. McCall, "The Lived Experience of African American Pastors" (EdD thesis, The Southern Baptist Theological Seminary, 2019), 103.

[34] Residential separation between Black and White households increased throughout most of the twentieth century and did not begin to decline until the 1980s. Despite some increases in urban diversification, 56% of African Americans remain in disproportionately concentrated neighborhoods in metropolitan areas where African Americans constitute more than 20% of residents. John Logan and Brian Stults, "Metropolitan Segregation: No Breakthrough in Sight: New Findings from the 2020 Census," Diversity and Disparities Project, Brown University, August 12, 2021, 2-5.

[35]Ana Hernández Kent and Lowell R. Ricketts, "Has Wealth Inequality in America Changed Over Time?," Federal Reserve Bank of St. Louis, December 2, 2020, www.stlouisfed.org/open-vault/2020/december/has-wealth-inequality-changed-over-time-key-statistics. In 1995, the median household wealth of an African American household was 8% of a White household. Melvin Oliver and Thomas Shapiro, *Black Wealth/White Wealth* (Milton Park, UK: Routledge, 1995), 93. At current rate of growth, it would take African American families 228 years to close this disparity. Dedrick Asante-Muhammad et al., *Report: The Ever-Growing Gap*, Institute for Policy Studies, August 8, 2016, https://ips-dc.org/report-ever-growing-gap/. Attribution of this deficit to a lack of motivation among African Americans is widespread (62% of conservative Protestants, 51% of Whites), as is attribution of the deficit to perceived defects in African American culture and family structures. Emerson and Smith, *Divided by Faith*, 100-113, 173. Although culture, family structures, and individual agency certainly *do* play a role in economic mobility, limiting the contributing factors to family structures and lack of motivation fails to consider adequately the continuing impact of policies and practices that have prevented economic flourishing by limiting opportunities. Wages and hiring practices continue to be marked by disparities even when African American candidates possess equivalent qualifications. See Chi Mac, Chris Wheat, and Diana Farrell, "Small Business Owner Race, Liquidity, and Survival," JPMorgan Chase Institute, July 2020, www.jpmorganchase.com/institute/research/small-business/report-small-business-owner-race-liquidity-survival; Lincoln Quillian et al., "Meta-Analysis of Field Experiments Shows No Change in Racial Discrimination in Hiring over Time," *Proceedings of the National Academy of Sciences of the United States of America* 114, no. 41 (September 12, 2017): www.pnas.org/doi/10.1073/pnas.1706255114.

[36]In *Black Rednecks and White Liberals*, Thomas Sowell helpfully articulates the ways in which enslavement of Africans began in Africa and Arabia far earlier than the Transatlantic Slave Trade (111-16, 165-69). Sowell's analysis of contemporary disparities is, however, less helpful. Sowell attributes economic gaps to the assimilation of lower-class White "cracker" values in African American culture. The African American

assimilation of cracker values was transplanted into northern cities during the Great Migration, according to Sowell, and it was northern distaste for this culture that brought about urban segregation (48). Much of Sowell's argument depends on anecdotes in which connections are drawn between cracker culture and urban Black culture in everything from recklessness and laziness to sexual licentiousness, with evidence largely dependent on Grady McWhiney, *Cracker Culture* (Tuscaloosa: University of Alabama Press, 1988). These alleged similarities could be cultural assimilations, yet it is equally possible that they are broader characteristics of cultures generationally isolated from economic and educational opportunities. Even if the thesis of assimilation of cracker culture were to be granted, at least three claims that sustain Sowell's conclusions are inadequately supported: (1) *Sowell ascribes a deficient work ethic to African Americans and attributes this behavior to the importation of "black redneck" culture into northern cities* (*Black Rednecks and White Liberals*, 13-22). However, studies conducted in the early twentieth century when African Americans were moving into northern cities from the South revealed that when African Americans were placed in equivalent jobs with White workers, the majority performed equivalent work and practiced an equivalent work ethic. When turnover among African American workers was high, it was found that African Americans were overcrowded in substandard yet overpriced housing, due to already-existing practices of segregation. During this time, African American workers broke at least two world records for productivity. See George Haynes, "The Negro at Work in New York City: A Study in Economic Progress" (PhD diss., Columbia University, 1912), 78-89; and George Haynes, *The Negro at Work During the World War and During Reconstruction* (Washington, DC: Government Printing Office, 1921), 21, 62-63, 87, 92-93, 106-17, 130-33. Evidence for Sowell's alleged importation of "black redneck" culture into early twentieth-century cities is lacking. (2) *Sowell contends that single parenthood was not widespread among African Americans until a century after enslavement; this allows an attribution of the rise of Black single parenthood to urbanized "black redneck" culture and to policies promoted by White liberals* (*Black Rednecks and White Liberals*, 160-62). Without a doubt, single parenthood *did* increase at a far higher rate among African Americans than among Whites in the late twentieth century, and this may be attributable in part to a liberalization of sexual standards that coincided with strained family structures at a time when the values of the New Left were appealing to African Americans. Nevertheless, single parenthood was more frequent among African Americans far earlier than Sowell seems to recognize. In 1880, 29.9% of African American children lived without one or both parents, compared to 12.7% of White children; nearly 43% more African American households (11.7%) were single-parent households than White households (8.2%) at this time. Even in the North in the mid-nineteenth century, single parenthood was more frequent among freed Blacks than among Whites. See Steven Ruggles, "The Origins of African American Family Structure," *American Sociological Review* 59, no. 1 (February 1994): 140-44. Decades of deliberate rending of families, forcible breeding, and rape at the hands of White captors have been amply documented. See, e.g., Catherine Clinton and Michele Gillespie, eds., *The Devil's Lane* (New York: Oxford University Press, 1997), 205-62; Patricia Gay, "Slavery as a Sexual Atrocity," *Sexual Addiction and Compulsivity* 6, no. 1 (1999): 6-7; Tera Hunter, *Bound in Wedlock* (Cambridge, MA: Harvard University Press, 2017), 1-85; Tera W. Hunter, *To 'Joy My Freedom* (Cambridge, MA: Harvard University Press, 1998), 11-12, 126-28; Harriet Jacobs, *Incidents in the Life of a Slave Girl* (London: Tweedie, 1862), 44-48; Thelma Jennings, "'Us Colored Women Had to Go Through Plenty': Sexual Exploitation of African American Slave Women," *Journal of Women's History* 1, no. 3 (1990): 45-74; Stephanie Jones-Rogers, "Rethinking Sexual Violence and the Marketplace of Slavery," and Brenda Stevenson, "What's Love Got to Do with It?" in *Sexuality and Slavery*, ed. Daina Berry and Leslie Harris (Athens: University of Georgia Press, 2018). While the causes of elevated instances of single parenthood in African American communities are multifaceted, heinous sexual abuse and fracturing of family units should be taken more seriously as a factor. (3) *Even if Sowell's thesis is correct, it should be recognized that members of White cracker culture received opportunities to transition into the American middle class throughout the late nineteenth and twentieth centuries which were systematically withheld from African Americans.* These opportunities included access to land and loans through the Homestead Act, Federal Housing Administration loans, and GI Bill benefits.

[37]For further exploration, see George Yancey, *Beyond Racial Division* (Downers Grove, IL: InterVarsity Press, 2022), 69-71. For a helpful comparison of two families, showing the long-term effects of enslavement, segregation, and discrimination, see Liederbach and Lenow, *Ethics as Worship*, 335-37. When these disparities are coupled with habits in law enforcement that have disproportionately impacted African American communities, the distinctions grow increasingly stark. See Jennifer Cox, "Frequent Arrests, Harsh Sentencing, and the Disproportionate Impact They Have on African Americans and Their Community," *South Regional Black Students Association Law Journal* (2009): 26; Roland Fryer, "An Empirical Analysis of Racial Differences in Police Use of Force," *Journal of Political Economy* 127, no. 3 (June 2019): 38-40; Phillip Atiba Goff et al., "The Science of Justice: Race, Arrests, and Police Use of Force," Center for Policing Equity, July 2016, https://policingequity.org/images/pdfs-doc /CPE_SoJ_Race-Arrests-UoF_2016-07-08-1130.pdf; Rebecca Hetey and Jennifer Eberhardt, "The Numbers Don't Speak for Themselves: Racial Disparities and the Persistence of Inequality in the Criminal Justice System," *Current Directions in Psychological Science* 27, no. 3 (June 2018): 183-87; Arthur Lurigio, "The Disproportionate Incarceration of Minorities for Drug Crime: A Primer on Drug Addiction, Crime, and Treatment," *Research Reports* 26 (2008): 1-63; Ojmarrh Mitchell, "A Meta-Analysis of Race and Sentencing Research: Explaining the Inconsistencies," *Journal of Quantitative Criminology* 21, no. 4 (December 2005): 439-66; Cody Ross, "A Multi-Level Bayesian Analysis of Racial Bias in Police Shootings at the County-Level in the United States, 2011–2014," *PLoS ONE*, November 5, 2015; "Investigation of the Seattle Police Department," United States Department of Justice Civil Rights Division and the United States Attorney's Office Western District of Washington December 16, 2011, www.justice .gov/sites/default/files/crt/legacy/2011/12/16/spd_findletter_12-16-11 .pdf. Ethnic disparities are also present in applications of the death penalty. Frank R. Baumgartner, Amanda J. Grigg, and Alisa Mastro, "#BlackLivesDontMatter: Race-of-Victim Effects in US Executions, 1977–2013," *Politics, Groups, and Identities* 3, no. 2 (April 2015): 218-21; Jefferson E.

Holcomb, Marian R. Williams, and Stephen Demuth, "White Female Victims and Death Penalty Disparity Research," *Justice Quarterly* 21, no. 4 (December 2004): 884-99. It is important, however, not to overstate the statistics related to these disparities. For example, although the ethnicity of an individual does affect police responses in some respects, police are not consistently more likely to shoot African American targets when compared to White targets. Joshua Correll et al., "The Police Officer's Dilemma: Using Ethnicity to Disambiguate Potentially Threatening Individuals," *Social and Personality Psychology Compass* 8, no. 5 (May 2014): 201-13. For an analysis of disparities with recommendations for cultural change from a retired police officer, see Daniel Reinhardt, *Rethinking the Police* (Downers Grove, IL: InterVarsity Press, forthcoming). See also Michelle Alexander, *The New Jim Crow: Mass Incarceration in the Age of Colorblindness*, 10th anniversary ed. (New York: New Press, 2020) 298-303.

[38] For examples of disparities in opportunities even when the same work is performed, see Chi Mac, Chris Wheat, and Diana Farrell, "Small Business Owner Race, Liquidity, and Survival," JPMorgan Chase Institute, July 2020, www.jpmorganchase.com/institute/research/small -business/report-small-business-owner-race-liquidity-survival. Disparities are not wholly dependent on differences in capacities, qualifications, or efforts to obtain jobs. African American job applicants possessing the same qualifications as other applicants are still less likely to receive callbacks from employers regarding their job applications. Lincoln Quillian et al., "Meta-Analysis of Field Experiments Shows No Change in Racial Discrimination in Hiring over Time," *Proceedings of the National Academy of Sciences of the United States of America* 114, no. 41 (September 12, 2017): www.pnas.org/doi/10.1073/pnas.1706255114.

[39] Augustine of Hippo, *Enarrationes in Psalmos I–L*, Corpus Christianorum Series Latina 38, ed. Eligius Dekkers and J. Fraipont (Ghent, Belgium: Brepols, 1956), 18:12 (19:12).

6. LITURGIES OF LAMENT

[1] Korie Edwards and Rebecca Kim, "Estranged Pioneers: The Case of African American and Asian American Multiracial Church Pastors," *Sociology of Religion* 80, no. 4 (Winter 2019): 456.

[2] Edwards and Kim, "Estranged Pioneers," 457, 471.

[3]Dominique Dubois Gilliard, *Subversive Witness* (Grand Rapids, MI: Zondervan, 2021), 50-51.

[4]At first, wanting to believe the best about every person in this context, I tried to find some explanation for the shotgun shell and the note other than a racist threat; however, the conference host—who knew the context and the participants better than I did—identified it as the threat that it seems to have been.

[5]Experiences of stereotype management when presenting at conferences are not unique to church and denominational conferences. See Ebony McGee and Danny Martin, "'You Would Not Believe What I Have to Go Through to Prove My Intellectual Value!': Stereotype Management Among Academically Successful Black Mathematics and Engineering Students," *American Educational Research Journal* 48, no. 6 (2011): 1347-89; and Ebony McGee and Lasana Kazembe, "Entertainers or Education Researchers? The Challenges Associated with Presenting While Black," *Race Ethnicity and Education* 19, no. 1 (2016): 96-120.

[6]"Racial Reconciliation Debrief and Next Steps," ed. Ryan and Celina Delapp, with Nick Weyrens and Jamaal Williams, Sojourn Church Midtown, 2016.

[7]A later service of lament, during the demonstrations in the aftermath of the killing of Breonna Taylor, took these earlier failures into account and resulted in a time that was far more gospel-driven and unifying. See the sermon from Jarvis Williams, "Love One Another," The Gospel, Race, and Justice, Sojourn Church Midtown, September 2, 2020, www.sojournchurch .com/midtown/justice.

[8]Gilliard, *Subversive Witness*, 50.

[9]Mark Vroegop, *Deep Clouds, Deep Mercy* (Wheaton, IL: Crossway, 2019), 29.

[10]"Resolution on Racial Reconciliation on the 150th Anniversary of the Southern Baptist Convention," June 1, 1995, www.sbc.net/resource -library/resolutions/resolution-on-racial-reconciliation-on-the-150th -anniversary-of-the-southern-baptist-convention/. See also James K. Dew Jr. and J. D. Greear, "Statement on the Death of George Floyd," *The Baptist Record*, June 4, 2020, 5. *Systemic racism*, for the purposes of this book, refers to "the ongoing impact of racist perceptions and practices, past or present, in a society's habits and structures." This definition of

systemic racism represents a rejection of recent redefinitions of *systemic racism* in ways that describe the American social order in its entirety as a racist entity organized to sustain racial oppression, as in, e.g., Joe Feagin, *Systemic Racism: A Theory of Oppression* (Milton Park, UK: Routledge, 2013), 6-9, 16. From a Christian perspective, no individual should be seen as bearing personal guilt for systemic racism because, outside the imputation of sin to all humanity in Adam, every individual is and can only be responsible for his or her own sins (Jeremiah 31:30; Ezekiel 18:1-4, 19-20). Social systems can, however, develop in such a way that particular sinful patterns may be pursued with less resistance in certain social contexts and, thus, may develop more readily into individual habits of sin; systemic racism develops in social systems in which racist attitudes can provide social benefits or persist on a widespread basis with little resistance. Andrew Gottschall utilized "systemic racism" in 1970 to describe pervasive attitudes that perpetuated disparities by assuming poverty as the unavoidable fate of African Americans. Andrew Gottschall, "Something's Got to Give: A Report on Twelve Attitudes which Disable the Community," 116 Cong. Rec. 17624 (May 28, 1970). The US Navy utilized the term to describe systematic misuses of personal or organizational power that result in unequal treatment of persons on the basis of ethnicity. See Charles Rauch, "Navy Human Goals Plan," *Commanders Digest*, February 21, 1974, 3; Alan Shethar and Jim Stovall, "A Look at the Human Side: A Review of the Navy's Long Range Human Goals Plan," *All Hands* 682 (November 1973): 5. These and other similar early usages of *systemic racism* rightly recognized that social systems may function in ways which allow racism to be perpetuated more easily but that any guilt for racist actions or attitudes, whether intended or unintended, is to be ascribed to individual acts.

[11] Augustine of Hippo, "Exposition of Psalm 59," *Expositions of the Psalms*, vol. 3/17, ed. John Rotelle, trans. Maria Boulding (Hyde Park, NY: New City, 2001), 186.

[12] Much like the phenomenon of extended altruism, lament for those who cannot reciprocate in any beneficial manner is not well explained by evolutionary theories, because there seems to be no adequate biological

explanation for a pattern of unselfish avoidance of limbic system rewards. Lament for others, by its very nature, provides little or no pleasurable reward. See Timothy Shaw, "The Human Brain, Religion, and the Biology of Sin," *Investigating the Biological Foundations of Human Morality*, ed. James Hurd (Lewiston, NY: Edwin Mellen, 1996), 162.

[13] Anthony O'Hear, *Beyond Evolution* (New York: Clarendon Press, 1997), 143.

[14] Bobby Gilles and Rebecca Elliot, "Let Justice Roll," *New Again*, Sojourn Music, 2015. Used by permission.

7. SEEING BOTH SIDES OF THE BALL

[1] Rupen Fofaria, "Dudley Flood Is an Education Trailblazer, but He Isn't Finished Helping the State Chart Its Course," EducationNC, November 23, 2020, www.ednc.org/nc-education-revolutionary-dudley-flood-still-working-for-equity/. Information on Dudley Flood and integration of public schools in Hyde County, North Carolina, has been drawn from David Cecelski, *Along Freedom Road* (Chapel Hill: University of North Carolina Press, 1994), 40, 88-149; James Ford and Nicholas Triplett, *E(race)ing Inequities* (Raleigh: EducationNC, 2019); and Phoebe Judge, "Episode 180: The Boycott," *Criminal* podcast, January 14, 2022, https://thisiscriminal.com/episode-180-the-boycott-1-14-2022/.

[2] James Palmer, *The Impact of Private Education on the Rural South* (Austin, TX: National Educational Laboratory Publishers, 1974), 10-14.

[3] William E. Nelson Jr., "School Desegregation and the Black Community," *Theory into Practice* 17, no. 2 (April 1978): 127.

[4] "The fact of White privilege is not the basis of attack, envy, or dissension. On the contrary, the point of discussing White privilege is to help Whites see how God can use those advantages and freedom from certain burdens as a platform for blessing those without them. In other words, Whites may be missing opportunities to use their privilege redemptively in the broken world." Anthony Bradley, *Aliens in the Promised Land*, ed. Anthony Bradley (Phillipsburg, NJ: P&R, 2013), 152-53. For the initial exploration of this topic, see Peggy McIntosh, "White Privilege: Unpacking the Invisible Knapsack," *Peace and Freedom* (July–August 1989): 10-12.

[5] Jerry Himelstein, "Conflict Theory and Segregation Academies" (PhD diss., Louisiana State University, 1980), 30-36, 82-83. When desegregation began to be enforced in the city of Louisville in 1974 and 1975, at least

seven Christian schools were quickly formed to avoid integration. Walter Reichert, "The Growth of Private Schools in Jefferson County following the Desegregation of the Public School System" (MS thesis, Indiana University, 1977), 14. See also Charles Clotfelter, *After "Brown"* (Princeton, NJ: Princeton University Press, 2006), 109; David Nevin and Robert Bills, *The Schools That Fear Built* (New York: Acropolis, 1976), 28. Despite some suggestions to the contrary, however, desegregation was not the only factor in the flight from public education. In 1979, a representative of the Association of Christian Schools International testified before Congress that he took no issue with the IRS removing tax-exempt status from Christian schools that practiced segregation. "Hearing before the Subcommittee on Taxation and Debt Management Generally of the Committee on Finance, United States Senate Ninety-Sixth Congress First Session on 103, S.449, S.990, S.995," April 27, 1979, 114. Shifts toward secularity in public schools and the presumption of discrimination in Green v. Connally, 330 F. Supp. 1150 (D.D.C., 1971) were also factors in the movement toward Christian schooling. Nevertheless, a burden remains for Christians today to counterbalance past practices that contributed to segregated schools, especially since limited economic opportunities, prejudice, and discrimination prevented many African Americans from pursuing private education when they might otherwise have done so. Hunter Baker rightly recognizes: "The best answer may be for conservative Christians to find . . . ways to create greater access to their institutions for those from whom they are suspected of fleeing. It is a burden of history not easily shrugged off, even by generations who did not make the world in which they live. We inherit debts other than the kind governments incur on their balance sheets. But the racial unification of the American church might best begin in the Christian schoolhouse." Hunter Baker, "Christian Schools and Racial Realities," *Touchstone* magazine, September–October 2013, www.touchstonemag.com/archives/article.php?id=26-05-019-v.

[6]Moral evil can be social and structural. Cornelius Plantinga, *Not the Way It's Supposed to Be* (Grand Rapids, MI: Eerdmans, 1996), 25. Nevertheless, we have avoided terms such as *structural sin* and *social sin* in this book. In Scripture, though sin can certainly be *corporate* and *social*, sin is not committed by structures but by individuals, and guilt is not accounted to

structures but to individuals. Ascribing sin to systems or structures can enable individuals to evade responsibility for their own actual sins, whether intended or unintended. *Structures of vice* may be a better phrase than *structural sin* to describe the way in which a structure may function to sustain and to promote sinful actions. For *structures of vice* as a better alternative which resonates with the theological ethics of Thomas Aquinas, see Daniel Daly, "Structures of Virtue and Vice," *New Blackfriars* 92, no. 1039 (May 2011): 354; and Daniel Daly, *The Structures of Virtue and Vice* (Washington, DC: Georgetown University Press, 2021). See also the critique of *social sin* in Michael Landon, "The Social Presuppositions of Early Liberation Theology," *Restoration Quarterly* 47, no. 1 (2005): 15-24.

[7]Recognizing and valuing different perspectives does not imply a relativistic view of truth. Truth is transcultural, but truth is culturally expressed, and differing cultural expressions may highlight different aspects of the same truth. For this same truth expressed in the context of different disciplines, see James Sire, *Naming the Elephant*, 2nd ed. (Downers Grove, IL: InterVarsity Press, 2015), 140; Kevin Vanhoozer, "One Rule to Rule Them All? Theological Method in an Era of World Christianity," *Globalizing Theology*, ed. Craig Ott and Harold Netland (Grand Rapids, MI: Baker, 2006), 94.

[8]Christena Cleveland, *Disunity in Christ* (Downers Grove, IL: InterVarsity Press, 2013), 21.

[9]*Over the Grave*, Sojourn, 2009; *The Water and the Blood*, Sojourn, 2011; *New Again*, Sojourn Music, 2015. Used by permission.

[10]For sociological analyses of the impact of changes in worship style in churches, see Brad Christerson, Korie Edwards, and Michael Emerson, *Against All Odds* (New York: New York University Press, 2005), 56-57, 168. In 1868, First Baptist Church in Jackson, Mississippi, removed all African American members due in part to their exuberance in worship. Alan Cross, *When Heaven and Earth Collide* (Montgomery, AL: NewSouth, 2014), 135.

[11]"Simple, rhythmic repetition as a liturgical expression of piety is in no sense new; it is as old as the Gregorian chant or, for that matter, the four living creatures of Revelation 4:8." Willis Jones, "Five Perspectives on Music in Reformed Worship," *Reformed Review* 48, no. 2 (1994): 128-29. Of course, the appropriateness of repetition is also dependent on the

meaningfulness of the terms repeated and the theological integrity of the song. See Mary Conway, "Worship Music: Maintaining Dynamic Tension," *McMaster Journal of Theology and Ministry* 7 (2006): 149.

[12] *Therapy* derives from the Greek θεραπεύειν, which meant "to serve" (see, e.g., Proverbs 19:6; 29:26 LXX; Acts 17:25) but which acquired the senses of "to care for the sick" and "to cure" (see, e.g., Matthew 4:23; 9:35; Luke 7:21). *Therapy* in the sense that we are using it here refers to the comfort and healing of the soul that can occur during times of worship through songs. See Eric Johnson, *God and Soul Care* (Downers Grove, IL: InterVarsity Press, 2017), 450.

[13] Gerardo Marti, *Worship across the Racial Divide* (Oxford: Oxford University Press, 2012), 57.

[14] Joshua Holland, "The Average Black Family Would Need 228 Years to Build the Wealth of a White Family Today," *The Nation*, August 8, 2016, www .thenation.com/article/archive/the-average-black-family-would-need-228 -years-to-build-the-wealth-of-a-white-family-today/. The point here is not to attempt to address this gap; it is simply to recognize how social, cultural, and even financial situations may play a role in worship preferences.

[15] Anthony Pinn, "Spirituals as an Early Reflection on Suffering," in *Why Lord?* (New York: Continuum, 2006), 29.

[16] Timothy Paul Jones, "The Gospel and Diversity," Sojourn Network Leaders' Summit, October 2018.

[17] African American and White Protestants are largely of the same mind with respect to their beliefs about core doctrinal statements, but religious sensibilities differ deeply. See Jason Shelton and Michael Emerson, *Blacks and Whites in Christian America* (New York: New York University Press, 2012), 48-56.

[18] Jeff Diamant, "Blacks More Likely than Others in U.S. to Read the Bible Regularly, See It as God's Word," Pew Research Center, May 7, 2018, www .pewresearch.org/fact-tank/2018/05/07/blacks-more-likely-than-others -in-u-s-to-read-the-bible-regularly-see-it-as-gods-word/.

[19] Sarah Grimké seems to have seen this connection between prejudice, power, and *libido dominandi* in 1836: "The lust of dominion inevitably produces hardness of heart, because the state of mind which craves unlimited power, such as slavery confers, involves a desire to use that

power, and although I know there are exceptions to the exercise of bar-
barity on the bodies of slaves, I maintain that there can be no exceptions
to the exercise of the most soul-withering cruelty on the minds of the
enslaved." "An Epistle to the Clergy of the Southern States," in *On Slavery
and Abolitionism* (New York: Penguin, 2014), 27.

[20]The presence of privilege should not provoke guilt on the part of the
privileged; instead, those that are privileged should become aware of
their privilege so that it can be deployed for the good of others. See John
Perkins with Karen Waddles, *One Blood* (Chicago: Moody, 2018), 89.

8. HOW GOD MADE A HOLY MESS AND TURNED IT INTO A HEAVENLY MOVEMENT

[1]Martin Luther, *Der Brief an die Römer. D. Martin Luthers Werke: Kritische
Gesamtausgabe, Weimar Ausgabe* 56, ed. Gustav Bebermeyer (Weimar,
Germany: Hermann Böhlau und Nachfolger, 1938), 304-5.

[2]Augustine of Hippo, *Augustine: City of God: Books 1–3*, Loeb Classical Library 411, trans. George McCracken (Cambridge, MA: Harvard University
Press, 1957), 1:30. Lust for dominance begins with those in power and
then infects "the worn and wearied," reshaping social structures in ways
that oppress and enslave. For Augustine, enslavement of captives when
a city was sacked was, though customary, nevertheless an expression of
libido dominandi (1:4). Lust for dominance produces oppression when an
individual or group forces others to become participants in their ungod-
liness. For oppression as forcing others to participate in unrighteousness,
see Carl Ellis, *Free at Last?*, rev. ed. (Downers Grove, IL: InterVarsity
Press, 2020), 28.

[3]Augustine identified human language as the instrument by which *libido
dominandi* is exercised; he also connected Babel with the City of Man,
Augustine of Hippo, *Augustine: City of God: Books 16–18:35*, Loeb Classical
Library 415, trans. Eva Stanford and William Green (Cambridge, MA:
Harvard University Press, 1965), 16:4-5, 10.

[4]Huber Drumwright, "The Holy Spirit in the Book of Acts," *Southwestern
Journal of Theology* 17, no. 1 (Fall 1974): 3-17.

[5]Paul Mumo Kisau, "Acts of the Apostles," in *Africa Bible Commentary*, ed.
Tokunboh Adeyemo (Grand Rapids, MI: Zondervan, 2006), 1339.

[6]Rodney Woo, *The Color of Church* (Nashville, TN: B&H, 2009), 77.

[7] Jarvis Williams, *Redemptive Kingdom Diversity* (Grand Rapids, MI: Baker, 2021), 99-100.

[8] William Larkin, *Acts* (Downers Grove, IL: InterVarsity Press, 2011), 99.

[9] Rodney Woo, *The Color of Church* (Nashville, TN: B&H, 2009), 167-68.

[10] John Polhill, *Acts* (Nashville, TN: B&H, 1992), 181. See also Larkin, *Acts*, 101.

[11] David Peterson, *The Acts of the Apostles* (Grand Rapids, MI: Eerdmans, 2009), 234.

[12] Soong-Chan Rah, *Many Colors* (Chicago: Moody, 2010), 120.

[13] Chester Hunt and Lewis Walker, *Ethnic Dynamics* (Belmont, CA: Dorsey, 1974), 354. See also Michael Emerson and George Yancey, *Transcending Racial Barriers* (New York: Oxford University Press, 2011), 40-42; and Paul Morrison, *Integration* (Eugene, OR: Pickwick, 2022), 191-93.

[14] Daniel Hill, *White Awake* (Downers Grove, IL: InterVarsity Press, 2017), 50.

[15] Commission on Theology and Church Relations of the Lutheran Church—Missouri Synod, *Racism and the Church*, The Lutheran Church—Missouri Synod, 1994, quoted in Anthony B. Bradley, ed., *Aliens in the Promised Land* (Phillipsburg, NJ: P&R, 2013), 184.

[16] William Barclay, *The Letters to the Corinthians* (Louisville, KY: Westminster John Knox, 2017), 271.

[17] Commission on Theology and Church Relations of the Lutheran Church—Missouri Synod, *Racism and the Church*, The Lutheran Church—Missouri Synod, 1994, 26.

[18] Curtiss Paul DeYoung et al., *United by Faith* (New York: Oxford University Press, 2003), 165. Michael Emerson and George Yancey similarly call for the formation of a shared identity—a "common core"—that unites different ethnicities. See Michael Emerson and George Yancey, *Transcending Racial Barriers* (New York: Oxford University Press, 2011), 90-125. Because Emerson's and Yancey's goals in this particular book are broader than the Christian tradition, their core concept is a common-grace notion of freedom. Nevertheless, their work is helpful for considering the dynamics of how a church might develop a multiethnic kingdom culture. See also George Yancey, *Beyond Racial Division* (Downers Grove, IL: InterVarsity, 2022), 109-12.

[19] This celebration of a superordinate identity in Christ reduces intergroup conflict through *crossed categorization* and *recategorization*, in the

NOTE TO PAGE 81

verbiage of social-identity theory. In crossed categorization, persons
sharing different category membership in one respect (such as ethnicity
or socioeconomic status) begin to see themselves as members of the same
category in another respect (such as siblings in Christ and members of
his church) so that the commonality works against the initial differenti-
ation. In recategorization, two categories do not merely cancel one another out; instead, persons who were previously perceived as members
of an outgroup are subsumed into a new and larger category so that they
are no longer seen as part of an outgroup but as fellow members of an
ingroup. See Philip Esler, "Jesus and the Reduction of Intergroup Conflict:
The Parable of the Good Samaritan in Light of Social Identity Theory,"
Biblical Interpretation 8, no. 4 (2000): 345-49; and Philip Esler, "Social
Identity, the Virtues, and the Good Life: A New Approach to Romans 12:1–
15:13," *Biblical Theology Bulletin* 33, no. 2 (May 2003): 54. Our understanding of early Christian identity formation stands in contrast to the
perspective proposed by Love Sechrest and others. According to Sechrest,
Paul became "a former Jew" as his ties to the Jewish community weakened
and his ties to Christian communities grew stronger. Sechrest rightly
notes that, for early Christians, biology no longer determined primary
kinship and that faith stood as the necessary and sufficient basis for
kinship. However, this new kinship in Christ did not (as Sechrest seems
to suggest) require the constitution of a new racial or ethnic identity that
replaced previous ethnic identities. For the notion of Christians as a new
race or ethnicity in this sense, see Love Sechrest, *A Former Jew* (London:
T&T Clark, 2009), 5, 123-29, 159; Denise Buell, *Why This New Race?* (New
York: Columbia University Press, 2005), 7-10, 45, 108, 165; Denise Buell and
Caroline Hodge, "The Politics of Interpretation: The Rhetoric of Race and
Ethnicity in Paul," *Journal of Biblical Literature* 123, no. 2 (Summer 2004):
238, 249; Caroline Hodge, *If Sons, Then Heirs* (New York: Oxford University
Press, 2007), 33; Judith Lieu, *Christian Identity in the Jewish and Graeco-
Roman World* (New York: Oxford University Press, 2004), 118.

9. LITURGIES OF GIVING

[1]This quote comes from a conversation I (Jamaal) had in 2016 with Derwin
Gray, pastor of Transformation Church in Charlotte, North Carolina, and
Indian Land, South Carolina.

[2]White Christians are more likely to expect Asian, Latino, and African American Christians to join White churches to make them more diverse than they are to consider the possibility of joining a church in which most members are non-White. See Kevin Dougherty, Mark Chaves, and Michael Emerson, "Racial Diversity in U.S. Congregations, 1998–2019," *Journal for the Scientific Study of Religion* 59, no. 4 (December 2020): 9-10. And yet, as our friend and fellow pastor Andy Norris reminded us, an African American Christian who leaves a historically Black congregation is leaving the safety of a context where dignity has been affirmed on a regular basis, a context which was at one time in history one of the few places where an African American person could be called "brother" or "sister" instead of a demeaning or derogatory term.

[3]Timothy Keller, "The Sin of Racism," *Gospel in Life*, Redeemer Church, Summer 2020, https://quarterly.gospelinlife.com/the-bible-and-race/.

[4]For the missiological need for a multiethnic understanding of the early history of Christianity, see Vince Bantu, *A Multitude of All Peoples* (Downers Grove, IL: InterVarsity Press, 2020), 1-6.

[5]When Christians from different backgrounds enter robust and meaningful dialogue, Christians become more able to see aspects of truth that they may not have noticed previously. The result is greater objectivity, not less. See David Horrell, *Ethnicity and Inclusion* (Grand Rapids, MI: Eerdmans, 2020), 344-45.

[6]For a similar perspective from an African American church planter, see Lance Lewis, "Black Pastoral Leadership and Church Planting," in *Aliens in the Promised Land*, ed. Anthony Bradley (Phillipsburg, NJ: P&R, 2013), 36-43. See also Soong-Chan Rah, *The Next Evangelicalism* (Downers Grove, IL: InterVarsity Press, 2009), 162.

[7]Some Christians have mounted biblical and theological arguments for reparations; see, e.g., Duke L. Kwon and Gregory Thompson, *Reparations: A Christian Call for Repentance and Repair* (Grand Rapids, MI: Brazos, 2021). Other Christians have made a case against reparations, arguing instead for a mutual accountability approach grounded in social-identity theory in which collaborative conversations result in alternative means of ameliorating disparities; see, e.g., George Yancey, *Beyond Racial Gridlock* (Downers Grove, IL: InterVarsity Press, 2006),

105-8. Both approaches, however, recognize a responsibility for Christians to take tangible steps toward addressing disparities that have resulted from racially discriminatory policies and practices. For further consideration of responsibilities that accompany privilege, see Mark Liederbach and Evan Lenow, *Ethics as Worship* (Phillipsburg, NJ: P&R, 2021), 304.

[8]Lactantius, *L. Caelius Firmianus Lactantius: Divinarum Institutionum Libri Septem, Fascicle 3, Libri V et VI,* ed. Eberhard Heck and Antonie Wlosok (Berlin, Germany: De Gruyter, 2009), 6:12.

[9]E. Randolph Richards and Brandon J. O'Brien, *Misreading Scripture with Western Eyes* (Downers Grove, IL: InterVarsity Press, 2012), 189.

[10]*The Epistle to Diognetus (with the Fragment of Quadratus): Introduction, Text, and Commentary,* ed. Clayton Jefferd (New York: Oxford University Press, 2013), 7:9

[11]*The Epistle to Diognetus,* 10:2-8. The author seems to have been replying to a question that included some query related to the love of Christians for one another ("φιλοστοργιαν," 1:1). The benevolent love described in 9:2 ("φιλανθρωπίας," cf. Titus 3:4) suggests that the love of Christians for one another is grounded in the love of God for humanity; imitation of this love causes Christians to reach beyond their love for one another and to love their neighbors who are not yet Christians. For further discussion, see Juan Ignacio Ruiz Aldaz, "La Recepción del Concepto de *Philanthropía* en la Literatura Cristiana de los Dos Primeros Siglos," *Scripta Theologica* 42 (2010): 295-96.

[12]*The Epistle to Diognetus,* 10:5.

[13]Anthony O'Hear, *Beyond Evolution* (New York: Clarendon, 1997), 143.

[14]Rebecca Elliot and Bobby Gilles, "All I Have Is Yours," *Before the Throne,* Sojourn, 2007. Used by permission.

10. GOING TO WAR BY PASSING THE PEACE

[1]"Although in Paul's days kisses were a part of everyday life and also of correspondence, Paul used these kisses in his own way when he asked his addressees to greet one another with a holy kiss at the end of his letters." Rianne Voogd, "Is the Instruction to Greet One Another with a Holy Kiss a Pauline Transformation?," in *Rituals in Early Christianity,* ed. Nienke Vos and Albert Geljon (Leiden, Netherlands: Brill, 2021), 58.

[2]This kiss was "reserved for fellow Christians or for particular occasions" and "marked the family bond of those who believed in Christ." James D. G. Dunn, *Romans 9–16* (Nashville, TN: Nelson, 1988), 899. For the kiss of peace as participation in the Spirit, see Lawrence Phillips, "The Ritual Kiss in Early Christian Worship" (PhD diss., University of Notre Dame, 1992), 41-96. Although Phillips may overstate the possibility that early Christians perceived the kiss of peace as an actual conveyance of the Spirit, he rightly recognizes the connection between passing of peace and mutual participation in the Holy Spirit.

[3]Rianne Voogd identified four functions of the holy kiss: (1) epistolary, conveying a greeting from an individual who is absent by means of persons who are present, (2) theological, expressing a shared devotion to holiness, (3) familial, constructing the Christian community as a family, and (4) contra-hierarchical, upending and relativizing sociocultural rankings. See Rianne Voogd, *De betekenis van Paulus' oproep tot de groet met de heilige kus* (Middelburg, Netherlands: Uitgeverij Skandalon, 2016), 253-61; Rianne Voogd, "Is the Instruction to Greet One Another with a Holy Kiss a Pauline Transformation?," *Rituals in Early Christianity*, ed. Nienke Vos and Albert Geljon (Leiden, Netherlands: Brill, 2021), 62. By constructing the Christian community as a family, the kiss of peace contributed to the formation of a shared, superordinate identity which coexisted with ethnic and cultural identities.

[4]Augustine of Hippo, "Sermon 227: Preached on the Holy Day of Easter to the *Infantes*, on the Sacraments," *Sermons III/6 (184–229Z) on the Liturgical Seasons*, trans. and ed. Edmund Hill and John Rotelle (Hyde Park, NY: New City, 1993), 255.

[5]Even among early Christians, the commonness of the kiss as a greeting did not preclude more intimate implications. Christians were careful to prevent men from taking advantage of women in the church by prolonging or repeating a kiss of peace. According to Athenagoras, a man violates the rule of the church if he lingers in kissing a woman "because it gives him pleasure.... If [the kiss] is corrupted by defilement of thought, it excludes [him] from eternal life." Athenagoras of Athens, "Libellus Pro Christianis," *Libellus Pro Christianis: Oratio De Resurrectione Cadauerum*, ed. Eduard Schwartz (Leipzig, Germany: Hinrichs, 1891),

chap. 32. For the loss of the kiss of peace because of the Protestant emphasis on peace with God and a devaluation of physical rituals, see Craig Koslofsky, "The Kiss of Peace in the German Reformation," *The Kiss in History*, ed. Karen Harvey (Manchester, UK: Manchester University Press, 2005), 25-28.

[6]This multiplicity of signs may have diluted the meaning of the kiss of peace since the sign of peace changes based on one's relational closeness to the recipient, thus eliminating the equalizing impact of the act. See Lawrence Phillips, "The Ritual Kiss in Early Christian Worship" (PhD diss., University of Notre Dame, 1992), 269-73. This potential dilution of the meaning does not, however, negate all continuities between past and present expressions of this liturgical act.

[7]Christine Pohl, *Making Room* (Grand Rapids, MI: Eerdmans, 1999), 5-7.

[8]Esau McCaulley, *Reading While Black* (Downers Grove, IL: InterVarsity Press, 2020), 69.

[9]"It is better to assume that guests are angels and to act accordingly rather than risk treating worthy people unworthily." Donald Guthrie, *Hebrews* (Downers Grove, IL: InterVarsity Press, 1983), 268.

[10]Mike Cosper, "The Land of My Sojourn: Looking Back on Twenty Years," September 14, 2020.

[11]From an interview quoted in Korie Edwards, *The Elusive Dream* (New York: Oxford University Press, 2008), 65.

[12]Sharon Garlough Brown, *Sensible Shoes* (Downers Grove, IL: InterVarsity, 2013), 141.

11. WHITE IS NOT A NEUTRAL COLOR

[1]This conversation is a composite of encounters with three individuals, with some details altered to preserve confidentiality. For composite narrative methodologies in qualitative research, see Rebecca Willis, "The Use of Composite Narratives to Present Interview Findings," *Qualitative Research* 19, no. 4 (August 2019): 471-75.

[2]When majority-culture practices, ideologies, and social locations are perceived as normative, practices and understandings that diverge from this norm are seen as deviant; majority-culture individuals perceive themselves as cultureless while identifying ethnic minorities as

possessing distinctive cultural practices. See Korie Edwards, *The Elusive Dream* (New York: Oxford University Press, 2008), 10-11.

[3]When White cultural assumptions and preferences are treated as neutral, "White" becomes "a kind of unlabeled position that stands as universal, unmarked, unraced; a racialized identity not recognized as racial or racially particular by those deemed to inhabit it." David Horrell, *Ethnicity and Inclusion* (Grand Rapids, MI: Eerdmans, 2020), 313. See also Tony Evans, *Oneness Embraced*, rev. ed. (Chicago: Moody, 2022), 112-13.

[4]Sandra Maria Van Opstal, *The Next Worship* (Downers Grove, IL: InterVarsity Press, 2015), 40.

[5]When church members are unaware of the ways in which their culture shapes their preferences, preservation of their own cultural identities may prevent the cultivation of multiethnic kingdom culture. See Edward Gilbreath, *Reconciliation Blues* (Downers Grove, IL: InterVarsity Press, 2010), 85.

[6]John Piper, "Is Racial Harmony Disintegrating?" Desiring God, December 7, 2017, www.desiringgod.org/articles/is-racial-harmony-disintegrating.

[7]Edwards, *The Elusive Dream*, 11, 84, 88-89; Douglas Sharp, *No Partiality* (Downers Grove, IL: InterVarsity Press, 2002), 25-26.

[8]Edwards, *The Elusive Dream*, 10.

[9]When a pattern of thinking seems so normal that it is unnoticed, choices are no longer a result of thoughtful deliberation; as a result, individuals relying on these unnoticed patterns to build their perceptions may become unable to see weaknesses in their logic or conclusions. Such thinking can be shifted and changed through deliberative practices, conscious management of emotions, and cultivation of mental habits—all of which overlap significantly with what James K. A. Smith describes in liturgical terms. See Daniel Kahneman, *Thinking, Fast and Slow* (New York: Farrah, Straus, and Giroux, 2011), as well as the popularizations of Kahneman's research in Paul Gibbons, *The Science of Successful Organizational Change* (London: Financial Times, 2015); and Paul Gibbons, *Impact* (Portland, OR: Phronesis, 2019).

[10]God himself is the ultimate exemplar of impartiality (Deuteronomy 10:17; 2 Chronicles 19:7; Matthew 22:16; Mark 12:14; Luke 20:21; Romans 2:11; Acts 10:34; Galatians 2:6; Ephesians 6:9), and he commanded that neither

the powerful (Deuteronomy 16:19) nor the powerless (Exodus 23:3) were to be favored. The sin of partiality could be committed with reference to individuals (Deuteronomy 1:17; 16:19; 21:16; Proverbs 18:5; Colossians 3:25; 1 Timothy 5:21), but James seems to extend the principles to a group or type of person (James 2:1-9) as did Peter (Acts 10:34). See David Gowler, *James through the Centuries* (Hoboken, NJ: Wiley, 2020), 153-54.

[11]προσωπολημπτέω, as well as προσωπολήμπτης and προσωπολημψία, seem to have been coined as single words by Christian writers; these terms were formed by contracting the multiple-word Septuagint renderings of Hebrew phrases into single words. See, e.g., λήμψη πρόσωπον as translation of פְּנֵי נָשָׂא in Leviticus 19:15. See Walter Bauer et al., "προσωπολημπτέω," in *A Greek-English Lexicon of the New Testament and Other Early Christian Literature*, 3rd ed., trans. William Arndt and F. Wilbur Gingrich, rev. and ed. F. W. Danker (Chicago: University of Chicago Press, 2000).

[12]The implications of the text in James extend beyond making a place for every socioeconomic stratum and include welcoming persons from every ethnicity. For ethnic implications of this text, see Douglas Moo, *The Letter of James* (Grand Rapids, MI: Eerdmans, 2000), 113; and Russell Shedd, "Social Justice: Underlying Hermeneutical Issues," *Biblical Interpretation and the Church: The Problem of Contextualization*, ed. D. A. Carson (Nashville, TN: Nelson, 1984), 222. God created human beings to love one's own family and to rejoice in one's own culture without viewing one's own kin or culture as superior to or more valuable than others. The privation of creation introduced through humanity's fall into sin distorted this love, resulting in kinism, racism, and other forms of partiality.

[13]For the impact of depicting Jesus and other biblical characters as White, see Eric Mason, "Restoring Black Dignity," in *Urban Apologetics*, ed. Eric Mason (Grand Rapids, MI: Zondervan, 2021), 9.

[14]Isaac Adams, *Talking about Race* (Grand Rapids, MI: Zondervan, 2022), 101.

[15]George Yancey, *Beyond Racial Gridlock* (Downers Grove, IL: InterVarsity Press, 2006), 31-34.

202 NOTES TO PAGE 102

[16] For this correct and helpful judicial function of colorblindness, see the dissent of John Marshall Harlan in Plessy v. Ferguson, 163 U.S. 537 (1895): 559. The usage of this terminology in legal contexts for a refusal to discriminate based on color seems to have originated with early civil rights activist Albion Tourgée, who used the term in his brief to the court in *Plessy v. Ferguson.* See Mark Elliot, *Color Blind Justice* (New York: Oxford University Press, 2008), 3-4.

[17] Martin Luther King Jr., as quoted in Eric Sundquist, *King's Dream* (New Haven, CT: Yale University Press, 2009), 194.

[18] Some individuals have wrongly argued that Martin Luther King Jr. was a proponent of a comprehensive colorblind approach. See, e.g., Coleman Hughes, "Martin Luther King, Colorblind Radical," *Wall Street Journal*, January 17, 2019, www.wsj.com/articles/martin-luther-king-colorblind -radical-11547769741. However, King explicitly supported special ethnicity-based considerations that would enable African Americans to recover the progress that centuries of subjugation and segregation had precluded. See Martin Luther King, Jr., *Why We Can't Wait*, repr. ed. (Boston: Beacon, 2000), 158-59.

[19] See, e.g., Evan P. Apfelbaum, Michael I. Norton, and Samuel R. Sommers, "Racial Color Blindness: Emergence, Practice, and Implications," *Current Directions in Psychological Science* 21, no. 3 (June 2012): 205-9; Evan P. Apfelbaum, Samuel R. Sommers, and Michael I. Norton, "Seeing Race and Seeming Racist? Evaluating Strategic Color Blindness in Social Interaction," *Journal of Personality and Social Psychology* 95, no. 4 (2008): 918-32; Michael Emerson and George Yancey, *Transcending Racial Barriers* (New York: Oxford University Press, 2011), 33-40; Lindy Gullett and Tessa West, "Understanding Racial Color Blindness and Multiculturalism in Interracial Relationships," in *The Myth of Racial Color Blindness*, ed. Helen A. Neville, Miguel E. Gallardo, and Derald Wing Sue (Washington, DC: American Psychological Association, 2016), 71-75; Michael Norton et al., "Color Blindness and Interracial Interaction," *Psychological Science* 17, no. 11 (November 2006): 949-53; Jennifer Richeson and Richard Nussbaum, "The Impact of Multiculturalism Versus Color-Blindness on Racial Bias," *Journal of Experimental Social Psychology* 40 (May 2004): 417-23; Stacey J. Sasaki and Jacquie D. Vorauer, "Ignoring Versus Exploring Differences

Between Groups: Effects of Salient Color-Blindness and Multiculturalism on Intergroup Attitudes and Behavior," *Social and Personality Psychology Compass* 7, no. 4 (March 2013): 246-59; Andrew Todd and Adam Galinsky, "The Reciprocal Link Between Multiculturalism and Perspective-Taking," *Journal of Experimental Social Psychology* 48, no. 6 (November 2012): 1394-98; Maykel Verkuyten, "Ethnic Group Identification and Group Evaluation among Minority and Majority Groups," *Journal of Personality and Social Psychology* 88, no. 1 (January 2005): 121-38; Christopher Wolsko, Bernadette Park, and Charles M. Judd, "Considering the Tower of Babel: Correlates of Assimilation and Multiculturalism Among Ethnic Minority and Majority Groups in the United States," *Social Justice Research* 19, no. 3 (August 2006): 277-306. Although our objections to the colorblind approach are theological and not psychological or sociological, it should be noted that the dominant methods for assessing the impact of colorblind ideology have validly been critiqued and modifications to assessment methods have been recommended. See, e.g., Matthew C. Jackson, Vera Katelyn Wilde, and Phillip Atiba Goff, "Seeing Color Blindness," in *The Myth of Racial Color Blindness*, ed. Neville, Gallardo, and Sue, 125-40.

[20]Randy Woodley, *Living in Color* (Downers Grove, IL: InterVarsity Press, 2004), 21.

[21]Brenda Salter McNeil and Rick Richardson, *The Heart of Racial Justice* (Downers Grove, IL: InterVarsity Press, 2004), 35.

[22]Shai Linne, *The New Reformation* (Chicago: Moody, 2021), 133.

[23]For ecclesiological weaknesses of a colorblind approach, see Daniel Slavich, "That the World May Know" (PhD diss., Midwestern Baptist Theological Seminary, 2020), 219-27, 263, 268.

[24]Language alludes to Chris Williamson, "Shepherding Toward Racial Reconciliation," in *For God So Loved the World*, ed. Walter Strickland II and Dayton Hartman (Nashville, TN: B&H, 2020), 134.

[25]Esau McCaulley, *Reading While Black* (Downers Grove, IL: InterVarsity Press, 2020), 106.

[26]Multiculturalism may contribute positively to social cohesion in certain circumstances. Sara Watters and Jaimee Stuart, "Does Normative Multiculturalism Foster or Threaten Social Cohesion?" *International Journal of Intercultural Relations* 75 (March 2020): 82-94.

[27] In some circumstances, multiculturalism can also work against its own goals by strengthening the perception that specified characteristics are essential and intrinsic to certain ethnicities. Leigh S. Wilton, Evan P. Apfelbaum, and Jessica J. Good, "Valuing Differences and Reinforcing Them: Multiculturalism Increases Race Essentialism," *Social Psychological and Personality Science* 10, no. 5 (July 2019): 681-89. For further critiques of multiculturalism, see Michael Emerson and George Yancey, *Transcending Racial Barriers* (New York: Oxford University Press, 2011), 55-57.

[28] See the descriptions of racism as "omnipresent," "epistemologically embedded," and pervading "every vestige of our reality," in Robin DiAngelo, *White Fragility* (Boston, MA: Beacon Press, 2018), 72-73. Cf. also "integral, permanent, and indestructible," in Derrick Bell, *Faces at the Bottom of the Well* (New York: Basic, 1992), xxi. For an example of secular antiracism applied in the context of higher education, see Allison Ash et al., "Anti-Racism in Higher Education: A Model for Change," *Race and Pedagogy Journal* 4, no. 3 (2020). "Secular antiracism" is employed here to distinguish this flawed approach from the "faithful antiracism" in Christina Edmondson and Chad Brennan, *Faithful Antiracism* (Downers Grove, IL: InterVarsity Press, 2022). John McWhorter utilizes the term *third-wave antiracism* to describe what we have described as "secular antiracism." See John McWhorter, *Woke Racism* (New York: Portfolio, 2021).

[29] George Yancey, *Beyond Racial Division* (Downers Grove, IL: InterVarsity Press, 2022), 88-98.

[30] Thaddeus Williams, *Confronting Injustice Without Compromising Truth* (Grand Rapids, MI: Zondervan, 2020), 41-48.

[31] In the early church, identity in Christ redeemed and relativized ethnic identities without obliterating them, thus enabling each individual to live as part of a family constituted of persons from differing ethnicities, cultures, ages, and socioeconomic backgrounds. Loyalty to Christ overwrote previous civic and ethnic loyalties. For further exploration of multiple and nested social identities, see Philip Esler, *Conflict and Identity in Romans* (Philadelphia: Fortress, 2003), 74-76, 108, 140, 276, 335-65; Philip Esler, "Giving the Kingdom to an Ethnos That Will Bear Its Fruit: Ethnic and Christ-Movement Identities in Matthew," in *In the Fullness of Time: Essays on Christology, Creation and Eschatology in Honor of Richard*

Bauckham, ed. Daniel M. Gurtner, Grant Macaskill, and Jonathan T. Pennington (Grand Rapids, MI: Eerdmans, 2016), 177-96; Philip Esler, "Jesus
and the Reduction of Intergroup Conflict," *Biblical Interpretation* 8, no. 4
(2000); Philip Esler, "Judean Ethnic Identity and the Matthean Jesus," in
Jesus-Gestalt und Gestaltungen, ed. Petra von Gemünden et al. (Göttingen,
Germany: Vandenhoeck and Ruprecht, 2013), 208. See also William
Campbell, *Paul and the Creation of Christian Identity* (London: T&T Clark,
2006), 94-124; William Campbell, "Unity and Diversity in the Church:
Transformed Identities and the Peace of Christ in Ephesians," *Transfor-
mation* 25, no. 1 (January 2008): 24; Pamela Eisenbaum, "Jewish Perspec-
tives: A Jewish Apostle to the Gentiles," in *Studying Paul's Letters*, ed.
Joseph Marchal (Philadelphia: Fortress, 2012), 150; Kathy Ehrensperger,
Paul at the Crossroads of Cultures (London: T&T Clark, 2013), 158; Aaron J.
Kuecker, *The Spirit and the "Other"* (London: T&T Clark, 2011), 48, 66,
228-30; Stephen Louy, "The Origins of Christian Identity in the Letters of
Paul" (PhD thesis, University of Edinburgh, 2012).

[32] *The Epistle to Diognetus*, 1. I (Timothy) have rendered the Greek *genos* as
"genus" to avoid confusion with modern uses of "race" and "ethnicity." This
notion of a "new genus" did not indicate either "ethnicity" or "race" in the
sense that we have utilized these terms in this book. The new "genus" described in *Epistle to Diognetus* provided a superordinate identity that coexisted with ethnicity. See also Aristides, *Apology*, 2, 14-15, and Tertullian of
Carthage, *Quintile Septimi Florentis Tertulliani Ad Nationes Libri Duo*, ed.
Philip Borleffs (Leiden, Netherlands: Brill, 1929), 1:8, 20. For discussion of
Christianity as *tertium genus*, see Erich Gruen, *Ethnicity in the Ancient
World—Did It Matter?* (Berlin, Germany: De Gruyter, 2020), 201-14. What is
proposed here as a superordinate identity coexisting with ethnicity is
similar to the "dual-identity model" proposed by some social-scientific
theorists. See, e.g., Gullett and West, "Understanding Racial Color Blindness,"
79. By calling high-status groups to leverage privilege for the sake of lower-
status groups by means of the example of Jesus and the power of the Holy
Spirit, Christian communities are able to overcome many of the weaknesses noted in secular applications of dual-identity models.

[33] Regarding the need for distinctly Christian and ecclesial solutions to the
problems of racial tension and segregated lives, see Thomas Schreiner,

foreword to Jarvis Williams, *One New Man* (Nashville, TN: B&H, 2010), xxi; John M. Perkins with Karen Waddles, *One Blood* (Chicago: Moody, 2018), 84; George Yancey, *Beyond Racial Gridlock* (Downers Grove, IL: InterVarsity Press, 2006), 11-12. In the 1970s, Carl F. H. Henry similarly lamented the failure of Christian scholars in providing distinctly Christian solutions to social issues, rightly noting that one result of this oversight was a tendency among younger Christians to gravitate toward Marxist and socialist alternatives that are unworkable and anti-Christian. Carl F. H. Henry, *God, Revelation, and Authority*, vol. 4, *God Who Speaks and Shows* (Wheaton, IL: Crossway, 1999), 712. For the unworkability of socialist solutions as well as a helpful distinction between "democratic socialism" and "social democracy," see Kristian Niemietz, *Socialism, the Failed Idea That Never Dies* (London: IEA, 2019), 16-21. Part of the goal of this book is to present a distinctly Christian and ecclesial approach that shows the inadequacy of popular secular solutions to issues of racial and ethnic division.

[34]Habitual crosscultural hospitality reduces the potential for intergroup conflict through *decategorization*, in which repeated person-to-person contact disconfirms negative stereotypes and reduces or dissolves previously divisive category boundaries. Regarding decategorization in social-identity theory, see Esler, "Jesus and the Reduction of Intergroup Conflict," 349-50.

[35]Tony Evans, *Oneness Embraced*, rev. ed. (Chicago: Moody, 2022), 80. Martin Luther King Jr. similarly recognized that exchanging one ethnic power structure for another solves nothing. Martin Luther King Jr., "Where Do We Go from Here?" in *A Testament of Hope*, ed. James Washington (New York: Harper & Row, 1986), 251.

12. LITURGIES OF HOSPITALITY

[1]Christine Pohl, *Making Room* (Grand Rapids, MI: Eerdmans, 1999), 4.

[2]Julian, "22: Ἀρσακίῳ ἀρχιερεῖ Γαλατίας," *Letters. Epigrams. Against the Galileans. Fragments*, Loeb Classical Library 157, trans. Wilmer Wright (Cambridge, MA: Harvard University Press, 1923), 429-30. Cf. Julian's usage of φιλανθρωπία (ἡ περὶ τοὺς ξένους φιλανθρωπία) with *The Epistle to Diognetus* 9:2. Cf. also Julian's reference to care for the dead (ἡ περὶ τὰς ταφὰς τῶν νεκρῶν προμήθεια) with Aristides, *Apology*, 15.

[3] Augustine of Hippo, *Sermons on Selected Lessons of the New Testament*, Nicene and Post-Nicene Fathers, series 1, vol. 6, trans. R.G. MacMullen, ed. Philip Schaff (London: T&T Clark, 1993), 31:9.

[4] Stanley Hauerwas and William Willimon, *Resident Aliens*, ex. ed. (Nashville, TN: Abingdon, 2014), 83; Joshua Jipp, *Saved by Faith and Hospitality* (Grand Rapids, MI: Eerdmans, 2017), 2-3.

[5] Carolyne Call, "The Rough Trail to Authentic Pedagogy: Incorporating Hospitality, Fellowship, and Testimony into the Classroom," *Teaching and Christian Practices*, ed. David Smith and James K. A. Smith (Grand Rapids, MI: Eerdmans, 2011), 78.

[6] Pohl, *Making Room*, 61.

[7] C. S. Lewis, "Answers to Questions on Christianity," *God in the Dock*, ed. Walter Hooper (Grand Rapids, MI: Eerdmans, 1970), 52.

[8] Multiethnic interactions cultivate an awareness of variability within each ethnicity, which reduces prejudice by reducing reliance on stereotyping. Markus Brauer and Abdelatif Er-Rafiy, "Increasing Perceived Variability Reduces Prejudice and Discrimination," *Journal of Experimental Social Psychology* 47, no. 5 (September 2011): 871-81; Markus Brauer et al., "Describing a Group in Positive Terms Reduces Prejudice Less Effectively than Describing It in Positive and Negative Terms," *Journal of Experimental Social Psychology* 48, no. 3 (May 2012): 757-61; Abdelatif Er-Rafiy, Markus Brauer, and Serban C. Musca, "Effective Reduction of Prejudice and Discrimination: Methodological Considerations and Three Field Experiments," *Revue Internationale de Psychologie Sociale* 23, no. 2 (January 2010): 57-95.

[9] Malcolm Boyd, "Martin Luther King: Man, Mystery," *Washington Post*, January 20, 1974, C–3. This statement suggests the influence of Gordon Allport's contact hypothesis on King's thinking. According to Allport, "prejudice . . . may be reduced by equal status contact between majority and minority groups in the pursuit of common goals." Gordon Allport, *The Nature of Prejudice*, 25th anniversary ed. (New York: Basic Books, 1979), 280-81.

[10] Tom Strode, "Chicago Pastor Says 'Dinner Tables' Key to Racial Reconciliation," *Illinois Baptist*, February 24, 2022, https://illinoisbaptist.org /chicago-pastor-says-dinner-tables-key-to-racial-reconciliation/.

[11] Emmanuel Acho, *Uncomfortable Conversations with a Black Man* (New York: Flatiron, 2020), 182; Michelle Ami Reyes, *Becoming All Things* (Grand Rapids, MI: Zondervan, 2021), 110-11.

[12] Howard Thurman, *Jesus and the Disinherited* (Boston, MA: Beacon, 1996), 98.

[13] According to the contact hypothesis, prejudices diminish when close and ongoing contact occurs between individuals who have equal status, are noncompetitive, develop a close relationship, and are supported by relevant authority figures. See Philip Esler, "Jesus and the Reduction of Intergroup Conflict: The Parable of the Good Samaritan in Light of Social Identity Theory," *Biblical Interpretation* 8, no. 4 (2000): 349-50; and George Yancey, *Beyond Racial Division* (Downers Grove, IL: InterVarsity Press, 2022), 107-8. For the positive impact of working in close contact with persons from other ethnicities as well as participating in voluntary programs to diminish ethnic prejudices, see Frank Dobbin and Alexandra Kalev, "Why Diversity Programs Fail," *Harvard Business Review*, July–August 2016, https://hbr.org/2016/07/why-diversity-programs-fail.

[14] To encourage a discipline of listening on the part of privileged persons is *not* to imply that minority groups possess inherent epistemic advantages while dominant groups have distinctly illusory perceptions, as some theorists have claimed. For a modest example of this type of errant claim, see José Medina, *The Epistemology of Resistance* (New York: Oxford University Press, 2013), 40-46. In some cases, claims of epistemic advantage are coupled with a binary logic that categorizes persons as oppressed or oppressor by virtue of their ethnicity or social location, regardless of any action on their part. See, e.g., Beverly Tatum, "The Complexity of Identity: 'Who Am I?'" in *Readings for Diversity and Social Justice*, ed. Maurianne Adams et al. (Milton Park, UK: Routledge, 2000), 11. Such perspectives wrongly treat epistemic virtues as structures that are determined, at least in part, by an individual's status as oppressed or oppressor. In its worst practical expressions, this binary-logic perspective rejects challenges to the accuracy of claims made by oppressed persons based on supposed epistemic virtues that are presumed to characterize the reasoning of the oppressed. For an example of such thinking, see the claim that privileged persons are forbidden to "deny what these people are telling us," in

Conor Friedersdorf, "Anti-Racist Arguments Are Tearing People Apart," *The Atlantic*, August 20, 2020, www.theatlantic.com/ideas/archive/2020/08/meta-arguments-about-anti-racism/615424/. One's awareness and appreciation of a particular truth certainly may be enriched when that truth is described from a different cultural perspective, but it does not follow that anyone's social class endows him or her with epistemic virtues or that anyone's perception of reality is more likely to be accurate simply because of his or her status as oppressed. Christians are better served by taking "an inductive, critical realist approach, examining each situation carefully in light of historical facts, evidence, and warrants." Hak Joon Lee, "Community, Mission, and Race," in *Can "White" People Be Saved*, ed. Love L. Sechrest, Johnny Ramírez-Johnson, and Amos Yong (Downers Grove, IL: InterVarsity Press, 2018), 224.

[15] Augustine points out that pride despises equality among humans. "Instead of [God's] rule, it seeks to impose a rule of its own on its equals." *Augustine: City of God: Books 18:36–20*, Loeb Classical Library 416, trans. W. C. Green (Cambridge, MA: Harvard University Press, 1960), 19:12.

[16] Henri J. M. Nouwen, *Reaching Out* (Baltimore, MD: Image, 1986), 66-67.

[17] Derwin Gray, *Building a Multiethnic Church* (Nashville, TN: Nelson, 2021), 104.

[18] Mutual contact doesn't automatically produce unity. For limits and weaknesses of mutual contact as a means of reducing ethnic division, see Robert D. Putnam, *"E Pluribus Unum*: Diversity and Community in the Twenty-First Century," *Scandinavian Political Studies* 30, no. 2 (June 2007): 141-51.

[19] Anthony O'Hear, *Beyond Evolution* (New York: Clarendon Press, 1997), 144. See also 129-32. Evolutionary naturalism cannot adequately explain regard for others, yet this regard is necessary for us even to discuss abstract values and rights. Hospitality moves beyond abstract values and rights to require dispositions that do not contribute to winning or survival. These inclinations could be explained by an intrinsic human nature with inclinations that transcend naturalistic explanations, by a regenerative act by which natural inclinations are changed, or by some combination of these and other factors.

[20] Charlie Richardson, "There Is a Peace," *Before the Throne*, Sojourn, 2007. Used by permission.

13. KNOWING YOUR PLACE

[1] The church is a particular gathering of believers in the gospel who have committed themselves to intentional accountability and fellowship within which "the Word of God [is] sincerely preached and heard" and "the sacraments [are] administered according to the institution of Christ." John Calvin, *Institutio Christianae Religionis, Johannis Calvini Opera Selecta*, vol. 5, ed. Peter Barth and Wilhelm Niesel (Munich, Germany: Kaiser, 1957), 4:1:9. As used here, "sacrament" is meant in the sense of a sign participating in and pointing to saving grace that has already been effected through regeneration and enacted through repentance and faith. For this use of *sacrament* among early Baptists, see Michael A. G. Haykin, *Amidst Us Our Belovèd Stands* (Bellingham, WA: Lexham, 2022), 91.

[2] Martin Luther, *Martin Luthers Tractatus de Libertate Christiana 1520*, ed. Josef Svennung (Berlin, Germany: De Gruyter, 1932), 7-8.

[3] For the problem of "place" in the modern era, see Craig Bartholomew, *Where Mortals Dwell* (Grand Rapids, MI: Baker, 2011), 219-32.

[4] Kentucky State Data Center and Metro United Way, "Russell Neighborhood Profile," July 2017, http://ksdc.louisville.edu/wp-content/uploads/2018/06 /Russell.pdf; *Louisville Metro Health Equity Report 2017*, Center for Health Equity, 2017, 37-38.

[5] Segregation was not comprehensively or immediately practiced even after the demise of Reconstruction in 1877. In some sense, Jim Crow was born in the North and moved to the South. See C. Vann Woodward, *The Strange Career of Jim Crow*, commemorative ed. (New York: Oxford University Press, 2002), 17, 28-40.

[6] Joseph Trotter, *River Jordan* (Lexington: University Press of Kentucky, 1998), 107.

[7] Luther Adams, *Way Up North in Louisville* (Chapel Hill: University of North Carolina Press, 2010), 149, 151, 165-67.

[8] For further historical data on urban segregation, see Adams, *Way Up North in Louisville*, 17, 29-36, 63-64, 149-61; Raymond Mohl, "Planned Destruction," in *From Tenements to the Taylor Homes*, ed. John Bauman,

Roger Biles, and Kristin Szylvian (University Park: Pennsylvania State University Press, 2000), 226-45; Richard Rothstein, *The Color of Law* (New York: Liveright, 2017), 4-13, 21-24, 45-50, 68-72, 127-31, 152-75; Trotter, *River Jordan*, 95-108; George Wright, "The NAACP and Residential Segregation in Louisville, Kentucky, 1914–1917," *The Register of the Kentucky Historical Society* 78, no. 1 (Winter 1980): 39-47.

[9]Marshall v. Bramer, 828 F. 2d 355, Court of Appeals, 6th Circuit, 1987. The investigation discovered that more than half of the members of the local Ku Klux Klan were Jefferson County police officers. At least one of them was also a member of a secret society of law-enforcement officers known as the "Confederate Officer's Patriotic Squad" (COPS). At least two individuals who had belonged to these racist groups remained high-ranking members of the Jefferson County Sheriff's Office in 2021. Ewan Palmer, "Kentucky Sheriff's Officers Leave Following KKK Membership Revelations," *Newsweek*, November 11, 2021, www.newsweek.com/kkk-kentucky-jefferson-county-sheriff-officers-1648407.

[10]Tom Skinner and Spencer Perkins, quoted in John Piper, *Bloodlines* (Wheaton, IL: Crossway, 2011), 178.

14. BUILDING UP WALLS THAT JESUS ALREADY BROKE DOWN

[1]Blake Touchstone, "Planters and Slave Religion in the Deep South," *Masters and Slaves in the House of the Lord*, ed. John Boles (Lexington: University of Kentucky Press, 1988), 123.

[2]Dwight Perry, *Breaking Down Barriers* (Grand Rapids, MI: Baker, 1998), 16.

[3]Evelyn Simpson-Curenton, "I Know It Was the Blood," in *African American Heritage Hymnal*, ed. Delores Carpenter and Nolan E. Williams, Jr. (Chicago: GIA Publications, 2001), #267.

[4]Some portions of this chapter have been adapted from Jamaal Williams, "Reconciled Under the Lordship of Christ," in *Ministers of Reconciliation*, ed. Daniel Darling (Bellingham, WA: Lexham, 2021), 117-26.

[5]Frank Thielman, *Ephesians* (Grand Rapids, MI: Baker, 2010), 148.

[6]David Rhoads, *The Challenge of Diversity* (Philadelphia: Fortress Press, 1996), 2.

[7]For more on how to approach conversations on race and justice see George Yancey, *Beyond Racial Division* (Downers Grove, IL: InterVarsity,

2022), 36-39. Yancey's "mutual accountability model" does not suggest that the responsibilities of every ethnicity and race are identical (36). Instead, Yancey contends that everyone in the conversation should have a capacity to be part of the conversation and no one is cut off, thus cultivating community through dialogue and relationships (39).

[8]Francis Schaeffer, *25 Basic Bible Studies* (Wheaton, IL: Crossway Books, 1996), 139.

[9]Theresa Walker, "Can We All Just Get Along? Rodney King's Question Still Matters," *Mercury News*, April 30, 2017, www.mercurynews.com/2017/04/30 /can-we-all-just-get-along-rodney-kings-question-still-matters/. I (Jamaal) first heard this question asked in a sermon by H. B. Charles Jr., "Tearing Down the Dividing Wall: How the Gospel Shapes Racial Reconciliation," Ethics and Religious Liberty Commission of the Southern Baptist Convention, April 17, 2018, https://erlc.com/resource-library/erlc-podcast -episodes/tearing-down-the-dividing-wall-how-the-gospel-shapes-racial -reconciliation/.

[10]Juan Sanchez, "The Chosen People and Racial Reconciliation," *Ministers of Reconciliation*, ed. Daniel Darling (Bellingham, WA: Lexham, 2021), 128.

[11]Christina Edmondson and Chad Brennan, *Faithful Antiracism* (Downers Grove, IL: InterVarsity Press, 2022), 16, 86-106.

[12]"White Christians Have Become Even Less Motivated to Address Racial Injustice," *Race Today*, Barna, September 15, 2020, www.barna.com /research/american-christians-race-problem/. See also Edmondson and Brennan, *Faithful Antiracism*, 17.

15. LITURGIES OF COMMUNION

[1]For distinctions between *honestiores* and *humiliores* in the Roman social order, see Peter Garnsey, *Social Status and Legal Privilege in the Roman Empire* (Oxford, UK: Clarendon, 1970), 221-67; Wenhua Shi, *Paul's Message of the Cross as Body Language* (Tübingen, Germany: Mohr Siebeck, 2008), 105-6; Ben Witherington III, *Conflict and Community in Corinth* (Grand Rapids, MI: Eerdmans, 1995), 259-60.

[2]Calvin Roetzel, *The Letters of Paul*, 2nd ed. (Louisville, KY: Westminster John Knox, 1982), 56-57.

[3]Richard Hays, *1 Corinthians* (Louisville, KY: Westminster John Knox, 2011), 194.

4 Anthony Thiselton, *The First Epistle to the Corinthians* (Grand Rapids, MI: Eerdmans, 2000), 882

5 Augustine of Hippo, "Sermon 227: Preached on the Holy Day of Easter to the *Infantes*, on the Sacraments," *Sermons III/6 (184–229Z) on the Liturgical Seasons*, trans. and ed. Edmund Hill and John Rotelle (Hyde Park, NY: New City, 1993), 254.

6 Michael Emerson with Rodney Woo, *People of the Dream* (Princeton, NJ: Princeton University Press, 2006), 159.

7 Russell Moore, *Onward* (Nashville, TN: B&H, 2015), 8.

8 Whitney Bozarth, "Come and See," *Anchor for My Soul*, Whitney Bozarth, 2014. Used by permission.

BENEDICTION: A BLESSING FOR THE ROAD

1 Jon Tyson, *The Intentional Father* (Grand Rapids, MI: Baker, 2021), 231, 232.

AFTERWORD

1 To see these three themes worked out more comprehensively, see Jarvis Williams, *Redemptive Kingdom Diversity* (Grand Rapids, MI: Baker, 2021).